WAR FILMS

virgin

film

WAR FILMS

James Clarke

For David Bayly, who always believed in my writing
and who was a great family friend.

First published in Great Britain in 2006
by Virgin Books Ltd
Thames Wharf Studios
Rainville Road
London
W6 9HA

ISBN 0 7535 1094 4
ISBN 9 780753 510940

Typeset by TW Typesetting, Plymouth, Devon
Printed and bound in Great Britain by Mackays of Chatham PLC

Contents

Acknowledgements

A big thanks to Ben Bowden for samurai backup on the *Ran* chapter and also to my friends and staff in the film department and library at the University of Gloucestershire. And a tip of the hat to Gemma Watters.

Thanks to my editor Gareth Fletcher and special thanks as always to Kirstie Addis for commissioning the book and to my agent Laura Morris.

Introduction

In his stunning novel *Three Soldiers*, about three disparate American troops fighting in the First World War, John Dos Passos writes, 'Men were more humane when they were killing each other than when they were talking about it . . . So was civilisation nothing but a vast edifice of sham, and the war . . . was its fullest and most ultimate expression.' War stories have always had to deal with a conflict of morality, and with an increasingly complicated sense of what war means. Finally, the war film must visualise and dramatise some sense of a world twisting out of recognition when war strikes. Men find it hard to emote and express frailty, so perhaps the war film creates opportunities for them to acknowledge their insecurities in a world apparently without reason. This way of presenting the distorting effect of combat and violence is never far from the minds of the filmmakers featured in this book.

We tell stories to one another, and always have done, as a means of confronting the frayed ends of life; with its painful and traumatic untidiness. This is magnified, intensified and most concentrated in the war story.

Many of the war films that have made their mark on the imaginations of the viewer have been stories of characters moving from innocence to experience in a way that corresponds with the strongest of myths and ancient stories. It seems fair to say that it is rare for a war film to engage only with the particular details and issues surrounding a specific conflict. Instead, war is frequently used in cinema as a means by which to dramatise the enduring issues that all of us face – mortality, frailty (physical and emotional), community and courage.

Since the early years of the twentieth century, war films have captivated audience interest with incredible force and consistency, many of the films becoming iconic frames of reference for a large number of us. In certain instances these films have made great efforts to express some of the trauma of war. Other films have gone all out to counter any imagined sense of excitement around combat. Tellingly, as David Lean entered preproduction on his action-drama *The Bridge on the River Kwai* in 1956, he observed that war was anything but the adventure that stories might often portray it as. Lean commented that 'War is not fun except in bad films and bad books . . . These ideas are false . . . War is the greatest plague on earth. I don't think this is a time to minimise its horror and film it in false colours.'

Undoubtedly, the war film is often a variation on the action movie in part or whole. The war film has provided many of cinema's most popular and accomplished directors with the opportunity to tell their stories using the arena of combat to open audiences' eyes, hearts and minds to the toll war takes and sometimes to those conflicts that have been forgotten.

For the majority of viewers it is the Hollywood-made, popular American cinema version of warfare that is most widely known. In an incisive article written in 2003 Guy Westwell commented, 'In the last few years, Hollywood has produced a distinct and commercially successful cycle of war movies . . . These films work hard to renew America's self-belief, to reclaim faith in war as a valid mechanism of change and to reassert American moral rectitude.'

War stories have existed for as long as people have thrilled to storytelling and the idea of 'courage under fire' and for as long as people have mourned the wastefulness of combat. In other words, war stories have existed for as long as people have fought one another. Homer's epic *The Iliad* is a war story, as is the Babylonian epic poem *Gilgamesh*. Shakespeare set many of his most celebrated plays against the canvas of war, such as *Henry V*. The critical, and perhaps unsettling, issue to consider is how war can rightly be used as a subject for an art form geared around the concept of 'entertainment'. This might seem an uneasy alliance. Erich Maria Remarque's landmark novel *All Quiet on the Western Front* includes the following assessment of war, and surely most war films with any kind of guiding moral impulse serve in some way to do the same thing: '. . . war is a cause of death like cancer and tuberculosis and dysentery. The deaths are merely more frequent, more varied and terrible.' Stories about war reshape history and can newly shape our imaginative sense of what combat is about.

The war film has been a part of popular cinema since its earliest days and in the post-World War Two era has arguably assumed an even more prominent place in our collective movie memory. Cinema is both narcissistic and voyeuristic. The war film, then, is yet one more way of telling stories about the tragic and seemingly inevitable violence that humans continue to commit against one another and the world.

Some war stories serve a propaganda purpose, while others seek to suggest that there are no good wars, and never will be. Some seek to visualise the horror, both emotional and visceral, especially in more recent years, whilst others seek to acknowledge the heroism and twisted social and political backdrops.

History and cinema have not always made a comfortable fit. Dramatic impulse will often override fidelity to history; though history itself is a vast sea of stories that has never been, and never will be, objective. History is as dramatic as any 'fiction' and both are always offering us versions of reality; of what actually happened.

The war story can contain a variety of forms, styles and tones. From the intense realism of *All Quiet on the Western Front* (Lewis Milestone, 1930) and *Saving Private Ryan* (Steven Spielberg, 1998) to the comedy of *Dr Strangelove* (Stanley Kubrick, 1962) and *Three Kings* (David O Russell, 1999). It's obvious to note that there are more war films to watch than this book can hope to acknowledge.

It's obvious to say that there are so many more war films than this book can hope to acknowledge. British war films alone number in the hundreds and from this output we can namecheck a small handful such as *The Dam Busters* (Michael Anderson, 1954), *The Cruel Sea* (Charles Frend, 1953) and *Battle of Britain* (Guy Hamilton, 1969) all of which fused a sense of documentary and drama in their portrayals of British military effort and the bravery of its recruits.

Then, too, there is the war film as action-adventure spectacle. In many ways, maybe this is its most enduring incarnation. To some eyes, as early an effort as the ethically committed *All Quiet on the Western Front* is punctuated by moments of kinetic energy and jeopardy. Is it smarter, though, to look to those films made at a safe enough distance from the Great War and World War Two to begin understanding how they attached macho heroics to the context of international combat? The films of the 1940s and 1950s, still so close to both world wars and also the Korean War stepped with understandable reverence through the battlefields.

By the 1960s the genre had seen a shift towards a more straightforward action-film approach, typified by the hugely popular *The Great Escape* (John Sturges, 1963) and films such as *Where Eagles Dare* (Brian Hutton, 1968) in which Allied commandos set out to rescue an American general being held in a Nazi castle. *The Guns of Navarone* (J Lee Thompson, 1961) has also endured as a much-loved action story and is surely responsible for ushering in the undiluted action-adventure war film that characterised many of the 1960s films set during war.

In the two decades or so since the late 1960s the war film was particularly marked by depictions of the Vietnam War, and then starting in the late 1990s we have seen the 'resurrection' of the World War Two combat film. This very recent wave of stories rolled in with *Saving*

Private Ryan and was soon followed by *When We were Soldiers* (Randall Wallace, 2002) and *Windtalkers* (John Woo, 2002). Alongside these titles, television featured the miniseries *Band of Brothers*, which was received with real enthusiasm for its accuracy and seriousness of purpose.

As I sat about to watch **War of the Worlds** (Steven Spielberg, 2005) a conversation started between the man sitting next to me and his wife. He had fought in the Korean War and he said something that continues to stick with me. He started talking about the fact that in combat ordinary people do 'the weirdest things'. Just that morning I had been writing of how war films show the sense of the ordinary slipping away during war. Watching a number of war films in close succession had expressed that fact with real clarity. Those films were made all the more real and acute by the real-life memory from the quiet man alongside me.

War films, like all films, show us worlds. If the job has been done effectively films immerse us in their realities and, as such, they have an immediacy that the written word can perhaps never possess. A war film can powerfully indicate the physical cost of war and its grimy, desperate scramble for survival with a vivid closeness that tends to supercede the written word. Where literature has the advantage is in charting the internal feeling and response to combat.

Russian filmmaker and writer Sergei Eisenstein, who was critical to the development of both film theory and film practice in cinema's early years, proved that literature and film are mutually enriching endeavours. Eisenstein had begun his lifelong work with drama and storytelling with the Proletkult Theatre which, rather than focus on an individual hero in its stage plays, would instead make the mass of people the hero. Dialogue was not considered the centre of dramatic meaning, but instead ideas and values were communicated through a montage of effects: and in film this included lighting, camera position, editing patterns, sound, music and acting. This concept of montage found rich expression in his expansive and critical war film *Battleship Potemkin*. In keeping with Eisenstein's socially inclined and politicised filmmaking, we can look to more recent efforts such as *The Battle of Algiers* (Gillo Pontecorvo, 1965), which was a highly inflammatory film that sided with the Marxist revolutionary opinion in its depiction of Algeria's fight for independence from France. In keeping with the work of the Italian director Roberto Rossellini in the 1940s, Pontecorvo's film made a rigorous attempt at realism. The film features only one professional actor and uses actual people and locations from the events it depicts. The film has been praised for being unflinching in confronting the harder, more complex aspects of that particular battle for freedom.

The twenty-first-century experience of the world is becoming ever more mediated through moving pictures, but it is perhaps images of World War Two that continue to endure in our imagination. As Jeanine Basinger discusses in her stunningly thorough book *The World War Two Combat Film*, 'the World War Two combat film . . . has almost magically regained its audience appeal . . . For Hollywood, the combat film is perfect. It provided ready-made conflicts . . . easily simplified and clarified – and reversed.'

The birth of film coincided with the end of the nineteenth century, a time when battles seemed very distant geographically to most audiences. Cinema brought images of the world to people's local neighbourhoods. The Boxer Rebellion of 1900 and the Boer War (1898–1902) both received their share of cinematic coverage. In his writing about the beginnings of depictions of war in cinema Robert Murphy writes, 'The high casualty rates among those who fought in the First World War made it difficult to either celebrate or condemn the war.' Murphy notes that the earliest motion-picture images of war showed soldiers disembarking and doing drill exercises, and so more 'exciting' versions of reality were produced such as *Attack on a China Mission* (James Williamson, 1900) or *Peace with Honour* (Cecil Hepworth, 1902).

With their focus on combat, war films have very much become ever more allied with the aesthetic of the action film, so that a war film of the early twenty-first century could have as much in common with the kinetic patterns of a film like *Die Hard* (John McTiernan, 1988) as with a film such as *A Walk in the Sun* (Lewis Milestone, 1945).

For more than half a century now the war film has developed a range of story elements that audiences expect to see regardless of the combat scenario. When we watch a war film of the most accepted and 'conventional' kind we will expect (or at least unconsciously anticipate) seeing a story that centres on one heroic soldier in relation to the unit of soldiers he is a part of (professional or otherwise). We might expect to see a range of ethnic backgrounds represented. We would also expect a scene in which the soldier receives mail from home, and another based around the men using their weapons. Maybe too we expect to see the soldiers quietly and anxiously anticipating the fury of the battle ahead. And we expect to see acts of bravery amidst terror. War films aim to satisfy audience expectations as much as any other film. Across a wide and varied span we see images repeat, character formations echo and the heart and soul of these stories reverberate in similar ways, even though on the surface they may appear very different in their historical reference points. Looking at things this way *Paths of Glory* (Stanley Kubrick, 1957) isn't so far removed from the drama of *Casualties of War* (Brian De Palma, 1989), even though the former film is set in First World War France and the latter in the jungles of Vietnam.

War has always involved the exercise of technology. Cinema is also about displaying, in part, the technological tools at the disposal of the filmmaker. In the modern age, war has often been dominated by images of machinery clashing with humans, and our sense of war and military campaigns has almost assumed the quality of a film itself, with images endlessly streamed to us via television and the Internet. Computer games that pitch the player in the firing line suggest war is a game. Yet films are equally able to portray war as hell, and war as the way to a nobler self. War as a potential character-building experience is the idea that shoots through the chaos.

Obviously certain films reach for a more mature and grounded sense of communicating what battle zones and wartime are about than others. To go from *Rambo: First Blood Part Two* (George Pan Cosmatos, 1985) or *The Great Escape* to the cinema of Italian feature film *Rome, Open City* (Roberto Rossellini, 1945) or the generous and gentle anti-war film *La Grande Illusion* (Jean Renoir, 1937) is a long journey, striking in its contrast. *Rome, Open City* marks the beginning of Italian Neo-Realism, that is to say an approach to cinema that strips away, by choice or circumstance, the established artifice of the medium. Location filming was critical to this stylistic development, and Rossellini's film was shot on the streets of Rome during the final days of its Nazi occupation, when the city was anything but open. The city was in a state of destruction and Italy was on the verge of economic and social collapse. Rossellini found himself battling for resources and would buy raw film stock to shoot on from street photographers. This situation in turn created a particular and startling aesthetic that was seen to be 'real' and without gloss, as none of the film stock was of consistent quality. The voices of actors and ambient sound were added after filming, but Rossellini was keen to stress that his presentation of war-torn Rome was not a series of invented episodes spontaneously conjured 'on the spot'. Yes, the project was impacted by the situation, but all along there was a clear commitment to telling a particular story.

Italy was not the only country to continue producing films during Nazi occupation. France, too, was occupied by the German Army and, intriguingly, during their period of invasion and occupation over 350 films were produced. The invading force saw value in making films in the French language in order to underline the efforts of the occupation. One such film to be produced under these conditions, and thus have its production affected directly by the occupation, was the classic feature *Les Enfants du Paradis* (Marcel Carné, 1945).

What is it, then, that the most affecting war films achieve? Is it to amaze us with how cinema is able to recreate gruesome reality? Is it to remind us of moments of human compassion amidst the fury and desperation of the world, or to remind us that war is wasteful? Is it to compel audiences to wish they had been war heroes, to encourage viewers to sign up, literally or ideologically? We can only hope that war films individually, and in sum, serve to compel viewers to acknowledge the waste of war in a tangible and an emotional sense. For writer Louis Menand, 'I have always thought that what makes war appalling isn't the possibility that someone will maim or kill you; it is that possibility that you will maim or kill someone else.'

It seems fair to say that our prevailing sense of what a war film is for, and how it functions, stems from the vast number of American and British films about combat in the First and Second World Wars, and more recently the Vietnam War. Inevitably, perhaps, these dramatic takes on combat have been more powerful in shaping a public sense of war than more journalistic documents and dispatches. But there's a pretty fine line between fact and fiction when you look more closely. Certainly for younger audiences, films articulating the American experience in Vietnam and World War Two have a particular clarity and familiarity. In the American context, 'Warfare . . . offers another opportunity for a return to versions of the American "frontier" experience.' For sure, British war films have been produced over recent years, such as *Memphis Belle* (Michael Caton-Jones, 1990), *Regeneration* (Gillies MacKinnon, 1997) and *The Trench* (William Boyd, 1999), but none of them have had the marketing backup and distribution to get them far and wide to audiences.

For early Hollywood, busily building its reputation and galvanising the way in which it viewed the world and reflected it back to audiences, there was not only the horror of the First World War battlefield but also the chance to use big conflicts as a backdrop for big stories of love, romance and heroism. Hence the Oscar-winning film *Wings* (William Wellman, 1927) and later the more downbeat World War One flying movie *The Dawn Patrol* (Howard Hawks, 1930). An interesting, and somewhat bizare, detail of Hollywood's relationship with the First World War was demonstrated when film director DW Griffith (who had begun filming his inflammatory and ethically stunted American Civil War drama *Birth of a Nation* in 1914) was the only director authorised to go to the battlefields of that conflict, whereupon he voiced disappointment at what he saw. There wasn't enough spectacle and action for him. Movie reality and 'real' reality are two very different things. You might think that a big-shot film director would be the first to understand that, but then again, perhaps not.

For American cinema the war that proved especially prescient was the country's own Civil War (1861–65). Whilst Griffith's film stands as the most memorable (we cannot ignore his contributions to developing cinematic language) several hundred silent films were produced. Towards the middle of the twentieth century America had other, more recent wars to look to, though it continued to occasionally produce Civil War pieces, notably *The Red Badge of Courage* (John Huston, 1951), *Gone with the Wind* (Victor Fleming, 1939) and *Major Dundee* (Sam Peckinpah, 1965). More recent notable American Civil War titles have been *Glory* (Ed Zwick, 1989), *Gettysburg* (Ronald Maxwell, 1993) and *Cold Mountain* (Anthony Minghella, 2003). Steven Spielberg has recently begun work on a film about the last five years of Abraham Lincoln's life as the Civil War raged, based on the recently published book by Doris Kearns Goodwin entitled *Team of Rivals: The Political Genius of Abraham Lincoln*.

America was not the only territory, though, in which war was conceived on a large movie canvas. France in the 1920s displayed a real enthusiasm for historical epics and none was more distinctive than Abel Gance's film *Napoleon* (1927). The epic tradition and the war story have always fitted well together in cinema, and the film is a stunning testament to this compelling relationship between history and artistry. Gance's film took three years to make and was initially to have told the story of all of Napoleon's life. Gance was a sort of 'Epics R Us' of the time and French cinema in the 1920s was notable for its big film output. The great British film historian Kevin Brownlow spent twenty years compiling the most comprehensive version of the film yet shown, running to five hours. Francis Coppola presented the film in America as a three-hour version. As a young filmmaker in the early 1960s, Kevin Brownlow had made *It Happened Here* (1966) on location in Radnorshire in the UK. Brownlow's film imagined a Great Britain that the Nazi forces had successfully invaded. One of its leading actors was Sebastian Shaw, who many years later would portray ageing Anakin

Skywalker in the intergalactic war film *Star Wars Episode 6: Return of the Jedi* (Richard Marquand, 1983).

Whilst alluding particularly to the Vietnam War, in a comment at the start of an all-encompassing collection of film essays entitled *From Hanoi to Hollywood* the editors observe that war films have a 'power to make war and to destroy lives. Explicitly, it is about the power to make images that may displace, distort and destroy knowledge of the history in which those lives ... participated.' This acknowledgement readily carries over to so many other wars that cinema has chosen to interpret, dramatise and reimagine.

World War One, World War Two and the Vietnam War are the combat subjects that have most evidently shaped the public imagination of what war might look and sound like. Of course, playing its part in this aesthetic is also the relationship between literature and movies, with many novels and journalistic pieces serving as starting points for feature films about war. In turn, one generation of stories will reinvent and redefine the generations that came before.

Even now, sixty years after the end of World War Two, many films are made set during that period, almost as though its images, motifs and reference points have become a shorthand for our understanding of combat. The Second World War resulted in films being produced during the conflict that served as propaganda much of the time, in pieces such as *Objective Burma* (Raoul Walsh, 1945), *They Were Expendable* (John Ford, 1945), *The Story of GI Joe* (William Wellman, 1945) and *A Walk in the Sun*. These films simplified issues of 'good' and 'evil', with the enemy presented as barbaric and the US intervention in war as totally justified. For Jeanine Basinger, Ford's film is particularly worthy of our interest because '(the) visual power of *They Were Expendable* extends the genre and proves it through its eloquent comment on established patterns. With its sense of dignity and truth and its rejection of false battle heroics, *They Were Expendable* is almost an anti-genre film.'

Then there are the World War Two movies made after the end of war when the outcomes were known, and finally in the 1960s there were the large-scale epic films that purported towards being some kind of docu-drama projects, and films like *The Longest Day* (Ken Annakin, Bernard Wicki and Andrew Marton, 1962) and *Tora! Tora! Tora!* (Richard Fleischer, 1970) come immediately to mind. Also from the 1960s movies such as **The Great Escape**, *The Dirty Dozen* (Robert Aldrich, 1967), *Play Dirty (*Andre de Toth, 1968*), Kelly's Heroes (*Brian G Hutton, 1970*)* and *Devil's Brigade* (Andrew V McLaglen, 1970) were made, wherein the heroes were a little less upstanding and more prone to cynical behaviour. *Devil's Brigade* featured a gold heist behind enemy lines and anticipates the plot of *Three Kings* (1999). Even the western *The Wild Bunch* (Sam Peckinpah, 1967) had much in common with these war-movie escapades. At the time of writing, Quentin Tarantino is developing his long-talked-about potentially two-part movie *Inglorious Bastards*, which he has described as his 'World War Two men on a mission' film in the spirit of films such as *The Dirty Dozen* and *Where Eagles Dare*. The proposed cast for Tarantino's film may well prove the film's most interesting aspect, with the following names being raised as possibilities: Eddie Murphy, Adam Sandler, Michael Madsen, Tim Roth, Bruce Willis and Sylvester Stallone.

Fantasy and the war movie also exist readily together, perhaps never more so than in one of the great British movies, *A Matter of Life and Death* (Michael Powell and Emeric Pressburger, 1943) in which a British fighter pilot apparently dies in his flaming fighter plane over World War Two England. The film was produced, in part, as a propaganda piece, but with Powell and Pressburger at the helm the film becomes a dazzling fantasy and dramatisation of metaphysical issues that to some degree sit well alongside *A Guy Named Joe* (Victor Fleming, 1943) and the much more recent film **The Thin Red Line** (Terrence Malick, 1998). With *A Matter of Life and Death*, the directors used fantasy to suggest the dynamics of a post-war world. Other films of the period also took the cinematic road less travelled in dealing with war. *Went the Day Well* (Alberto Cavalcanti, 1942) dramatised the possibility of an English village invaded 'quietly' by German soldiers, and was based on a Graham Greene short story *The Lieutenant Died Last* that had been published in June 1940 in America. There is an intensity to the Cavalcanti film and the action includes a suitably chilling moment in which the postmistress kills one of her German soldier lodgers with an axe. Powell and Pressburger also made *A Canterbury Tale* (1944), which is, despite its surface appearance as a slightly eccentric real-world fantasy, a propaganda film with a spiritual edge. The film is set during the war but the concept of the film is to celebrate a spiritual Englishness that, at the time at least, was intended to articulate the contrast with the awful materialism of fascism.

With its great liberty to refract the present through imagined futures or alternative presents, science fiction has memorably collided with the subject of war over the years. Consider the longevity of HG Wells's novel *War of the Worlds* and its cinematic iterations, or the film project

Things to Come (William Cameron Menzies, 1953), based on the same author's work. Look also at *The Postman* (Kevin Costner, 1998) which is both western and war film. Major Russian filmmaker Andrei Tarkovsky made *The Sacrifice* (1986), in which the prospect of nuclear war propels the action in a world without a strong spiritual sense.

The war film can assume many kinds of combat scenario, from the most expected re-creations of the two world wars through to an epic samurai feud, to the outer-space 'grunts' going one on one with bio-mechanoid aliens. Some films favour the simple, straight-ahead approach, whilst others go for a more confidently expressed sense of moral complexity.

As the decades have passed, the combat war film has morphed from telling strongly fictional accounts of combat, to other films more committed to finding ways to document an actual event through the use of drama, and then to films that have found ways to reimagine battle and launch a critique of history from a 'safe distance'.

In many instances the war film is a subset of the action genre, but the war film has also been able to graft onto it a range of other generic devices so that it can be an action-adventure such as *The Guns of Navarone* or *Rambo: First Blood Part Two*, a philosophical soul piece such as **The Thin Red Line** or even a fantasy such as *Lord of the Rings: The Two Towers* (Peter Jackson, 2002) and **Aliens** (James Cameron, 1986).

By the 1960s the function of the war film was, in part at least, to dramatise the valour of the soldier. Some films began to tell war stories that presented soldiers whose values and intentions were not as clean-cut and heroic as they had been, for instance *Kelly's Heroes* and *The Dirty Dozen*. Then there was the film *M*A*S*H* (Robert Altman, 1970), set during the Korean War, which was notable for its subversion of the war film idiom, though depicting combat was not its central narrative line. The reverential approach to the war story was replaced by something rather more sceptical. Perhaps one exception to this was the film *Patton* (Franklin J Schaffner, 1970). By the late 1970s, though, the most prominent war-themed films had reverted to a super-seriousness of purpose, as shown by **The Deer Hunter** (Michael Cimino, 1978), *Coming Home* (Hal Ashby, 1978) and **Apocalypse Now** (Francis Ford Coppola, 1979) most notably. *A Bridge Too Far* (Richard Attenborough, 1977) was far more in the spirit of the 1960s docu-drama mode.

In an age when audiences are more prepared to question those 'in power', cinema has found pockets of opportunity to question the established order and consider the cost of wars fought and possible wars to come. British television offered up *Threads* in its consideration of what would come of a nuclear war when that threat seemed to hang in the air throughout the 1980s. In the early 1990s British television produced an affecting drama about the Falklands War, but still there has been no major British cinema release to explore this conflict.

In very recent years, perhaps the most high-profile mainstream films set within very recent war zones have been **Welcome to Sarajevo** (Michael Winterbottom, 1996) and *Three Kings* (David O'Russell, 1999), an action film based in the period immediately after the end of the Gulf War in the early 1990s.

Certainly, audiences expect a certain kind of tone in a war film and when honour and dignity are subverted by satire and dissent this often does not rhyme with the popular feeling. There are, of course, exceptions, as borne out in a film such as *Dr Strangelove*, produced at the height of the Cold War. Consider also the hyperkinetic comedy of *1941* (Steven Spielberg, 1979) and the small-scale satire of the more recent *Wag the Dog* (Barry Levinson, 1997) in which the American administration hire a Hollywood producer to stage a fictional war in a generic eastern European state using the latest filmmaking technology in order to boost ratings for the administration. Certainly one can object to the decision of going to war when diplomacy appears not enough to resolve a conflict, but one can only offer support and empathy to those who have gone to the battlefield.

It would be inaccurate and ignorant to think that the only wars that get screened, recorded and reimagined are the two world wars and Vietnam. Undoubtedly these films constitute a significant portion of the body of work we label as war films, and as such our general expectation is tied to our familiarity with these films. Other terrains, other conflicts and other ways of *looking* at conflict have been taken up by the cinema. For Australia, the war film has offered several key opportunities to express reservations about Australia's ties to Britain, notably in **Gallipoli** (Peter Weir, 1981) and also the film *Breaker Morant* (Bruce Beresford, 1979), which centres on a court martial during the Boer War.

We are familiar with Afghanistan as a backdrop for hyped-up Hollywood heroics in *Rambo III* (Peter McDonald, 1988) but what of films produced in that war-torn, beleaguered country that seek to explore the cost of war? Consider films such as *Baran* (Majid Majidi, 2001) and *Delbaran* (Abolfazl Jalili, 2001) both of which are set on the Iran–Afghanistan border. Perhaps the most well-known film to come out of Afghanistan recently has been *Kandahar* (Mohsen Makhmalbaf, 2001). Another film is *Jung* (Rama Rao Tatineni, 1996) that, like *Kandahar*, explores life lived under the rule of the Taliban. *Jung* is notable for its images of land-mine victims in this film about two Western doctors' efforts to create an effective medical response to the casualties.

Whilst this book considers 'fiction' films, it is worth noting that alongside these creative efforts is a vast world of documentary film about war, such as Ken Burns's vast documentary about the American Civil War. The Vietnam War was dissected in documentaries such as *In the Year of the Pig* (Emile de Antonio, 1968) and *Dear America: Letters Home From Vietnam* (Bill Couturié, 1988), and not to be overlooked is Claude Lanzmann's nine-hour documentary *Shoah* (1985) about the Holocaust. All of these films offer perspectives on the cost of conflict. These films all testify to the tensions and tragedies, cultural confusions, hatreds, mistrust and murder that have always formed part of human experience, and which show no sign of abating.

More recently, conflicts in Europe of the early 1990s have been taken on by filmmakers, for instance in **Welcome to Sarajevo** and the Oliver Stone produced *The Saviour* (Peter Antonijevic,1998). Less widely known by a fairly long way is the stunning and artful *Ulysses Gaze* (Theo Angelopoulos, 1995), one of the greatest films of the last twenty years, in which a filmmaker (portrayed by Harvey Keitel) returns to his home country and takes a road trip through the war-torn Balkans. The film exists somewhere between war film and road movie and explores the pains and costs of conflict in a way very different from most films that take war as their setting and subject. *Ulysses Gaze* lacks the hysteria that marks many war films and instead favours a thoughtful stillness, yet never avoids contemplating the violence and destruction that war creates.

Peace is the proclamation of so many war stories. Not every war film has to take place on the battlefield though. For some real homefront drama and exploration of post traumatic stress, watch *The Best Years of Our Lives* (William Wyler, 1946), *Coming Home* (Hal Ashbury, 1978), *Birdy* (Alan Parker, 1985), *Gardens of Stone* (Francis Ford Coppola, 1987), *Hope and Glory* (John Boorman, 1987) and *Forrest Gump* (Robert Zemeckis, 1994).

Sometimes the less combat we see the more room there is to measure the cost of that combat on those separated from their loved ones. Other settings have been used to make memorable comments on the futility of war but also on the bravery of those who fight. Thankfully not every war film has to be some kind of gung-ho exercise in jingoistic flag waving and macho derring-do. Even films that are ostensibly far removed from Vietnam engage with it. Travis Bickle in *Taxi Driver* (Martin Scorsese, 1976) is a threatening ex-combat soldier at war with himself and New York city, and Scorsese has often claimed that this is his Vietnam film, commenting, 'Travis Bickle was affected by Vietnam; it's held in him and then it explodes . . . any second the time bomb might go off again.'

War films suggest a loss of faith in paternal authority, social institutions and commonly held beliefs around what constitutes 'decent' human behaviour. They are about unity, terror, romance, perhaps even love lost and found.

Men and war films seem synonymous, but what of war stories with women at their heart? We can look to *So Proudly We Hail* (Mark Sandrich, 1943), *Cry Havoc* (Richard Thorpe, 1943), *This Happy Breed* (David Lean, 1943) and *Flight Nurse* (Allan Dwan, 1954) as especially memorable examples of this narrow division of the war movie during and just after World War Two. More recently Britain produced *The Land Girls* (David Leland, 1998), and *Hope and Glory* (John Boorman, 1987) and *Gardens of Stone* (Francis Coppola, 1987) all feature women as focal characters. The science-fiction combat of **Aliens** focuses on a woman at war and the Polish film **Kanal** (Andrzej Wajda, 1957) features a young woman who does all she can to pursue her freedom as Warsaw is purged by the Nazis.

For better or worse, modern war has been inextricably linked to the development of cinema and visual, dramatic storytelling. Is it not a touch unsettling to hear war zones described as theatres of war? In his book *War and Cinema*, French academic Paul Virilio writes, 'War can never break free from the magical spectacle because its very purpose is to produce that spectacle: to fell the enemy is not so much to capture as to "captivate" him, to instil the fear of death before he actually dies.'

Is it more likely that older battles will be resuscitated in the name of 'entertainment'? Historian JM Roberts talks about how mass emotion is very easily roused by mass media in the forms of the cinema, television and the press.

Whilst films set in combat zones form the focus of this book, it is worth recalling how effective films set far from the battlefield can be in defining the impact and cost of war, and the emotional wars that are waged for survival on the 'battleground of the soul', to quote Greek writer Nikos Kazantzakis. Films in this category include *Gardens of*

Stone (Francis Ford Coppola, 1987), the last third of *The Deer Hunter* (Michael Cimino, 1978), *Coming Home* (Hal Ashbury, 1978), *Hope and Glory* (John Boorman, 1987) , *This Happy Breed* (David Lean, 1944) and the second half of **Born on the Fourth of July** (Oliver Stone, 1989).

The use of the 'home front' or just the home as a means of projecting the horror of combat is a powerful storytelling device, because the terrible impact of the combat zone is brought right into the location that we are most familiar with. The sense of loss and permanent damage is powerfully, unequivocally clear. How can we forget the storyline of Steven in **The Deer Hunter**? For all of the intensity and pain such narratives can bring, these acts of cinematic remembrance and witnessing are ultimately to be thanked, for it is in these quieter stories that the rage of war perhaps makes the most sense to the audience. Oliver Stone, one of the most accomplished movie chroniclers of the Vietnam War spoke on behalf of many, if not all of the filmmakers whose work is explored in this book when he made the comment some years ago that, 'You have to make films as an idealist. You've got to make them to the greater glory of mankind.'

In this book many of the titles one might expect to see included are present front and centre, but there has also been a conscious decision to explore films a little less expected or known. There is not the space to deal with every major war film, so the task has been to indicate assured examples of the form and to suggest other film titles worth viewing. For example, in picking only one film to dramatise the American Civil War, one is immediately inclined to investigate other films about the internal American conflicts as dramatised in *The Last of the Mohicans* (Michael Mann, 1992), *The Patriot* (Roland Emmerich, 2001), *Drums Along the Mohawk* (John Ford, 1939), *Revolution* (Hugh Hudson, 1985) and *Gettysburg* (Ronald F Maxwell, 1995) to name just several key films.

At a time where film plays such a part in shaping and defining public imagination and understanding of the world, the war film has been significant in exploring the trauma, complexities and heroism that find their place in every conflict.

The war film, consciously or not, carries a significant responsibility in reimagining conflict. In his book on John Ford, Scott Eyman writes: 'For many Hollywood filmmakers, the war was a thorny psychological problem . . . For a man like John Huston, the problem was more intellectual than psychological – to hate it and glory in it simultaneously.' This is the tension that surely underscores war films even today.

Evidently, war films have long been a cornerstone of popular cinema and continue to be so with films such as *Black Hawk Down* (Ridley Scott, 2001), **Saving Private Ryan** and the recently released *Jarhead* (Sam Mendes, 2005) all pulling in the multiplex crowds. With his *Star Wars* (itself a war story) series now over, George Lucas plans his follow-up to be a war movie called *Redtails*, set in World War Two and charting the airborne endeavours of the African-American Tuskegee airmen. Clint Eastwood is currently adapting the book *Flags of Our Fathers* for the movies, telling once more of the American World War Two soldiers at Iwo Jima.

At its best the war film has been a crucible in which to pour a range of wider social issues and concerns about what it is to be human and humane. Certain films have endured with their anti-war messages, such as Abel Gance's 1938 film *J'Accuse*, one of the earliest pieces of cinema to function in this way. Gance paved the way for countless other efforts, including *The Cranes Are Flying* (Mikheil Kalatozishvili, 1957).

From the thunderous jungle adventure of **Apocalypse Now** to the cocky, juvenile bravado of **The Great Escape**; from the mournful **Kanal** to the patriotic fervour of **In Which We Serve** (Noel Coward and David Lean, 1942) the war film is global. As we know, with regret sometimes, history is typically written by the victors, and this situation never seems to go out of fashion.

For all its claims of fidelity to historical truth and detail the war film is ultimately one more way to deal with stories about human experience in which the drama plays out the possibilities and limitations of human action. Whatever the tone, style, genre or subject, films remain obsessed with one key issue – human behaviour.

With the recent popular success of several war films the genre continues to hold its place in the popular imagination. Spielberg, Malick, Coppola, Lean, Stone, Scott, Kurosawa, Weir, Wajda, Renoir, Ford. All these filmmakers and more have made war films, frequently bringing a range of other generic qualities to stories of the battlefield. Do women ever feel inclined to use film to dramatise war.

As cinema audiences look into the projector of the future, what stories of war seem to stand most strikingly on our fractured horizon? In a world where terrorism and covert combat is perhaps becoming ever more the norm, the lines between good and evil become more indistinct and we realise that the word evil is an immature and inappropriate term that denies the historical and cultural complexities that source so much conflict.

What will the American campaign in Iraq of 2003 yield cinematically over the next ten years, and will we ever see a movie scaled like *Apocalypse Now* on such a subject?

The most recent war to find a dynamic and compelling movie rendition was depicted in *Black Hawk Down*, directed by Ridley Scott from Mark Bowden's account of the combat in Mogadishu to depose the local warlord. The film, produced by Jerry Bruckheimer (an aesthetic influence not to be underestimated), is kinetic in a way that says much for the influence of *Saving Private Ryan* and, by extension, of audience familiarity with news footage from combat zones over the last thirty years. *Black Hawk Down* can be praised for its suggestion of moment-to-moment life at combat level, but perhaps fails to explore enough the political context. This is the tightrope that the war film walks, as it attempts to offer a range of expected thrills and visuals with some sense of cultural subtlety.

This book makes an attempt to consider some of the most engaging and available war films, taking into account their strength as works of cinematic expression but also their fidelity or otherwise to a specific historical moment. It charts the missions to make these notable films, considering their development, their production histories and their reception by critics and the public. It puts a number of classic war movies in the spotlight whilst also recalling less-celebrated films well worth revisiting or discovering. From Weir's *Gallipoli* to Malick's *The Thin Red Line* to the Polish classic *Kanal* and the epic pacifist drama of *All Quiet on the Western Front*, the reader will embark on a global journey through visions of conflict and images of heroism; of dangerous worlds and moments of hope, promise and understanding.

At best the war film can remind us of the trauma and warped reality that combat creates. In an age that is ever more visually orientated, where we live in a global culture where images can transcend barriers of spoken and written language, there is an opportunity to be seized for us to understand one another better. There is, of course, the human tendency to transmit images that play to our fascination with flashes of anger and violence. Surely, to borrow a phrase from American President Abraham Lincoln, the angels of our better nature can prevail. We know that our animal instinct leads to war. Our instinct also leads to re-experiencing and trying to understand the trauma of conflict. People need stories because stories help all of us carry the burden of life's pains and sorrows. The role of stories, of art, is to find ways to suggest better ways of living, or at least of ways of coping with those unavoidable conflicts.

Our job as an audience, bringing meaning to every film we watch, is to invest the imaginary worlds on our screens with an unspoken sense of futility and desperation. The war films that endure create moments amidst the fury that ignite our faith in attempts at peace, love and understanding. What we long for when we watch a war film is a sense of emotional legacy, to find the value and hope that can be picked out of the rubble.

The French director Francois Truffaut objected to the idea of making anti war films, regarding it as an impossibility because films could not help making war and combat look exciting. Images that show the horror of war in an effort to remind us of its immense tragedy have always formed a part of human expression. For example, consider the sketches and paintings that the artist Goya made.

Ultimately, this is a book about films that explore the nature of courage. Courage under fire. Courage in the shadow of death. Courage in the face of corruption. Courage in the midst of a world where reason and kindness seem to have been eradicated. These films, like so many enduring stories, remind us of how there is always the possibility that destruction and intolerance will be countered and challenged by heroic efforts to restore some trace of honour and integrity to a world sliding towards its end in which 'goodness' seems such a fragile ideal.

How this Book Works

The Virgin Film Guide: War Films selects a very small number of titles from an absolutely enormous range of possibilities. The attempt is to cover a number of films that all engage with the subject and setting of war in vivid, cinematic ways. The hope is that the films covered all provide visually arresting examples of the war film, but also of films that are rich with characterisation, ideas and emotional power.

The first three sections cover films set during the Great War (or First World War, as we more commonly refer to it today), the Second World War and the Vietnam War. Of course, there are many other wars that have been covered by films, but these three seemed to be the most fundamental and obvious places to start. A final section, simply entitled Wars in Other Worlds, widens the view to conflicts such as the American Civil War, feudal Japan and beyond.

Each film selected for this book is explored within a range of sections titled as follows:

WAR STORY: a summary of the film's storyline and key plot points.

CONCEPT/THE MISSION: a look at the circumstances in which a film was developed. Also a consideration of the creative processes and influences that came into play.

CASTING/RECRUITMENT: those who made the mission in front of the camera, with information on the casting process and listings of other films a given actor has appeared in.

BACKUP: a consideration of the crew involved in bringing the film to life.

PRODUCTION/IN THE TRENCHES: an overview of the conditions under which the film was made, including especially remarkable moments in the making of the movie.

MARTIAL MUSIC: a look at the music created or found for the film.

REIMAGINING REALITY: a consideration of the film's representation of the historical incident it depicts or draws inspiration from.

HEART OF BATTLE: a consideration of the thematic heart and soul of the film, looking at how the film has relevance and resonance beyond the surface details.

CHARACTER: a look at how the characters express themselves, the bigger ideas of the film and how they relate to one another and to the audience.

STYLE: information about the qualities that are interesting in terms of what we see and what we hear.

CRITICAL CROSSFIRE: a selection of reviews for the film encapsulating the spirit in which the film was received.

MEDALS OF HONOUR: a list of awards and honours bestowed on the film.

OTHER BATTLEFRONTS: a look at other films that relate in some way to the film being discussed in detail.

THE HOMEFRONT: notes about the film's availability on DVD.

FINAL BRIEFING: an evaluation of the film's merits, interest and impact.

FINAL SALUTE: a closing comment from a cast or crew member or someone connected to the film that honours the film.

The Great War/World War One

It is often considered inaccurate to refer to the 1914–18 war as World War One, as it is felt that other wars preceding it had a claim to be the first global conflict. It is often referred to more appropriately, especially by those who fought in it, as the Great War.

By the late nineteenth century, Europe was the dominant world power but a number of complex and interrelated social strains were beginning to emerge. For example, whereas much of Europe had advanced with the modern age, Russia had not been as progressive, and there was a sense of imminent revolution there. World War One was the Great War not in moral terms, but because of the geographical scale of the combat. The central issue of the Great War came to centre on countering and controlling the rise of German power within Europe. Many consider that 1914 ushered in what was effectively a European civil war that lasted until 1945.

The Great War had a far more convoluted genesis than that which brought World War Two into being. It began with the murder of Austro-Hungarian Archduke Franz Ferdinand on 28 June 1914 in Sarajevo. He was killed by an organisation called The Black Hand, a Serbian nationalist society that operated in secret. Immediately the Austrian government ordered that the murderers be brought to justice, and very swiftly Austria-Hungary declared war on Serbia. Serbia, though, had ties with Russia, who offered military support. In turn, Germany (eager to become more of a player on the global stage) declared war on Russia because of Germany's alliance with Austria-Hungary. Next in the chain was France, who, because of its treaty with Russia, found itself at war with Germany. Soon German soldiers were heading for Paris. Great Britain had a looser treaty with France but a moral obligation to support it in war. Other countries such as Turkey and Italy were inevitably drawn into the conflict. The United States only entered the fray in 1917 when its commercial trade routes across the Atlantic were threatened by German submarines.

All Quiet on the Western Front (1930)

127 minutes

Universal Pictures
Producer: Carl Laemmle Jr
Director: Lewis Milestone
Screenplay: George Abbott from the novel *All Quiet on the Western Front* by Erich Maria Remarque
Cinematographer: Arthur Edeson and Karl Freund
Sound: C Roy Hunter
Editor: Edgar Adams, Edward L Cahn and Milton Carruth
Music: Sam Perry (non-dialogue version), Heinz Roemheld (sound and non-dialogue version)
Art Direction: Charles D Hall, William R Schmidt
Visual Effects: Frank H Booth and Harry Lonsdale
Dialogue Director: George Cukor

CAST: Louis Wolheim (*Katczinsky*), Lew Ayres (*Paul Baumer*), John Wray (*Himmelstoss*), Arnold Lucy (*Kantorek*), Ben Alexander (*Franz Kemmerich*), Scott Kolk (*Leer*), Owen Davis Jr (*Peter*), Walter Rogers (*Behm*), William Bakewell (*Albert*), Russell Gleason (*Muller*), Richard Alexander (*Westhus*), Harold Goodwin (*Detering*), Slim Summerville (*Tjaden*), G Pat Collins (*Lt Bertinck*), Beryl Mercer (*Mrs Baumer*), Edmund Breese (*Herr Meyer*)

RATING: PG

TAGLINE: At last – the motion picture!

WAR STORY: A German town in 1914. Soldiers march off to the front accompanied by cheers and celebrations from the townsfolk. In a boys' school classroom looking out onto the main street where the soldiers march by, an ageing schoolmaster extols the apparent virtues of combat and invests all his energy in encouraging his pupils to sign up for the war. Sure enough, the boys are stirred and they quit the class for the army. One of the boys is Paul Baumer, who will emerge as the hero of the film.

The young men arrive at their army barracks and commence their relentless training programme, which strips them of their individuality.

Eventually the troops enter the combat zone, and find themselves in a village that immediately comes under attack from bombs. Making camp in the buildings of the wrecked community, the new soldiers meet the veteran troops for the first time, and the gulf between innocence and experience is there for all to see. The new troops are hungry, but food has been short for days, so one of the more charismatic soldiers, Katczinsky, goes to see what he can find. Sure enough, he returns with a dead pig over his shoulders.

The soldiers then head out for the western front and once in the battle zone begin the task of constructing barbed-wire defences on open ground. War for the foot soldier is very much about physical labour. In the barrack room underground, behind the trenches, the soldiers listen as bombs fall. Several of the younger soldiers cannot handle the pressure, but others are furious with impatience at having to wait to fight.

Battle is imminent. The men line the trenches ready to fight, the signal is given and they charge into battle. After the battle the survivors gather for food and rest, talking and joking and trying to understand why the war has come about.

Paul decides they should go and visit their injured comrade, Kemmerich, in the field hospital, but when they arrive at the converted church they find their friend has had his leg amputated. Paul stays with the despairing soldier, attempting to calm his anxieties, and encourages him to remain hopeful.

Another battle comes and Paul finds himself in a foxhole, where a French soldier attacks him. Paul kills the soldier but is then engulfed by remorse for what he has done and tries to seek forgiveness from God. He spends the rest of the battle sheltering in his foxhole.

The soldiers relentlessly march on. Paul and several of his comrades bathe in a river and talk to three French women on the riverbank. At night the soldiers go back to visit the women and Paul ends up in bed with one of them.

The army prepares for another offensive, and in the ensuing battle Paul is injured and hospitalised. He is then granted leave and so heads home to see his mother and sister. While there Paul returns to his former school, and finds the same teacher there encouraging the latest class of boys to sign up to fight. The teacher is thrilled to see Paul and asks him to share his heroic war stories with the class, but he explains there are no such stories to tell. The class are astonished and Paul leaves.

Paul returns to the front line and finds that his company is seriously depleted. He goes for a walk with his friend Katczinsky, who is injured when a bomb drops nearby, and Paul has to carry him back to base.

Paul returns to the battlefield. As he prepares to fight he sights a beautiful butterfly and reaches out to touch it. In that moment a French rifleman sights Paul and kills him. Paul's fingers fall lifelessly to the earth, just out of reach of the butterfly.

CONCEPT/THE MISSION: Erich Maria Remarque's novel is a classic anti-war text and perhaps the definitive novel about the Great War. Remarque wrote other novels but *All Quiet on the Western Front* is the one for which he is best remembered; a semi-autobiographical bestseller, its popularity was never equalled by any of Remarque's other books. The novel sold two million copies in 1929 under its native title of *Im Western nichts Neues.*

Director Lewis Milestone (Lewis Milstein originally, from the Ukraine) came to America in 1917 and served in World War One. His adaptation of *All Quiet on the Western Front* became a major popular cultural phenomenon at the time of its release, proving the degree to which cinema can occasionally make contact with the zeitgeist. The film won the Oscar for Best Picture and Best Director and raised the standing of Universal in Hollywood. Milestone went on to direct movies set during the Second World War, such as *A Walk In The Sun* (1945) and *Pork Chop Hill* (1959), which tended to be less anti-war than his acknowledged classic directorial debut.

When *All Quiet on the Western Front* was released to cinemas internationally it had a mixed reception. Released in Germany as an edited-down version, the film was attacked by the Nazi party and led to riots in the streets. Unsurprisingly, the film was banned. This same fate befell the film in Hitler's home country of Austria. By contrast, the film was very well received in Britain, though the bedroom scene, in which Paul takes a break from the horror of war and spends the night with a French woman, was abbreviated.

CASTING/RECRUITMENT: Lew Ayres famously confirmed his pacifist leanings after his involvement in the film (he was later dropped from the *Dr Kildare* TV series when his pacifist views were seen as potentially problematic). During the Second World War, Ayres became a real-life hero when he served as a medic. His film career, though, never really took off. But perhaps one great film is enough for any actor, and *All Quiet on the Western Front* ultimately stands as Ayres' defining cinematic moment. He went on to star in a number of *Dr Kildare* films between 1938 and 1945, and was Oscar nominated for his role in *Johnny Belinda* (Jean Negulesco, 1948). He also appeared in *Iron Man* (Tod Browning, 1931), and *The Carpetbaggers* (Edward Dmytryk, 1964).

In 2003, 93-year-old Arthur Gardner related his experiences of being involved in the making of the film to journalist Duncan Campbell in an interview with the *Guardian* newspaper. Gardner, who played one of the students in the classroom in the early scenes, recalled how committed everyone was to making the anti-war film.

Another young man who appeared as an extra in the movie was Fred Zinneman, who went on to direct classics such as *High Noon* (1952), *From Here to Eternity* (1953), *A Man For All Seasons* (1966), *Julia* (1977) and *Day of the Jackal* (1973).

BACKUP: Director Lewis Milestone had worked for the Photographic Division in the US Signal Corps. This role involved making training films and also photographing and indexing limbs sent from field hospitals. The influence of this experience can clearly be seen in Milestone's sense of reportage and immediacy, qualities that are apparent in *All Quiet on the Western Front*. Milestone went on to direct a number of Hollywood films, notably *Rain* (1932), *Of Mice and Men* (1939), *Pork Chop Hill* (1959) and *Mutiny on the Bounty* (1962), all of which concern units of men in one context or another. For many, Milestone's other landmark film was *A Walk in the Sun* (1945), a piece that memorably dramatised the frailties of men under pressure to achieve their mission. The year previously, Milestone had made a more overtly patriotic film called *The Purple Heart* (1944) that contrasted with the more thoughtful tone of *A Walk in the Sun*.

Milestone's 'co-director' of sorts, George Cukor, went on to direct *Camille* (1936), *Holiday* (1938), *The Women* (1939), *The Philadelphia Story* (1940), *A Star is Born* (1954), and *My Fair Lady* (1964). Whilst Milestone engineered the shots on *All Quiet on the Western Front*, it was George Cukor who rehearsed with the actors, who were often inexperienced young performers getting used to the specific demands of speaking for a sound film. Cukor would direct them in terms of line readings and gesture. To some degree, perhaps, the Milestone–Cukor collaboration was a forerunner to the similar relationship between co-directors Noel Coward and David Lean on the 1942 British World War Two film *In Which We Serve*.

PRODUCTION/IN THE TRENCHES: *All Quiet on the Western Front* was a lavish production for Universal Studios and director Lewis Milestone spared no technical or logistical expense. Much of the filming took place atop a mesa in California as the terrain was similar to that of northern Europe. Appropriately, filming began at 11 a.m. on 11 November 1929 and production lasted four months. The key locations were the Irvine Ranch, the Pathe back lot for the filming of the river sequence, and Sherwood Forest in the San Fernando Valley for the first journey to the front. The Universal back lot was used for the creation of the German village. Milestone also made use of Universal's huge crane camera, which was perfect for creating expansive shots that emphasised the scale of destruction and lost lives. Milestone also remained committed to using only one camera, and used a silent camera set up for all the film's memorable tracking shots. With sound recording still in its infancy at the time, this mobile camera constantly frustrated the sound department.

To ensure historical authenticity a former German army officer served as adviser on the project, and the practice of involving a consultant in filming has been taken up by many war films since then. Milestone and Cukor's effort to recreate a physical and emotional reality succeeds brilliantly. From all accounts, though, the pursuit of realism during filming occasionally went a little too far, and on one occasion the use of pyrotechnics caused actual injury on set, after which the crew took to wearing helmets for protection (Milestone was knocked unconscious by one blast).

The extant extra, Arthur Gardner, who had been an extra in the film, recalled how the German adviser exhibited a definite anti-Jewish view, slightly ironic given that Milestone and Cukor were both Jewish.

Several endings for the film were shot but it was ultimately the cinematographer Karl Freund who devised the symbolic final scene.

Perhaps the most poignant detail about production is that five hundred veterans of the First World War were hired to play the soldiers. Of this reality/fantasy fusion, Arthur Gardner commented in 2003, 'These guys thought they were back on the battlefield.'

MARTIAL MUSIC: The film's musical score is sparse and its absence only serves to further the sense of realism that the film is committed to.

REIMAGINING REALITY: The historian JM Roberts has suggested of World War One that the fact that 'whole societies were engaged in warfare brought with it the realisation that whole societies could be targets for warlike operations'.

All Quiet on the Western Front clarified and confirmed this sense of potential mass carnage and loss with an unsettling starkness. The film's many wide shots accentuate bombed-out villages and the images are busy with vast numbers of soldiers marching by, being tended to by nurses, or hunched over in groups gathering for the march to war.

A *Punch* magazine cartoon of 25 April 1917 showed an image of the Kaiser talking to a German recruit saying, 'And don't forget that your Kaiser will find a use for you – alive or dead.' The Kaiser is pointing the young soldier to look out of a window at the corpse factory, where even dead soldiers have a use. It is a chilling cartoon that acknowledges the brutality of war in an industrial age and the cartoon is entitled 'Cannon Fodder – And After'.

HEART OF BATTLE: Of *All Quiet on the Western Front*, Jeanine Basinger has written that 'scenes suggest that war is hell and we shouldn't be doing it, as opposed to World War Two's war is hell but we should do it and win.'

The film begins with a title card based on the text at the start of the source novel, explaining: 'This story is neither an accusation nor a confession . . . death is not an adventure.' Clearly there is a distinct point of view at work.

The film also emphasises the tedium of combat as the soldiers become frustrated at apparently waiting for ever to fight. It is a sentiment repeated in the submarine drama of *Das Boot* (Wolfgang Petersen, 1981) and many other war films where the 'mundane' is punctuated by the intensity and unreality of combat. Milestone's film is especially impressive in dramatising the loss of youth in war and also the tragedy of soldiers who don't quite understand what they are fighting for in the larger scheme of things. *All Quiet on the Western Front* is notable for being the first attempt by a non-German film to humanise the German soldiers of World War One. This effort to acknowledge that beneath national identity, helmets and foxholes hide human beings is still somewhat rare to this day, and enemies are often rendered as stereotypes or as more symbolic than actual.

When *The Deer Hunter* was released in 1978 it was widely criticised for somewhat demonising the Vietcong, though for Michael Cimino, writer/director of that film, the specifics of war are perhaps less important than the emotional, universal implications of combat and returning home from a war zone. Indeed, many war films deal more with the general than the specific aspects of a given conflict.

CHARACTER: Paul Baumer is the young protagonist who, in the course of the film, goes from innocence to experience, recognising the awfulness of war that he had previously considered to be a grand adventure. Baumer's critical moment, his epiphany if you like, comes when he experiences deep remorse on the battlefield after killing a French soldier. As Baumer lies in the foxhole next to the dead body he asks for the corpse's forgiveness and also for the forgiveness of God, asking, 'Why should they send us to fight each other?'

Paul is essentially still a boy and as such the experience and tragedy of war is felt all the more acutely. At the very end of the film, when Paul returns to his company and looks at the faces of the exhausted soldiers, it is their youth that is most striking.

Baumer embodies both the political and the spiritual side of war. Midway through the film he struggles to understand, along with his fellow soldiers, why there is a war at all, and what it is that starts wars. Is it that one country offends another? One soldier says war benefits manufacturers and industry. The plight of these soldiers seems all the more tragic due to their ignorance of the cause of their fighting.

Towards the end of the film, as Paul addresses the class of boys, he essentially delivers a monologue on the futility and waste of war. For Paul, what is most sickening about his experience is not the battlefield but the inculcation of young minds with the idea that war is glorious. Paul says to the teacher in the class, 'You still think it's beautiful and sweet to die for your country, don't you? It's dirty . . . now they're sending babies . . . every day a year, every night a century.' The truth, as we have seen, is that the experience of war is miserable, arduous, angst-ridden and soul-destroying.

Paul Baumer is the first in a long line of pacifist war film characters that leads all the way to the transcendentally minded Witt in *The Thin Red Line* (Terrence Malick, 1998), the gentle, intellectual Corporal Upham in *Saving Private Ryan* (Steven Spielberg, 1998), Chris Taylor in *Platoon* (Oliver Stone, 1986), Ron Kovic in *Born on the Fourth of July* (Oliver Stone, 1989), and the idealist Dave in *Land and Freedom* (Ken Loach, 1995). For all the varied territories and nationalities, the war film often re-explores the same sense of how a young adult grows into an awareness of life's hard truths. Thus the experience of going to war becomes a metaphor for life in general.

The schoolteacher represents the danger of indoctrination, persuading the boys to enlist, telling them they are 'the life of the Fatherland'. He is a pompous buffoon at the start of the film, and by the end he is revealed as ignorant and crass.

The source of the new recruits' anger and frustration is the pompous ex-postman turned sergeant, who tells the new recruits to 'Forget everything you ever knew.' Sure enough, the sergeant's efforts to discipline the newly enlisted soldiers, many of whom he knows from his home town, are met with derision.

As with all war films, the combat unit is a mixture of innocence and experience. The gruff, middle-aged Katczinsky embodies the experienced soldier, his initial cynicism giving way to a warmth and ragged paternalism that we can trace from here right through to films such as *In Which We Serve, Das Boot, The Thin Red Line* and *Saving Private Ryan.*

STYLE: *All Quiet on the Western Front* is striking in its ambition, the scale of its set design and the 'luxury' of its frequent backward-tracking shots to reveal the sheer size of a location. Perhaps the most affecting shot early in the film is the wide shot of the classroom, with its window framing the street beyond as the mass of German soldiers march by en route to war, anticipating the later clash of these two worlds as the boys sign up for battle.

All Quiet on the Western Front was one of the first war movies to benefit from the advent of sound. Indeed much of the action is made all the more forceful by what we hear, notably the sound of bombs falling and guns firing. As Paul lies in a foxhole it is the sound of shelling that most terrifies him. In *La Grande Illusion* (Jean Renoir, 1937) a similar comment is made about noise being the source of greatest terror and unease.

The battle sequences are marked by a dirty, grimy quality and also a startling energy as the camera tracks over the trenches and alongside the soldiers as they hurtle into battle. These sequences are particularly chilling and foreshadow the battle scenes at the beginning of *Saving Private Ryan*, a film that makes a point of showing the same griminess and dirtiness of war we see in Milestone's film.

All Quiet on the Western Front, along with countless other titles that followed, also shares certain affinities with the horror film. During one of the massive battle scenes there is a throwaway detail that stays in the mind. A soldier is blown up and the shot holds for the smoke to clear to reveal just the soldier's hands remaining, hanging onto a strip of barbed wire. The film unflinchingly shows the horror of amputation and surgery. Even Paul screams out as he is taken to surgery, shouting out that he will not die.

Alongside the fury and bloodshed of battle Milestone's film also plays up the quiet, desperate moments such as when the young soldiers in the bunker are terrified by the sounds of bombs and explosions. By contrast the film's closing, lyrical image places new life and death in the same gentle moment as Paul reaches out to a butterfly on the field of battle. Paul's young life is as brief and bold as the life and colour of a butterfly.

CRITICAL CROSSFIRE: For the *Time Out Film Guide* 'the film's strength now derives less from its admittedly powerful but highly simplistic utterances about war as waste', whilst *Variety* felt that it should 'be shown to every nation every year until the word war is taken out of dictionaries'. *Leonard Maltin's Movie and Video Guide* commends the film for being a 'vivid, moving adaptation of Erich Maria Remarque's eloquent, pacifist novel'.

MEDALS OF HONOUR: *All Quiet on the Western Front* won the 1930 Academy Awards for Best Director and Best Picture and was nominated for Best Cinematography and Best Screenplay. In 1990 the film was included in North America's National Film Registry of films preserved by the American Congress.

OTHER BATTLEFRONTS: *All Quiet on the Western Front* marks a moment in cinema when there was recognition of the need to communicate the reality of combat. Milestone's film took a distinctly pacifist stance, as did two other films that followed soon after, *Journey's End* (James Whale, 1930) and *Westfront,1918* (Georg Pabst, 1930). The 1920s had been marked by a kind of 'romanticism', a tendency to use the Great War as a backdrop for a wartime romance in titles such as *Woman to Woman* (Graham Cutts, 1923, and Victor Saville, 1929) and *Mademoiselle from Armentieres* (Maurice Elvey, 1926). The other kind of story that war films of the 1920s often dealt with (and understandably so) was to explore the experience of men struggling to cope with life after combat in films such as *Blighty* (Adrian Brunel, 1927) and *The Guns of Loos* (Sinclair Hill, 1928). *All Quiet on the Western Front* brought an end to a decade of such films by aiming for a more graphic depiction of soldiering life. The Great War continued as a subject for

Hollywood films right through to the early 1940s. The film *Sergeant York* (Howard Hawks, 1941) starred Gary Cooper as country boy Alvin C York who goes off to fight in World War One and learns why it is necessary to go into combat. The film was the top-grossing Hollywood film of the year.

Towards the end of the twentieth century and into the early years of the twenty-first, the Great War has continued to appear as a war-film setting. In 2004 a French romantic epic was released entitled *A Very Long Engagement* (Jean Pierre Jeunet, 2004). Jeunet's film was popular worldwide with its story of a young woman tirelessly searching for her fiancé who has gone missing from the battlefields of the Somme. *A Very Long Engagement* substantiates the observation that war films are often ways of framing a range of other genres and the film harks back to the romance war films of the 1920s. When Ernest Hemingway's novel *A Farewell to Arms* was transferred to the screen by Frank Borzage in 1932 he was angry by the film's positive ending after it had been depicting the travails of an Italian ambulance corps. The British film *Regeneration* (Gilles Mackinnon, 1997) was a compelling film that failed to find a wide audience. There were also *The Trench* (William Boyd, 1999) and *Deathwatch* (Michael J Bassett, 2002).

Milestone's own World War Two film, *A Walk in the Sun*, again examines the pressures of warfare on a unit of men and often uses sound more powerfully than images to express the intensity, violence and rupture of battle. *A Walk in the Sun* benefits from a supremely simple story that covers a six-hour period as an American unit land on the Italian coast and then make their way to secure a farmhouse. The trek, the odyssey, becomes a journey of the heart and, without depending on rhetoric, quietly offers up its pacifist, anti-war message.

THE HOMEFRONT: War films have always been popular and the film was a huge success when initially released, breaking box-office records in its first week and making back its $1.2m very swiftly. The film's success also encouraged the film industry to invest ever more in synch sound.

For the re-release of the film in 2003 the Library of Congress in the United States restored the film, stripping away additional music and sound effects that had been added to the soundtrack, and the muddled sound of bomb blasts and gunfire. In Britain, the 2003 release was the first time the complete, coherent film had been issued.

All Quiet on the Western Front is available on DVD at a running time of 129 minutes. The film was reissued in the 1940s and for television with 35 minutes cut from the original running time. In 1998, based on the wishes of the late Lewis Milestone who died in 1980, Universal Pictures restored thirty minutes of material. The non dialogue version of the film was restored by America's Library of Congress.

FINAL BRIEFING: *All Quiet on the Western Front* is a bleak film (consistent with its source material) that so clearly charts the journey from promise to despair. It confidently balances the larger sequences with the quieter ones and reminds the audience of how emotionally fragile humans become under combat, how easily crushed and warped the soldier is by the battlefield. The film also succeeds in visualising that essential reality: the vast number of young men who were churned out as cannon fodder.

All Quiet on the Western Front is just one of many stories and narratives derived from World War One. Poetry has a particular associaton with this war in the words of Wilfred Owen (1893–1918). Owen died at the Somme just a week before the armistice. Rupert Brooke was revered as a poet during the conflict, notably for 'The Soldier', one of his five 'War Sonnets'. Brooke died of blood poisoning. The American poet TS Eliot wrote his epic poem *The Wasteland* partly in response to the Great War.

All Quiet on the Western Front creates a mood and sensibility of romanticism around the young men lost to war. This image of lost youth, of forlorn hope you could say, frames the film, its central portion committed to capturing the visceral and unrelentingly grim and earthy battlefield with an immediacy that to some degree steps away from the artifice of a Hollywood film. The closing image of *All Quiet on the Western Front* shows the soldiers looking over their shoulders back at us. The soldiers have become ghosts, haunting us so we never forget. The film's sincerity is present from start to finish and even though some of its proclamations might now appear very simplistic, the film is successful in relentlessly describing the exhaustion of war.

FINAL SALUTE: 'And our bodies are earth. And our thoughts are clay. And we sleep and eat with death.' Paul Baumer, portrayed by Lew Ayres.

La Grande Illusion (1937)

117 minutes

World Pictures Corporation
Producer: Frank Rollmer and Albert Pinkovitch
Director: Jean Renoir
Screenplay: Jean Renoir and Charles Spaak
Cinematographer: Christian Matras and Claude Renoir
Editor: Marguerite Marthe-Huguet
Music: Joseph Kosma
Production Design: Eugene Lourie
Sound: Joseph de Bretagne
Costume Design: Decrais (René Decrais)

CAST: Erich von Stroheim (*von Rauffenstein*), Jean Gabin (*Marechal*), Pierre Fresnay (*Boeldieu*), Marcel Dalio (*Rosenthal*), Julien Carette (*The Actor*), Gaston Modot (*The Engineer*), Jean Daste (*The Teacher*), Georges Peclet (*French soldier*), Jacques Becker (*English officer*), Sylvain Itkine (*Demolder*), Dita Parlo (*Elsa*), Werner Florian (*Sergeant Arthur*)

RATING: U

WAR STORY: French pilot Marechal is off duty at his airbase when he is given a mission to go and take a series of photos of enemy territory. Marechal takes off with his captain, Boeldieu, and the next time we see them is at a German airbase, having been shot down and captured. The German commandant invites his prisoners to share a meal with his men. The Frenchmen accept and are then transported to a German prisoner-of-war (POW) camp.

The new prisoners are instructed about the kind of behaviour and discipline expected of them, and life in the barracks quickly falls into a routine. Marechal and the captain are then told by some veteran prisoners that they are digging an escape tunnel. Although it seems well planned, it goes wrong and one prisoner is shot for trying to escape.

A variety show is staged by the men for their fellow POWs. During the production Marechal, who is behind the scenes, reads a newspaper and learns that a French city, Douamont, has been retaken from the Germans by the French. Marechal interrupts the entertainment, tells the news and then leads the soldiers in singing the 'Marseillaise', to the disgust of the German soldiers.

Marechal is put into a cell for a while for his defiance of camp rules and he rages at the guard. On his release the camp guard informs the prisoners that they are to be transported to another camp.

The new camp is a high mountain fortress in deepest Germany. The commandant of the camp is the very soldier whose men had shot down Marechal and the captain during their surveillance mission. Marechal, Boeldieu and another prisoner (Demolder) are addressed by the commandant about their numerous previous escape attempts. He speaks to the men with respect, but warns them that this fortress will not be escaped from.

The men begin to plan an escape from the fortress, a scheme that revolves around distracting the guards by getting the prisoners to play music loudly on flutes. The plan kicks into action and, sure enough, the guards confiscate them. There is then a roll call and all prisoners are marked present. Another round of singing occurs fifteen minutes later and the guards react again. This time Marechal and Rosenthal (another POW) escape. Boeldieu defiantly plays the flute while the commandant warns him to stop, an act of defiance that leads the German to shoot him.

Boeldieu, seriously injured by the gunshot, is treated by a nurse in the commandant's chambers but dies there, the commandant standing by the bedside.

In the German–Swiss borderland, Marechal and Rosenthal sleep in ditches and bicker their way across the hills and fields. Marechal eventually leaves the struggling Rosenthal but then returns to help him continue. The men reach a hilltop farmhouse and are taken in by a widow and her young daughter. The men soon become part of daily domestic life, helping out on the farm, and Marechal falls in love with the woman. Eventually he and Rosenthal must leave. They push on through the snow and are spotted by German soldiers. As they are about to gun the men down, their commander orders them to stop – the fugitives have crossed the border into neutral Switzerland. Marechal and Rosenthal run on.

CONCEPT/THE MISSION: Jean Renoir is universally considered one of the greatest filmmakers of all time. His work is defined by both great humanism and an understated visual brilliance and fidelity to realism. Renoir's father was the painter Auguste Renoir, and Jean Renoir appears in some of his paintings as a child. As a young man, Renoir had fought directly in World War One in the dragoons. He was seriously injured by a sniper and a surgeon was about to amputate his leg, but Renoir's mother was so insistent this did not happen that the surgery was not performed and Renoir limped for the rest of his life. Having recuperated, Renoir returned to battle, this time as a pilot.

The concept for *La Grande Illusion* came from a story that Renoir heard from a French soldier who had escaped eight times from prisoner-of-war camps. Renoir interviewed other prisoners of war and devised the scenario with his regular writing collaborator Charles Spaak. The other key source for the film was an experience that Renoir had when shooting his film *Toni* (1935) near a French airbase. Renoir's filming was hindered by the sound of aircraft and when Renoir met the base commandant he discovered that he had been the pilot who had often provided fighter cover for Renoir's reconnaissance plane during the war.

Film producers were not especially keen on Renoir's proposed anti-war project. It took three years for him to secure finance for the film and the backing eventually came from Rollmer and Pinkovitch, neither of whom were involved in the French film industry. One thing that eventually helped raise the money was the interest of major French film star Jean Gabin, who was to play Marechal. The film had in fact been entitled *Les Evasions du Capitaine Marechal*. In an early draft of the screenplay, the story concluded with a rendezvous at Maxim's in Paris arranged after the war to which nobody comes.

Despite Renoir's experiences and injuries as an aviator in the First World War, he had not directly experienced life in the trenches. By the 1930s cinema and culture was already in the process of finding a sense of nobility and honour in the Great War and *La Grande Illusion* plays its part in that cultural expression.

When *La Grande Illusion* was premiered in 1937 at the Venice *Biennale* festival, Joseph Goebbels attempted to persuade Mussolini to stop the film winning a prize. As a reaction to this the jury created the International Jury Prize to award the film instead. Goebbels was so irritated by *La Grande Illusion* that he called the film 'cinematographic enemy number one'. For its German release, Rosenthal, the Jewish soldier, was edited out, as the film presents him sympathetically and in human terms. The film was shown at the New York exhibition in 1939 and then more widely across America, with President Roosevelt urging people to see it for its democratic impulse. The film was a huge popular success and in 1958 was released for the third time in France in its definitive form.

CASTING/RECRUITMENT: Renoir worked with a number of regular French actors and his films have always been celebrated for the richness and subtlety of their performances. When Eric von Stroheim came on board the commandant's role was minor, occupying not even five minutes of screen time. When Renoir learned that von Stroheim wanted to be involved, he immediately developed the role to the point of significance and meaning it now carries. Renoir, Spaak and Jacques Becker 'secretly' rewrote the script whilst filming was under way so that the character featured more powerfully. It was von Stroheim who suggested the character should have a neck brace.

Jean Gabin also collaborated with Renoir on *La Bete Humaine* (1938), based on the Emile Zola novel of the same name, and also starred in *Pepe Le Moko* (Julien Duvivier, 1937) and *Le Chat* (Pierre Granier-Deferre, 1971).

Julien Carette worked with Renoir again in *La Bete Humaine* and *La Regle de Jeu* (1939), a story of romance and the French aristocracy. Pierre Fresnay appeared in countless films throughout a long career.

Eric von Stroheim had an enduring career as a star actor and director. Perhaps his most famous film as director was *Greed* (1924), adapted from the novel by the late, great (and barely known, it seems) Frank Norris. Von Stroheim had appeared in films since 1915 after starting out as an extra, and famously appeared in *Sunset Boulevard* (Billy Wilder, 1950).

BACKUP: The cinematographer on *La Grande Illusion* was Christian Matras, for whom the film was a major early career project. Matras went on to shoot films until the early 1970s in France. Amongst his many credits are *Le Dernier Tournant* (*The Last Turn*, Pierre Chenal, 1939) and *Le Beau Voyage* (Louis Cuny, 1947).

Charles Spaak, Renoir's co-screenwriter on the film, wrote *Le Dernier Tournant* and *Le Pere Goriot* (Robert Vernay, 1945).

PRODUCTION/IN THE TRENCHES: *La Grande Illusion* was shot between late January and April 1937. The scenes in Germany were filmed at Alsace, at the barracks at Colmar, Neuf-Brisach and the castle at Haut Koenigsburg. Filming in the studio at Billancourt and the 'clair Stuidos, Epinay followed.

MARTIAL MUSIC: The film uses music sparingly and it is most fully used to underscore journeys to the prison camps and also the final sequences of the film at the hillside farmhouse. The composer Joseph Kosma went on to score *La Bete Humaine*.

REIMAGINING REALITY: The film's incidents were inspired in part by research that Renoir undertook and, whilst set during the Great War, reflects the tensions of the mid-1930s that would eventually lead to World War Two. At the time of the film's production there was a hope that perhaps Germany would not want to 'retaliate' for its loss in the First World War. In 1937, Renoir proudly stated his pacifist stance and could not stand the aggression of Hitler.

HEART OF BATTLE: *La Grande Illusion* is an incredible film and provides an exciting opportunity to see a different kind of war movie.

Just like Kubrick's later ***Paths of Glory*** (1957), also set during World War One, *La Grande Illusion* extensively explores and dramatises the class divisions that wartime can accentuate. What Renoir's film dwells on most powerfully is the attempt by individuals in war, even when in opposition to one another, to maintain respect. The film celebrates the potential for human kindness and generosity. When Marechal rages in his cell the guard comes in and just sits and talks with him, leaving his harmonica behind for Marechal to play.

Music and art (performance, illusions) are ways of easing the pain and maintaining some decency in the world of war, as well as providing a means of escape. When Marechal and Rosenthal find solace in the German farmhouse they prepare for Christmas and play music on the gramophone, and the trauma of war temporarily ceases to exist. For a moment, at least, they create a perfect world.

Human pettiness and politics are finally discussed as Marechal and Rosenthal prepare to make one last bid for freedom. Rosenthal observes, 'Man invented frontiers, not Nature,' when Marechal notes how the landscape all looks the same. The film's plea for unity and an attempt to understand our common bonds is expressed from the first moment to the last.

CHARACTER: *La Grande Illusion* uses the prison camp setting as a microcosm of the world. It's an age-old device and it continues to work brilliantly. Working-class men live and survive alongside aristocratic soldiers. Marechal is the focal character of the film, with whom the audience is encouraged to identify, and he makes the film's rallying cry when he says, 'We've got to finish it off, this damned war . . . even though we hope it's the last.' Marechal also becomes the romantic hero of the film in its final movement when he falls in love with the widow. As he leaves her he painfully tells Rosenthal that if he looks back at her he may never get away. Marechal also makes a keen and understated observation about the most haunting aspect of prison life: 'It's not the music or instruments that get you, it's the marching feet.'

Given how often German commandants and soldiers are stereotyped in the film canon of the Great War, it is interesting that *La Grande Illusion* abandons national pigeonholing and puts the more specific context of war aside, exploring instead the issue of how people's values are defined by their class.

The commandant is reluctant to serve as the terrifying overlord and instead goes out of his way to conduct himself humanely, in part as a sign of his aristocratic lineage. His commitment to gentility and civilised behaviour is never more touching and quietly celebrated than in the scene where he talks with Boeldieu about the bloom of just one flower that is able to grow within the fortress. The flower comes to symbolise the possibility and hope for friendship and understanding. The commandant even comments that 'My men are not young but they enjoy playing soldiers.' He feels disgusted by the job he has and, as Boeldieu lies dying, the commandant asks him for forgiveness for having shot him. To which the captain replies, 'I would have done the same. Duty is duty.' Like the commandant, Boeldieu is of aristocratic descent; he acknowledges the courage of the 'enemy' and does all he can to avoid violence. The men's relationship is based on this shared understanding of the social class they have been shaped by.

Throughout the film different characters are marked by their social status but there is still a sense that unity, or at least understanding, can be achieved. Perhaps Boeldieu's most insightful comment comes as he watches the young German soldiers marching whilst the French prisoners he is with prepare to put on a show. He remarks, 'On one side children playing at soldiers, on the other soldiers playing like children.' His overriding rule is that 'sentiment has no place in war'.

In such a male-dominated film, the one female character endures in the memory. A war widow, she longs for male company and very reluctantly says goodbye to Marechal.

STYLE: Of his approach to the film Renoir commented that 'I toed the line absolutely, and technically sought no innovation. The only innovations are in the style of the actors . . . in pushing further . . . a kind of semi-improvisation . . .'

Film writer Raymond Durgnat has commented that the film 'deploys a European complexity of symbolism with an American speed'.

The film has momentary similarities with *The Great Escape* (John Sturges, 1963) in the way it presents the men's efforts to dig their way out and how they get around being discovered as they make their tunnel.

For the tender love that emerges between Marechal and the widow there is a moving shot as Rosenthal watches them from a doorway, not wanting to interrupt their fleeting, precious time together.

The film uses a lot of comedy to weave through its more tragic narrative aspects, none more comic than the energetic bits of business during the POWs' efforts to go unseen as they dump the soil from the tunnel. And there is humorous dialogue, such as when Boeldieu observes that just as a golf course is for playing golf, and a tennis court for playing tennis, then so too a prison is for escaping from.

Another expressive image that tellingly shows the emptiness that war brings to bereaved families is the shot of the German girl sitting at the family table. She is alone, and two chairs are upturned, never to be filled.

CRITICAL CROSSFIRE: For Pauline Kael, '*La Grande Illusion* has an immediate, idealistic aim . . . *La Grande Illusion* poetry . . .' For the *Time Out Film Guide*, 'The Grand Illusion, often cited as an enigmatic title, is surely not that peace can ever be permanent, but that liberty, equality and fraternity is ever likely to become a social reality rather than a token ideal.' Similar praise is awarded by *Leonard Maltin's Movie and Video Guide*, which says of the film, 'Beautiful performances enhance an eloquent script.'

MEDALS OF HONOUR: Renoir's film won Best Overall Artistic Contribution at the Venice Film Festival. In 1938 the film won the National Board of Review (USA) award for Best Foreign Film. *La Grande Illusion* was Oscar nominated for Best Picture in 1939.

OTHER BATTLEFRONTS: *La Grande Illusion* was released at a time when Europe was becoming aware of the growing threat of fascism. The Spanish Civil War had proved the dangers of expanding right-wing activity and the need to resist it in order to protect democracy. The 1930s and early 1940s were marked by a range of films designed to remind audiences of the threat of fascism. The film *Espoir Sierra de Ternel* (*Days of Hope*, directed by Andre Malraux, 1939) warned audiences of the impending danger of another huge war. In Hollywood, films such as *Escape* (Mervyn Le Roy, 1940) *Foreign Correspondent* (Alfred Hitchcock, 1940) and *The Great Dictator* (Charlie Chaplin, 1940) were made as anti-war films. In Russia, Sergei Eisenstein, who had directed *Battleship Potemkin* (1925) made *Alexander Nevksy* (1938), which was, beneath the surface drama, an anti-Nazi piece. At the same time, in Germany the famous and notorious film *Triumph of the Will* (Leni Riefenstahl, 1935) had been released. Riefenstahl's *Triumph of the Will* uses the backdrop of the Olympics to create images of physical perfection and accomplishment that could be seen as consistent with the drive at the time under Hitler to create a perfect Aryan race.

THE HOMEFRONT: *La Grande Illusion* is available in the UK as one of three Renoir films on DVD. In North America, the film is available on DVD featuring a newly restored digital transfer, a rare theatrical trailer and even an essay by Erich von Stroheim about Renoir.

FINAL BRIEFING: *La Grande Illusion* is characterised by its humanity and the subtlety of its message that human kindness is possible in a world of differences. It has its moments of excitement, but the truly spectacular effects are of the heart and mind. The film is celebratory of humanity yet does not avoid showing the cost of war and conflict. It does so quietly by not showing the field of combat but rather the impact of war on the sidelines and in the home.

This film makes immense (and successful) efforts to portray both sides as human and capable of respect and integrity. This is perhaps the gentlest war film ever made and, whilst it shows hardly any violence at all (the only visible bloodshed coming towards the end), the film is always mindful of the cost of war. However, it also emphasises that life goes on, with all its sadnesses, friendships and loves found and lost. Rather like the Polish film *Kanal* (Andrzej Wajda, 1957), Renoir's film seems sadly lost to the younger film audiences of the new millennium. Both of them are compelling stories of escape and human endurance.

FINAL SALUTE: For Jean Renoir the film in part countered the terror of the Nazis who 'almost succeeded in making the world forget that the Germans are also human beings'.

Film scholar Andre Bazin wrote that Renoir 'has inherited from the literary and pictorial sensibility of his father's era, a profound, sensual and moving sense of reality'.

The film director and all-round moviemaking wunderkind Orson Welles commented that: 'If I had to save only one film in the world, it would be *La Grande Illusion.*'

Paths of Glory (1957)

86 minutes

United Artists
Producer: James B Harris, Kirk Douglas
Director: Stanley Kubrick
Screenplay: Stanley Kubrick, Calder Willingham and Jim Thompson (based on the novel *Paths of Glory* by Humphrey Cobb)
Cinematographer: Georg Krause
Editor: Eva Kroll
Music: Gerald Fried
Production Design: Ludwig Reiber
Costume Design: Ilse Dubois
Visual Effects: Erwin Lange

CAST: Kirk Douglas (*Colonel Dax*), Ralph Meeker (*Corporal Paris*), Adolphe Menjou (*General Broulard*), George Macready (*General Mireau*), Wayne Morris (*Lieutenant Roget*), Richard Anderson (*Major Saint-Auban*), Joseph Turkel (*Private Arnoud*), Timothy Carey (*Private Ferol*), Peter Capell (*Colonel Judge*), Susanne Christian (*The German Girl*)

RATING: PG

TAGLINE: It explodes in the no-man's land no picture ever dared cross before!

WAR STORY: The setting is a chateau in France. It is 1914, France is embroiled in the early months of the Great War and French troops are immersed in attempting to repel the German forces. General Broulard arrives at the chateau to meet with General Mireau. Broulard wants Mireau's men to begin their next counteroffensive and take the German-held ground, the Anthill. Mireau is uneasy about this, but when he is told by Broulard that he is being considered for promotion to oversee the 12th Corps, Mireau instantly shifts from appearing doubtful to being certain that his men can take the difficult Anthill target.

In the trenches the French soldiers are visited by General Mireau, who has arrived to see them prepare for their assault on the Anthill. The general meets Colonel Dax and explains the Anthill mission to him. Dax is unhappy about the mission, especially as Mireau explains that he will not be able to offer Dax's troops any initial backup, and it is noted that more than half of Dax's men could be killed. Dax's scepticism grows. He challenges Mireau's plans and unsettles him with his articulate, low-key subversion. Mireau informs Dax that he is so lacking in confidence he will be relieved of his post, so Dax then says that he and his troops will take the Anthill. Dax goes to his subordinates and wishes them luck for the mission to be undertaken the next day.

That night three soldiers go on a reconnaissance mission towards the Anthill. One of them, Lejean, is accidentally killed by Lieutenant Roget. The drunk Roget, realising that he has killed one of his fellow soldiers, flees back to base where he is confronted by the other officer he was with, who insists that Roget explains what has happened. The lieutenant says he will cover up the death in the paperwork to avoid taking the punishment for the death of Lejean. When Dax asks Roget how Lejean was killed, he tells him that machine-gun fire was responsible.

Dax briefs his soldiers on their mission, telling them they will have to hold the Anthill all day before reinforcements can be sent in. As they wait for the attack to begin one very philosophical soldier, Private Arnoud, talks to another about fear of death and fear of pain, and reasons that the fear of pain is more frightening than the idea of death.

The next morning General Mireau is present as the attack on the Anthill is to begin. Dax blows his whistle and leads his men over the top of the trenches to make their assault. However, many troops, realising how dangerous the mission is, remain in the trenches. In his anger, and wanting to avoid any embarrassment on his part, Mireau orders his battery commander to begin firing on the French troops who remain in the trenches. The battery commander refuses to do so without a written order.

Realising that his men are not attacking, Dax runs back to the trench to see what is happening. Lieutenant Roget tells him it is an impossible mission to undertake because of the casualties they will incur. As it becomes impossible to stop the soldiers retreating, Mireau demands a court martial for what has occurred that morning.

At the chateau Dax is questioned on the actions of his men. Broulard is less insensitive than Mireau, who refers to the soldiers as 'scum'. Mireau wants to shoot a hundred men as an example, but Dax says that he should be the one to be shot. Eventually, Mireau agrees to the suggestion that only three soldiers be taken to court martial. Dax asks to be counsel for the accused.

Paris, Arnoud and Ferol are the three soldiers selected to be court-martialled, for showing cowardice in the face of the enemy. Dax goes to see them and explain the severity of the situation. Mireau then talks to Dax and wants him to drop the case, saying that Dax is acting disloyally.

In the chateau the court martial proceeds with alarming speed. Dax challenges the process as a sham and unjust, and pleads for mercy on the men's behalf, but they are sentenced to be shot.

The three condemned men are visited by a priest, but tensions flare and Arnaud is concussed in a scuffle. Paris then breaks down. Dax appoints Lieutenant Roget to be in charge of the firing squad as a means of getting back at Roget for his drunken irresponsibility and cowardice the night before the doomed attack on the Anthill.

Dax then learns of Mireau's plan to have shelled his own soldiers in the trenches. Dax tells General Broulard of Mireau's desperate intention, and hands over the battery commander's signed statement confirming it.

The next morning the three soldiers are marched out to face the firing squad. Mireau watches smugly as the men are shot dead.

Back at the chateau Broulard informs Mireau that he knows of his attempts on the battlefield to gun down the 'cowardly' soldiers, and tells him he will now be brought before an enquiry. Broulard then offers Dax the post that Mireau held, but he rejects the offer.

Dax goes into town where he sees his soldiers relaxing in a bar, where a beautiful young German woman sings for them. Dax receives instructions that it is time for the men to return to duty. He goes to his office to prepare to fight another day.

CONCEPT/THE MISSION: *Paths of Glory* was based on a novel of the same name by Humphrey Cobb, which had been a bestseller in 1935. The title comes from a line in the poem 'Elegy Written in a Country Churchyard' by Thomas Gray, which reads 'The paths of glory lead but to the grave.' With his earliest films, such as *The Killing* (1956), Stanley Kubrick had shown profuse evidence of his skills as a director, in terms of both technical assurance and an engagement with the human elements of a story. *Paths of Glory* elevated his standing yet more and would lead to the larger-scale projects that began in 1960 with *Spartacus* (though Kubrick does not regard *Spartacus* as a personal film).

For Kubrick, *Paths of Glory* was a test of confidence in his commitment to the film. He was finding it hard to raise the necessary funding, but had a breakthrough when Kirk Douglas read the screenplay and agreed to star in the film.

The novel centres on the three young soldiers throughout, but the film takes Dax as the protagonist – the soldiers only appear in the last third of the film as Dax does all he can to save them from a desperate fate. The film was banned for political reasons from being screened in France for eighteen years.

CASTING/RECRUITMENT: By the time that Kubrick made *Paths of Glory*, Douglas had begun to establish his film career and the 1950s and 1960s were his richest period. He had appeared in *The Glass Menagerie* (Irving Rapper, 1950), *The Bad and the Beautiful* (Vincente Minelli, 1952), *20,000 Leagues Under the Sea* (Richard Fleischer, 1954), the fabulous *Lust for Life* (Vincente Minelli, 1956) and *Gunfight at the O.K. Corral* (John Sturges, 1956) before *Paths of Glory*, and went on to make *The Vikings* (Richard Fleischer, 1958), *Spartacus*, *Lonely are the Brave* (David Miller, 1962), *The Heroes of Telemark* (Anthony Mann, 1965) and *The Fury* (Brian De Palma, 1978).

Adolphe Menjou had acted in films since the silent era and *Paths of Glory* was one of his last features. He also appeared in *Gold Diggers of 1935* (Busby Berkeley, 1935) and *Pollyanna* (David Swift, 1960).

George Macready appeared in many films over a long career, including *Vera Cruz* (Robert Aldrich, 1954), *Taras Bulba* (J Lee Thompson, 1962) and *Tora!Tora!Tora!* (Richard Fleischer, 1970).

Joe Turkel later puts in an appearance as the bartender in Kubrick's adaptation of the Stephen King novel *The Shining* (1980).

BACKUP: Kubrick's writing partners Calder Willingham and Jim Thompson were both relatively new to cinema at the time *Paths of Glory* was produced. As a result of their work on the film they both developed their writing careers. Willingham had a short tour of duty in the development of the script for *The Bridge on the River Kwai* (David Lean, 1957) but Lean did not take to Willingham's contributions. Willingham went on to script *The Vikings* and did uncredited work on the screenplay for *Spartacus*. He also wrote *The Graduate* (Mike Nichols, 1968), *Little*

Big Man (Arthur Penn, 1970) and *Thieves Like Us* (Robert Altman, 1973).

Jim Thompson went on to become a successful novelist, writing two books that both eventually became films. One was *The Getaway*, which Sam Peckinpah adapted into a 1972 film starring Steve McQueen and Ali McGraw, and the other book was *The Grifters*, brought to the screen by Stephen Frears in 1990.

PRODUCTION/IN THE TRENCHES: When Kirk Douglas came onto the project he wanted to star in the film as Dax, and with his name attached United Artists Corporation forwarded one million dollars towards the film's small budget. The film was shot entirely in Germany, with interiors shot at Geiselgasteig Studios in Munich and the chateau and battle scenes filmed forty minutes from there. When Kubrick was faced with 600 extras for the battle scenes, rather than direct them en masse he divided them into segments and told them to die in their allocated zone. For the soldiers, Kubrick enlisted German police.

MARTIAL MUSIC: The film begins with a military drum and then the playing of the 'Marseillaise' with pomp and circumstance. Throughout the rest of the film music is not used to characterise the drama any further. Only in the film's closing moments does music return and with powerful effect.

REIMAGINING REALITY: Kubrick's film is made vital and authentic by its location work. The battlefield sequence, though quite brief, sits well alongside the recreation of the First World War battlefield of *All Quiet on the Western Front*. Where Kubrick's film presents French soldiers, Milestone's focuses on Germans, but there is barely any difference in the moral dilemmas they face. They are all the same soldier.

HEART OF BATTLE: For *Paths of Glory* war is presented as an issue of class, of hierarchies in battle with the 'working class' (the troops in the trenches) being exploited. In his book *The Penguin History of the World*, JM Roberts observes that 'There are even signs that many Europeans were bored by their lives in 1914 and saw in war an emotional release purging away a sense of decadence and sterility.' Certainly the chateau is a place of plenty and comfort, not to say decadence, for the military commanders. Like Milestone's film, too, there is no effort to muddy the clear storytelling by having the actors mimic French and German accents. The class tensions hinted at in Kubrick's film also recall some of the issues at play in *La Grande Illusion*.

Paths of Glory can be readily compared with *All Quiet on the Western Front* in that both films grapple with national identity via dealing with foreign combatants. Savage decisions are made and savage, inhumane opinions are expressed within the chateau, an emblem of civility and delicacy.

There is something perhaps surprisingly spiritual at work in the film. The image of the three soldiers as sacrifices is somehow made most telling in the character of young soldier Arnoud, who is actually tied to the post whilst lying on a stretcher. There is something especially Christlike about his buckled, battered body at this moment, and the sight of the three men attached to posts recalls images of the Crucifixion.

The film's conclusion, as the soldiers sit singing, recalls the line of the German writer Goethe, who observed that 'Where there is music there is no evil.'

CHARACTER: The central character is Colonel Dax who, prior to serving in the French army, was once a first-rate criminal defence lawyer. The skills of his past are about to become part of his present. Dax's battle does not take place in the trenches but in the court martial, and with his immediate superiors as he undertakes a very personal mission to ensure that justice and humanity are upheld in a time of war. This moral mission is echoed much later in film history in the film *Casualties of War* (Brian De Palma, 1989). In that film a young soldier persists in challenging his superiors and reports the gang rape of a Vietnamese girl by the other men in his unit. A court martial ensues.

Dax finds himself compromised throughout his experience and his resolve to counter the *Schadenfreude* and absence of decency is his heroic act. Dax finds himself negotiating in a world where people are unable to see beyond blind adherence to the rules. Discipline and order are only good up to a point, the logic of orders and commands only as valuable as the morality driving them. Dax is a humanist who confidently and quietly confronts Mireau's cruelty towards the soldiers. This confrontation forms the bedrock of the drama that unfolds as Dax strives to retain, if not restore, a basic sense of respect for human life within the context of his immediate military surroundings. Dax makes a stand against the corruption he perceives around him, making a number of impassioned statements throughout the film. Quoting Samuel Johnson, Dax tells Mireau, 'Patriotism is the last refuge of the scoundrel.' Mireau is angered by Dax's quiet, educated, liberal intelligence. In the court martial Dax expresses his shame at being a human and calls the proceedings a 'stain' and a 'disgrace' on the integrity of the military.

General Mireau is undoubtedly the clearly defined 'villain' of the piece. He is a man whose concern for his troops is secondary to his pursuit of military glory. Early in the film, though, when offered the possibility of career advancement if successful in the mission, Mireau replies to Broulard, 'What is my ambition against that.' It is false humility, as the film will reveal. Mireau's inflated sense of self will be his undoing.

General Broulard is an apparently affable officer who ultimately is riddled with a corrupt outlook on life. Broulard tells Dax that 'one way to maintain discipline is to shoot a man now and then'. Broulard will not confront the failings of the military. Indicative of the film's strain of black humour, Mireau's visit to the troops in the trenches early in the story is both terrifying and starkly comic. When Mireau is confronted by a soldier with shellshock, he says, 'I won't have any brave men contaminated by him.' When he realises the troops do not want to make the assault on the Anthill he rather comically rages, 'If those little sweethearts won't face German bullets, they'll face French ones.' After the firing squad have done their work, Broulard perversely and sadistically comments to Mireau that 'your men died very well'.

The soldiers who are put on trial are very much victims of corruption. One is easy in his thinking about the distinction between fear of death and fear of pain. Another is something of an innocent and the other is a man who for all his stoicism is ultimately as fragile as anyone. Feraud, one of the three soldiers put on court martial for cowardice, makes the telling comment that he is a soldier who outside of the army is considered a 'social undesirable'. It's a throwaway comment that says so much and echoes a similar line of thought in *Platoon*.

STYLE: *Paths of Glory* is rendered with a precision and thoughtfulness that integrates sound and vision, character and theme. According to critic Alexander Walker, 'The fact that some favourably compared the film to the work of Max Ophuls is one measure of Kubrick's growth as an artist.' The camera deals indirectly with events in the chateau to reflect the indirect dealings of the commanding staff with the situation.

The savage mindsets of Mireau and Broulard are emphasised by their contrast with the delicacy and civilised surroundings and décor of the chateau.

For all the dynamism of the battle and trench scenes and the austerity of the court martial, perhaps the most affecting and beautiful image is the peaceful tableau-like image of Ferol on his knees at confession with the priest as sunshine falls onto him through the window of the barn. There is an immaculate quality to the light that contrasts with the grime and desperation of the trench and the corruption of the chateau.

Kubrick's celebrated camera tack through the trenches offers us a point of view of the anxious, desperate soldiers as Dax passes them. There is a grim inevitability to this shot design, as though Dax is being inexorably pulled along towards death. A similar sense of how the camera can be used is at work in the Polish war film *Kanal*. Late in *Paths of Glory* the tracking point-of-view shot is used again as the three soldiers approach the place where they will be shot by the firing squad.

Fundamentally a small-scale character piece, Kubrick's film opens out visually in the battle sequence. The scene in which the soldiers assault the Anthill is notable for the tracking shot that carries the audience across the battlefield. The black-and-white photography recalls documentary footage of the First World War, images that audiences would have been familiar with. During the night scene, when the wrong-headed reconnaissance mission is undertaken, the battlefield is appropriately apocalyptic but also bizarre (Kubrick's 1987 film, *Full Metal Jacket*, would amplify this unreal aspect of war zones). Jutting out of the earth is a mysterious object, the identity of which the soldiers are unsure of, later revealed as a fallen fighter plane. War turns the world into something unreal both physically and emotionally. All is distorted.

Despite the expanse of the battlefield and the opulence of the chateau, the most striking scenes in the film are often played out in the shadow and half-light of bunkers and stables. An arresting close-up of Dax late in the film expresses his intensity of feeling. In the final moments of the film we are also offered a close-up of a soldier shedding a tear as he sits listening to the German woman singing. The soldier is no more than a boy.

CRITICAL CROSSFIRE: *Paths of Glory* was released on 25 December 1957. For Bosley Crowther of the *New York Times* the film carried 'an impact of hard reality . . . a frank avowal of agonising, uncompensated injustice is pursued to the bitter, tragic end'. Looking back, the *Time Out Film Guide* raves, saying the film is 'unusually trenchant for its time . . . The critique of military hypocrisy and misguided strategy is laid out in an ultra-lucid exposition.' The hits keep coming with *Leonard Maltin's*

Movie and Video Guide saying that this 'shattering study of the insanity of war has grown even more profound with the years'.

MEDALS OF HONOUR: The film was nominated in the category of Best Film at the BAFTAs in 1958. It was also nominated for Best Screenplay at the Writers Guild of America Awards in 1958. Perhaps most tellingly the film was included on the National Film Register by the National Film Preservation Board (USA).

OTHER BATTLEFRONTS: *Paths of Glory* served as Kubrick's breakthrough film. It connected with a more mainstream audience and it further proved his value to the studio system in Hollywood. It would, though, be thirty years before Kubrick returned to the subject of modern warfare with *Full Metal Jacket*. Released just twelve months after Oliver Stone's **Platoon**, which had been considered a watershed moment in the cinema of Vietnam, Kubrick's very different approach to the same conflict perhaps lost some of its impact as a result. Kubrick, as with all his films (and he only ever made thirteen features in all), had been in development on *Full Metal Jacket* for some years. Michael Herr has recalled how intrigued Kubrick had been by the term Full Metal Jacket in an arms catalogue. The director found the term 'poetic'.

Full Metal Jacket is notable for its intense coldness of emotion, especially in its first part where the recruits go through the hell of boot camp. Adapted from a slim novel called *The Short Timers* by Gustav Hasford, Kubrick suggested a title change, as many would not appreciate the military lingo for the period of time for a Vietnam tour of duty in which every day was marked off with a Magic Marker pen on a calendar. The title *Full Metal Jacket* refers to the copper casing for lead bullets, allowing them to feed better into a gun and also to stop the lead expanding inside the body as per the ruling of the Geneva Convention on war.

Full Metal Jacket is notable for also interpolating some of Michael Herr's journalism. Herr, of course, made a very significant contribution to **Apocalypse Now** (Francis Ford Coppola, 1979). *Full Metal Jacket* was shot in southeast England (Kubrick was famous for not being keen on travelling far afield with his films). In Beckton, east London, a former gas works site became the city of Da Nang for the combat sequences, and the training camp sequences that begin the film were shot at Enfield. *Full Metal Jacket* filmed for five and a half months, and hundreds of Vietnamese were brought in as extras and tropical plants were imported and distressed appropriately. The film's production designer was Anton

Furst, who went on to create the sets for *Batman* (Tim Burton, 1989). Intriguingly, Kubrick had planned to follow *Paths of Glory* with another combat film about a lost patrol called *Fear and Desire*.

In the early nineties Kubrick considered making a film called *The Aryan Papers*, based on the novel *Wartime Lies* by Louis Begley. The narrative was a World War Two story in which a mother and her son attempt to escape the Holocaust. However, Kubrick abandoned the project, feeling that Spielberg's *Schindler's List* (1993) had already covered much of this subject. Joseph Mazello, the little boy from Spielberg's *Jurassic Park* (1993) had been due to play the boy with possibly Julia Roberts or Uma Thurman playing the mother. Perhaps most famously, the war film project that Kubrick put into development but got no further during the 1960s and 1970s was his proposed epic about Napoleon, for which he had written a 186-page screenplay in 1969 and then collaborated further with Napoleon expert Professor Felix Markham of Oxford University. The project never came to light, even though Kubrick had committed to much research and pre-production planning around costumes and the logistics of such a huge production. In an interview with Joseph Gelmis in 1969, Kubrick explained that Napoleon's battles as described in written history and art were 'so beautiful, like lethal ballets'. Equally compelling to Kubrick would have been the prospect of dramatising Napoleon's obsession with Josephine. Obsession, of course, characterises many Kubrick protagonists.

THE HOMEFRONT: *Paths of Glory* is readily available on DVD and includes the original theatrical trailer for the film.

FINAL BRIEFING: *Paths of Glory* is astonishing for the skill of its image making and structure, but also for its combination of spectacle and small-scale, intense human conflict. The film, for all its desperation of character, is marked too by several blackly humorous lines that do much to indicate the film's criticism of military hierarchy and corruption. The film carries a liberal message without sentimentality. The courtroom drama sequence fits so well with both the scenes of combat and the scene dealing with the three soldiers' reactions to their fates. The film assumes a spiritual dimension not immediately signalled and its black-and-white photography complements the shadings of good, evil and compromise.

This is surely one of the most assured and thoughtful of war films. It is not really concerned so much with the First World War but far more with the archetypal human issues that war stories can express. It is the same kind of approach that characterises a wide range of other movies including such disparate titles as *The Cruel Sea* (Charles Frend, 1953), *The Deer Hunter* (Michael Cimino, 1978) and *The Thin Red Line* (Terence Malick, 1998). Kubrick is often tagged a cold filmmaker, but *Paths of Glory* is rich with humanity, acknowledging its capacity for kindness, but also for cheap cruelty and inhuman behaviour.

On the day that Stanley Kubrick died in March 1999, Steven Spielberg screened a sequence from *Paths of Glory* for friends as a tribute at his house.

FINAL SALUTE: For Kubrick, 'The soldier is absorbing because all the circumstances surrounding him have a kind of charged hysteria . . . It's difficult to say who is engaged in the greater conspiracy – the criminal, the soldier or us.'

Gallipoli (1981)

110 minutes

Paramount (Australia)
Producer: Rupert Murdoch, Robert Stigwood and Patricia Lovell
Director: Peter Weir
Associate Producers: Martin Cooper, Ben Gannon, Su Armstrong
Screenplay: David Williamson (based on a story by Peter Weir)
Cinematographer: Russell Boyd
Editor: William Anderson
Music: Brian May
Production Design: Wendy Weir
Art Direction: Herbert Pinter
Costume Design: Terry Ryan and Wendy Weir
Visual Effects: Chris Murray
Military Adviser: Bill Gammage

CAST: Mel Gibson (*Frank Dunne*), Mark Lee (*Archie Hamilton*), Bill Kerr (*Uncle Jack*), Bill Hunter (*Major Barton*), Frank Dunne (*General Gardener*), Harold Hopkins (*Les McCann*), Ronnie Graham (*Wallace Hamilton*), Heath Harris (*Stockman*), Gerda Nicholson (*Rose Hamilton*), Robert Grubb (*Billy*), Tim McKenzie (*Barney*)

RATING: PG

TAGLINE: From a place you've never heard of . . . a story you'll never forget.

WAR STORY: Western Australia, May 1915. Eighteen-year-old Archie is being trained by his Uncle Jack in preparation for an athletics competition later in the week. Jack psyches Archie, up telling him to 'run like a leopard'. Archie's hero is the Australian athlete Harry Lasalles.

Working on the farm, one of the farmhands, Les, mocks Archie for his running interest. Archie bets that he can beat Les on his horse across the farmland in a race – as Archie runs barefoot, so Les must ride bareback. Les is thrown from his horse late in the race and Archie wins, his feet torn to shreds by the cross-country run. His Uncle Jack is angry at Archie for injuring himself so close to race day. The subject of the war comes up and Archie tells his uncle that he wants to enlist, but Jack reminds him that he is too young, and anyway Jack doesn't want him to.

The scene changes to a camp for railroad workers. A group of young men sit around talking about the little they know about the war going on in Europe. They all want to enlist except Frank Dunne, but eventually he tags along, saying that going to war is probably better than being stuck in the middle of nowhere on the railroad.

Frank arrives in town and competes in the sprint that Archie has come to race in. Archie wins, and the next day he meets Frank and they strike up a friendship. Archie has not been allowed to enlist in the Light Horse Brigade because he is under age. Frank says that if he went to Perth he could try to enlist there, so they jump a train, but find themselves marooned in the desert, fifty miles from the nearest habitation. Frank is quite prepared to wait two weeks for the next train to come by, but Archie is not and begins walking the desert. Frank follows and eventually they find a farmhouse, clean themselves up and head into Perth. Archie enlists, but Frank does not make it into the Light Horse Brigade, so he signs up for the infantry.

The scene changes to July 1915, the Australian training camp in Cairo, Egypt. In the shadow of the pyramids Frank undergoes training. They are marched into the desert and stage a mock training battle with the Australian Light Horse, where he meets Archie again. Frank asks to be transferred so that he can serve alongside his friend and his wish is realised.

The newly arrived Australian troops sail into the beach at Gallipoli where Australian and New Zealand soldiers are already in action. Frank and Archie soon get used to the military battlefront routine. Archie is asked by his commanding officer, Major Barton, to be a messenger because of his speed as a runner, but Archie declines, saying he wants to fight in the imminent battle. Frank is charged with the position of messenger instead. Battle comes and the Australian soldiers are slaughtered by the Turkish forces. There is tension between the commanding officers in the trench and their superiors who cannot see what a bloodbath is going on. Frank takes a message to explain how desperate the situation is. A senior officer considers calling the attack off, but the message does not arrive in time. Frank realises it is too late as Archie and hundreds of young soldiers advance on the Turks. Archie rushes across the battlefield.

CONCEPT/THE MISSION: The film *Gallipoli* derives its narrative from the book *The Broken Years* by Bill Gamage and the *War Histories* of CEW Bean. *The Broken Years* was an anthology of letters and diary entries of Australian soldiers.

For director Peter Weir, *Gallipoli* marked his career shift from art-house features to mainstream acknowledgement. Taking on such a nationally recognised and resonant subject as the ANZAC (Australian and New Zealand Army Corps) defeat in Turkey during World War One when the British enlisted troops from their empire (now the British Commonwealth) to fight, Weir had the backing of media entrepreneurs Rupert Murdoch and Robert Stigwood. Weir developed the screen story and Australian playwright David Williamson wrote the script with Weir's involvement. The story focused on the moment during the Great War that prompted the growth of Australian resentment towards Great Britain. Of the approach that he and Williamson took to dramatising this historic event Weir has said, 'By approaching the subject obliquely, I think we had come as close to touching the source of the myth as we could.'

Gallipoli capped the explosion of new Australian filmmaking that had begun in 1970 when, under John Gorton, the government established the Australian Film Development Corporation. For Weir, *Gallipoli* was his 'graduation film'. Prior to this film he had made dreamy, offbeat movies such as *The Cars that Ate Paris* (1974), *Picnic at Hanging Rock* (1975) and *The Last Wave* (1977). *Gallipoli*, in depicting a military disaster in the First World War, carries echoes of **Paths of Glory**.

In 1975 Weir took a drive to Gallipoli to see the site of the battlefield, where he walked through the trenches and found belts, buttons, and an Eno's Fruit Salts bottle. These details all find a home in the subsequent film.

Initially Weir and Williamson developed a first draft of the screenplay, which began with enlistment in 1914 and ended with the evacuation of Gallipoli at the end of 1915. But Weir felt that this approach was not 'getting at what this thing was, the burning centre that had made Gallipoli a legend'. When Weir could not construct the story around a number of specific historical moments, he and Williamson decided to create a fictional account of how two young men meet in the months immediately before they go into combat.

The Light Horse regiment was chosen for the film because they had fought at the Battle of the Nek, which is the battle referenced in the film's ending.

One of Weir's compelling traits to the film enthusiast has been his willingness to talk about his influences, frames of reference and 'inspiration'. When being interviewed at the time of *Gallipoli*'s release, Weir discussed how the writing of Carl Jung (*Man and His Symbols* et al.), Thor Heyerdahl and Emmanuel Velikovsky (*Worlds In Collision*) had all been important to his sense of the spiritual.

CASTING/RECRUITMENT: *Gallipoli* provided Mel Gibson with one of his earliest major roles. He had recently appeared in *Mad Max* (George Miller, 1979), a performance that had inspired Weir, and went on to appear in its sequels *The Road Warrior* (George Miller, 1982) and *Beyond Thunderdome* (George Miller/George Ogilvy, 1985). The romantic, epic tone of *Gallipoli* has in more recent years become a feature of two of Gibson's own directorial efforts: *Braveheart* (1995) and *The Passion of the Christ* (2004). As an actor Gibson has starred in *The Year of Living Dangerously* (Peter Weir, 1982), *The River* (Mark Rydell, 1984), *Lethal Weapon* (Richard Donner, 1987), *Forever Young* (Steve Miner, 1992) and *The Man Without a Face* (Mel Gibson, 1992). Gibson's performance in *Gallipoli* is lively and moving and exhibits his taste for the goofy expression for comic effect.

Mark Lee had won the role of Archie as a result of a photo call for a Gallipoli brochure. Unlike Gibson, Lee had not appeared in a feature film previously.

BACKUP: The cinematographer on *Gallipoli* was Russell Boyd, whose other credits include *The Last Wave*, *The Year of Living Dangerously*, *Tin Cup* (Ron Shelton, 1996) and *Master and Commander: The Far Side of the World* (Peter Weir, 2003).

The film represents the only film that Rupert Murdoch ever produced.

PRODUCTION/IN THE TRENCHES: The *Gallipoli* battle scenes were filmed at Port Lincoln in Australia and the sequence set around Archie's rural homestead was filmed at Beltana in Western Australia. En route by plane to Beltana, Weir spotted Lake Torrens, which was subsequently used for the West Australian desert scenes.

The film was not shot entirely in Egypt because of the logistical problems of getting white extras. The film features around 4,000 extras, though for the battle scenes themselves around 700 extras were used. Military advisers worked on the film and they drilled the actors and extras in how to clean weapons, wield their guns and march. On set Weir would supply extras with notes about the specifics of the battle they were recreating.

During his visit to the battleground sites at Gallipoli, Weir swam in the sea off the coastline and felt a sense that soldiers swimming there would be somehow below the battlefield in a world separate and unaffected by human conflict. There is a brief sequence in the film where the soldiers swim in the water and it has the quality of a dream, of an unreal moment. In some ways, Weir's conception of the natural environment as part of the characters' odyssey in *Gallipoli* is echoed in the work of filmmaker Terrence Malick in his film *The Thin Red Line*.

MARTIAL MUSIC: As with all of Peter Weir's films, music is richly deployed, whether material composed specifically for the film or sourced from elsewhere. *Gallipoli* combines an original score by Brian May with a number of recognisable pieces of music, primarily classical. Weir uses these pieces to heighten the tragic tone of the later scenes of battle and the anticipation of conflict. This very romanticised use of the music rhymes with the visuals.

The music that the film uses includes *Oxygene* by Jean Michel Jarre, a very modern piece of synthesised music, the *Adagio in C Minor for Strings and Organ* by Albinoni, *The Pearl Fishers* by Bizet, and *Tales from the Vienna Woods* and *Roses from the South* by Strauss. Nicolo Paganini's *Centore di Sonata* also features.

REIMAGINING REALITY: The battle that Weir's film builds towards was the Battle of Sari Bair (also known as the Battle of the Nek) and it was fought from 6–10 August 1915. Forty-five thousand ANZAC troops were involved in action, but were overwhelmed by the terrain and intense heat. Seven Victoria Crosses were awarded to ANZACS for hand-to-hand combat with the Turks.

At Gallipoli the tragic cost of life numbered around 2,700 of the New Zealand troops and the Australian casualties numbered 26,000, including 8,000 killed. Soon after Gallipoli, ANZAC troops went to serve on the Western Front on the European field of war. For the Turks who fought against the Allied troops the death toll was around 87,000. Kemal, the Turkish hero of Gallipoli, went on to become the Founding President of The Turkish Republic. Alongside the tragic loss of life, Gallipoli served to further strengthen the bond between New Zealand and Australia.

The title *Gallipoli* has an emotional resonance for an Australian audience, rather in the way that the Alamo speaks of a tragic defeat to an American audience. The Gallipoli defeat is legendary in Australian military history and folklore, and the film dramatises the resentment that Australians felt towards being part of the British Empire and hence having to fight in a war by default. The character of Frank embodies this stance. Indeed, as a result of the Gallipoli tragedy, the Australian people voted 'No' to conscription twice in a referendum in 1916, and this is seen as a vital moment in Australia's emerging identity as a nation separate from the British Empire.

As Frank tells eager Archie, 'It's not our bloody war! It's an English war. It's got nothing to do with us.'

HEART OF BATTLE: At the heart of *Gallipoli* is a theme that appears in countless combat-set war movies, namely the bonding between young men. For some, David Williamson's screenplay offers a critique of Australian masculinity. Others have identified a suppressed homosexual relationship between the two men, which the film deals with by having Archie die.

The film's archly romantic story of young men (boys, really) moving from innocence to experience to death is a theme popular with certain World War One poets, such as Rupert Brooke and Wilfred Owen.

The theme of lost innocence was revisited by Weir in *Dead Poets' Society* (1989).

CHARACTER: The film's primary focus is the friendship between Archie and Frank. Archie is a patriotic and idealist character, qualities that provide the source of his life's tragedy. From the beginning of the film he is keen to enlist, seemingly unaware of the larger cultural clash between Australia and Great Britain, of which Frank has some understanding. Archie, like Michael in **The Deer Hunter**, is something of a nature boy, attuned to the turning of the earth and the land.

Frank is cocky, quick-thinking and cynical. Like Archie, his whole life is ahead of him and Frank does what he can to protect that. His anxious, desperate messenger sprints late in the film contrast with his playful, goofy behaviour earlier on as he and Archie cross the Australian desert on foot. The most telling gesture Frank offers in the film is his refusal to salute a British officer, an indication of Frank's frustration at British rule of Australia. 'I am not going to fight for the British Empire,' Frank protests early in the film to Archie. Both Archie and Frank are drawn as romantic young men.

Rather like Mireau in *Paths of Glory*, the commanding officer Robinson is relentless in ensuring his men attack, even though there are reservations about the wisdom of that.

STYLE: Weir's commitment to telling a war story in a highly accessible, realist and transparent manner is seemingly at odds with his typical lyricism. That said, *Gallipoli* engaged Weir with populist filmmaking, a skill he developed with *The Year of Living Dangerously* and then parlayed into one of the most distinctive American film-industry careers of the last twenty years. Weir went on to direct *Witness* (1985), *The Mosquito Coast* (1986), *Dead Poets' Society* (1989), *Green Card* (1992), the brilliant and almost always forgotten *Fearless* (1993), *The Truman Show* (1998) and, most recently, *Master and Commander* (2003).

Weir has always imbued nature with a sense of mystery and majesty. Early in the film Archie is associated utterly with the land, his face first seen in the glorious sunset as he trains to sprint with his Uncle Jack. Later in the film, Archie and Frank climb the pyramids at Cairo by sunset and sit on top of one in silhouette with a dazzling sunset sky behind them. Their characters become universal and their story of coming to understand the world and its desperate side through war is made common to all of us.

The arrival of the soldiers by night at the coast of Gallipoli has a muted quality to it, not filled with terror like the Omaha Beach landing in *Saving Private Ryan* or, indeed, any kind of excitement. Instead, it is an almost unreal moment.

The film's battle sequences have stillness and energy and movement to them. Like those in *Paths of Glory* and **All Quiet on the Western Front** they portray the claustrophobic and messy nature of the situation. By contrast, the image of the Australian defences arriving by night on the coast, rendered simply as dots of light with a trail of lights rising and falling across the ship moored just off the beach, is both dazzling and magical.

Weir has always favoured images over dialogue in communicating the biggest ideas. The farmhand, Les, who had been so cocky at work on the farm, stands next to Archie in the trenches crying as they prepare for battle. Before the soldiers go over the top into their final battle, they hang their watches and wedding rings from the swords they leave in the trenches. The watch symbolises the fleeting lives of its young, heroic characters. Like Archie and Frank's sprint, the lives of the young men are short-lived.

The film begins with the sound of Archie's breathing as he prepares to run. It closes with Archie motionless, captured in freeze-frame as he runs for his life. In the freeze-frame he is memorialised.

CRITICAL CROSSFIRE: Pauline Kael referred to the film in 1982, just a year after its American release, as 'a well executed academic exercise on the subject of the waste of war'. The *Time Out Film Guide* wrote at the time of the film's release that Weir's efforts were 'buoyed up by a fulsome nationalistic fervour . . . the Gallipoli reconstructions are impressively done'. For *Leonard Maltin's Movie and Video Guide* the film offers 'engrossing human drama with meticulous direction [and a] striking feel for period detail'.

MEDALS OF HONOUR: The film won the 1982 Australian Cinematography Society award for Best Cinematography and at the 1981 Australian Film Industry Awards the film swept the board, winning for Best Cinematography, Editing, Sound, Actor, Supporting Actor, Director, Screenplay and Best Film. At the 1982 Golden Globes the film was nominated for Best Foreign Film.

OTHER BATTLEFRONTS: The film that most readily comes to mind to reference to *Gallipoli* is *All Quiet on the Western Front*. Whilst stylistically very different, it invests the same energy in expressing the youthfulness of the soldiers who enlisted, often idealistically.

THE HOMEFRONT: *Gallipoli* is available on VHS and DVD.

FINAL BRIEFING: Weir's film is stunningly simple in its plot, typical of many war films, and the emphasis is on dramatising the mindset with which young men entered the First World War. In its story of young men having their innocence pulled from their hearts and minds the film has strong ties with the Vietnam-set *The Deer Hunter* and *Born on the*

Fourth of July. The film takes time to immerse us in the world of the characters, so that when we see them on the brink of combat we have a real sense of the world they are leaving behind, possibly for ever. Like *The Thin Red Line*, the film possesses a lyrical quality we might not normally equate with the pace and frenzy of most war films.

FINAL SALUTE: Peter Weir commented that 'I wanted to give the film that more abstract start – it was an interesting way to approach a great European war.'

World War Two

With Germany rebuilding and rearming itself after the 1914–18 war, it found itself ultimately more powerful still. Concurrent with this was the evidence that Japan was consolidating its position as an economic and industrial force. The key concern was whether a way could be found to control Germany without resorting to war. France and Britain opted for an economic blockade initially. Before its process of rebuilding, Germany had fallen into depression and nationalist and socialist interests came to the fore.

By 1930 the Nazis were demonstrating their power in Germany. There was growing support from them across the board, it seemed. Anti-communists supported them. Nationalists who wanted to rearm Germany supported them. Most disturbing at this point was that the Nazi party succeeded in eliminating the democratic institutions. The Nazi party controlled and intimidated its people just as it would go on to do the same across Europe in a chilling way that recalled pogroms of the Middle Ages.

Whether World War Two could ever have been avoided is still open to contention and debate. Starting in 1930 Hitler began to fulfil his ambitions to see Gemany supreme again. Fearing the might of Germany in central Europe, Mussolini made Italy an ally of Germany. Through the early 1930s Hitler sought to bring Germany to a point when it was ready and able to begin rearmament and he announced this process was underway in 1935. Things moved swiftly from there. Austria was annexed in 1938 and in 1939 Germany occupied Poland. Because Great Britain and France had promised to protect Poland against any invasion when the German forces moved into the country, Britain and France stood by their commitment and declared war on Germany.

In Which We Serve (1942)

115 minutes

Two Cities (UK)
Producer: Noel Coward
Director: Noel Coward and David Lean
Associate Producer: Anthony Havelock-Allan

Screenplay: Noel Coward, based on the experiences of Lord Louis Mountbatten
Cinematographer: Ronald Neame
Editor: Thelma Myers
Music: Noel Coward
Art Direction: David Rawnsley
Visual Effects: Douglas Woolsey

CAST: Noel Coward (*Captain Kinross*), John Mills (*Shorty Blake*), Bernard Miles (*Walter Hardy*), Celia Johnson (*Alix Kinross*), Kay Walsh (*Freda Lewis*), Joyce Carey (*Kath Hardy*), Michael Wilding (*Flags*), Penelope Dudley-Ward (*Maureen Fenwick*), Philip Friend (*Torps*), Derek Elphinstone (*Number One*)

RATING: U

TAGLINE: The greatest motion picture of all time!

WAR STORY: *In Which We Serve* begins with a montage of shots of the destroyer the *Torrin* being constructed. The crew are then shown on deck, with the flag being raised, as the ship is ready for service.

May 1941, off the coast of Crete. The *Torrin* is engaged in combat and the German ships are being defeated, when they take a hit from a German fighter. 'We got him, but I'm afraid he's got us too,' declares Kinross. The ship begins to sink, but a small number of the crew, including Kinross, swim to a dinghy and hold on for as long as they can. As they drift on the waves the crew remember their time serving on the ship and their time on land with their families and loved ones.

Kinross's recollections establish him as a family man whose paternal qualities carry over into his treatment of his crew.

Walter Hardy remembers his time at home with his wife Kath and his mother-in-law before the war, as Kath wonders whether or not war can be avoided.

Kinross is then shown addressing his crew and explaining how he aims for a happy and efficient ship. The crew are given three days to prepare it for sailing.

We then hear the prime minister's radio announcement declaring that Britain is at war with Germany.

In the present, as Kinross and his surviving crew float on and around the dinghy, they watch as their ship sinks further beneath the waves. Kinross recalls Christmas Day on the ship and we then see Shorty, Walter and Kinross celebrating their respective Christmas Days when the ship was in port for repairs.

The men continue floating on the dinghy as German planes fly over and take shots at them. Walter gets hit and sustains an injury. As he passes out he remembers the moment he met his future wife. The story then returns to Shorty's past and details how he and his wife, on their honeymoon, met Kinross on a train.

The next flashback is of the *Torrin* in combat at night, before it has to be towed home for further repair. Kinross thanks his crew for their hard work and admonishes one sailor for not staying at his post during combat. We see Freda and Shorty saying goodbye as he readies to leave shore once again.

The *Torrin* is then charged with picking up a number of soldiers from Dunkirk. Kinross insists on his crew showing respect to the Army, and to avoid the usual light-hearted jibes and putdowns about one service being better than another. The *Torrin*'s crew look after the troops and return them safely home.

In the Hardy household Kath refuses to move to the country in spite of the air raids. Staying with her is Freda, who is pregnant. A bomb strikes the house. Back on ship, Shorty receives a letter from Freda telling him he is now the father of a baby boy, but that Kath and her mother have died in the air raid. Shorty has to break the news to Walter.

Back in the present, the men watch the *Torrin* finally sink. A British destroyer passes by and picks up the survivors. Kinross tends to his wounded and dying men, taking their home addresses and promising to write home with news of fatalities.

At home, a telegram arrives from Shorty informing Freda that he is safe. Kinross's wife receives a similar telegram from her husband. As Kinross addresses his crew for the last time in Alexandria, he tells them he has come to say goodbye, and that the fight goes on.

The film concludes with shots of British Navy ships on the high seas as a voice-over celebrates the bravery of British sailors. Another ship is launched with Kinross at the helm.

CONCEPT/THE MISSION: *In Which We Serve* is distinctive not only as a major British war film of the Second World War, but also for being David Lean's directorial debut, on this occasion in collaboration with

Noel Coward. Lean had worked his way up to the role of director from the soundstage floor via the role of editor, a route that has often led to highly effective and visually economic and dynamic film directors. *In Which We Serve*, whilst adopting a typically British naturalistic approach, reveals a number of promising visual flourishes that Lean would develop over the next forty years. Lean would follow *In Which We Serve* with two more war-themed movies *This Happy Breed* (1944), about south London working-class family life over twenty years up to the Second World War, and then *Blithe Spirit* (1945). Lean went on to direct one of the most famous war films, **The Bridge on the River Kwai** (1957).

In Which We Serve was based on the service record of a British destroyer, the *Kelly*. The story of the *Kelly* was recounted initially to writer Noel Coward by Lord Mountbatten, whom Coward knew socially. Coward had been inspired by the Mountbatten couple for his one-act play *Hands Across the Sea* (1936). Coward was so moved by Mountbatten's recollections that he was sure it would form the basis of an affecting feature film, a format that Coward had not worked in before. The resulting film tells both the life of the ship from yard to seabed grave, whilst also exploring the human drama of the men staying afloat and remembering their wartime experiences. Rather surprisingly, the film was conceived as one of the many British and American propaganda films at the time and, understandably, an element of propaganda is evident throughout, right through to the end title card that reads, 'God bless our ships and all who sail on them.'

Noel Coward, who had established himself as a master of British theatre, was the driving force behind *In Which We Serve*.

Coward's first move in setting up the film was to approach Sir Gerald Campbell, the Director-General of the British Information Service in New York and then in London, to suggest the time was right for a naval propaganda feature film. Campbell liked the idea, even though the Admiralty had an aversion to publicity.

For his research, Coward visited Plymouth, the British naval base at Scapa Flow and HMS *Nigeria*. Coward then hooked up with producers Filippo Del Giudice and Anthony Havelock-Allan, who had what Coward did not, namely filmmaking experience. It was these producers who suggested Coward spend a little time observing David Lean and Ronald Neame at work on a current production, *One of Our Aircraft is Missing* (Michael Powell and Emeric Pressburger, 1942).

Coward's original title for what became *In Which We Serve* was *White Ensign*, and the original time span of Coward's proposed story was 1922–41. Lean and Neame had to explain to Coward that a narrative on this scale would result in a film ten hours long, leading Coward to narrow his focus significantly. When Mountbatten read the script he urged Coward to make the captain less obviously based on himself. Indeed, throughout the production Mountbatten had a sizeable amount of input to dialogue and was permitted to view the rushes footage and make comments about what had been filmed.

Interestingly, in 1953 Mountbatten wrote to Coward to explain how he had been criticised by the Admiralty for being involved in a 'vanity piece'.

CASTING/RECRUITMENT: Whilst Noel Coward was the star of the film, he had written the part of Ordinary Seaman Shorty Blake expressly for upcoming British actor John Mills to portray. Mills was to be a major actor in British cinema from the 1940s through until the early 1970s. His career continued beyond this but that period defined his greatest accomplishments in films that included *We Dive at Dawn* (Anthony Asquith, 1943), *This Happy Breed, Waterloo Road* (Sidney Gilliat, 1945), *Great Expectations* (David Lean, 1946), *Hobson's Choice* (David Lean, 1954), *Swiss Family Robinson* (Ken Annakin, 1960), *Oh! What a Lovely War* (Richard Attenborough, 1969) and *Ryan's Daughter* (David Lean, 1970). Mills won an Oscar for *Ryan's Daughter*, in which he played a man who could not speak.

To portray Kinross, Coward had to play down his theatrical acting style for the camera. In an effort to acknowledge Mountbatten as the inspiration for the character, Coward even wore his cap at the angle Mountbatten would have done.

The brilliant James Mason was rejected on account of his pacifist views.

BACKUP: The cinematographer for *In Which We Serve* was Ronald Neame, who went on to become a film director of titles including *Scrooge* (1970) and *The Poseidon Adventure* (1972). *In Which We Serve* was edited by Thelma Myers and David Lean. Lean, of course, went on to direct a number of major feature films, his last being *A Passage to India* (1984). Thelma Myers also edited *The Hill* (Sidney Lumet, 1965) and *Alfie* (Lewis Gilbert, 1965).

PRODUCTION/IN THE TRENCHES: *In Which We Serve* was the 1940s equivalent of today's mega-budget war-film spectacular. The film's original budget of £60,000 ballooned to £200,000 by the end, costing £1,000 a day to film.

When extras failed to impress Coward, real sailors who were recovering from war in the naval hospital at Haslar were brought onto the film.

Two advisers were brought onto the project to ensure authenticity. One was Lieutenant Commander IT 'Bushy' Clarke, who had been a destroyer commander, and the other was Able Seaman Terry Lawler, who had been Mountbatten's batman on the *Kelly*.

As a consultant to the project, Lord Mountbatten was able to secure steel for set building from the Board of Trade, who were not especially keen on contributing to the film. Mountbatten was even able to delay the call-up of first assistant director Michael Anderson, who went on to direct *The Dam Busters* (Michael Anderson, 1954).

The media were interested in the production of *In Which We Serve*, but reported it with a mixture of enthusiasm and reservation. The *Express* voiced concern at Mountbatten being portrayed, writing 'it is wrong to have a professional actor dressed in the peaked cap and gold braid of a British naval officer'.

Full-scale wooden replicas of the ships were constructed and the bridge, quarterdeck and front third of a K-class destroyer were constructed for the film, as were numerous smaller rooms and cabins.

The tank at Denham studios was used and, filled with the same water for weeks, began to stink. Camera operator Guy Green was sent to sea to shoot footage of real destroyers in the South Atlantic, and for the effect of bullets hitting the water, air-filled condoms were exploded just beneath the surface of the water.

MARTIAL MUSIC: Coward composed the music for the film, alternating from the heroic overture to something more jaunty and festive to accompany the building of the boat, to the use of the hymn 'For Those in Peril on the Sea'.

REIMAGINING REALITY: The film is effective not only in communicating life on board a destroyer ship and also the scope of battle, but also in charting the emotional lives of those left at home. The most dramatic of these home-front sequences is that during an air raid when the house of one of the naval officers is bombed, resulting in fatalities.

HEART OF BATTLE: Watching *In Which We Serve* sixty years after its release, the film's morale-boosting efforts are clear to see. Whenever Kinross addresses his troops, or indeed when certain other characters offer up 'sloganistic' turns of phrase, it is evident that the film is addressing the audience who would have been watching in 1942.

CHARACTER: Kinross is yet another of many father-figure characters who dominate so many war films. His fatherly, gentle approach, with a firm but fair attitude, puts him right alongside characters such as Captain Miller in **Saving Private Ryan** and the captain in **Das Boot**. Kinross is father, friend and even 'priest' at one point, when he leads the Christmas service on board the boat.

Kinross always has a witty reply. When coming on board the rescue ship after the *Torrin* has sunk, one of the crew comments to Kinross that he looks well. Kinross replies, 'Nothing like a good swim before breakfast.' Perhaps the most telling comment that Kinross makes, though, is early in the film when he and another crew member are talking about the sunrise. Kinross says how different a picture of sunrise is to the reality and comments, 'That is where art and reality part company.' For Noel Coward, *In Which We Serve* is art as a means of communicating reality.

A contrast to the 'aristocratic' Kinross is the character of Shorty Blake – the film's common man. Blake is by turns cocky, romantic, and supremely resilient and even witty under fire. When one sailor, as the ship comes under fire, says, 'Join the Navy and see the world,' Blake replies with, 'Looks like it's going to be the next world.'

The women in the film are strong-headed characters, none more so than Mrs Kinross, who gives a devastating 'speech' at her Christmas lunch on board the *Torrin*. She offers a melancholy portrait of the life of a naval wife, citing how the love of all naval men for their ship can seemingly exceed the love for their families.

The sequence near the end of the film where the wives receive telegrams is affecting, and when Kinross says goodbye to each and every crewman one by one it is rather like the film is paying homage to all those real sailors who died.

STYLE: *In Which We Serve* is a large-canvas picture that contrasts images of the comforts of home with the harshness of combat. Lean's economical visual style, developed surely in part from his editing experience, manifests itself in the montage of the ship's construction at the beginning of the film. The film amplifies its scope by interpolating documentary footage of battle and also of the ship being built.

A high-key lighting approach is favoured for the less intense sequences on deck, while high-contrast images are created for those scenes where an emotional intensity prevails, such as when the *Torrin* comes under fire at night or when Shorty and Freda sit drinking tea in a railway café (foreshadowing Coward and Lean's *Brief Encounter* in 1945). A number of wider shots reveal the film's scope in recreating reality, such as the shot of the army marching along the dockside having been evacuated from Dunkirk.

For all his confidence on deck and in battle, Kinross cuts a slightly pathetic figure in the moment when the camera pulls back to reveal him virtually alone, having said goodbye to his crew. The loneliness of command is a theme explored in **The Dam Busters**.

CRITICAL CROSSFIRE: *In Which We Serve* was a critical and commercial success, premiering in September 1942. *Picturegoer* magazine effused with, 'I wish I could find words adequate enough to convey the power and beauty, the pathos and the grandeur of *In Which We Serve*.' Ernest Betts in the *Daily Express* described the film as, 'Human, deeply moving . . . brutally faithful and exact.'

Looking back on the film from the distance of about thirty years, Roger Manvell wrote, 'If this in so many respects admirable film had an Achilles heel, it was the uncomfortably middle-class way in which it bound all classes together . . . through the uniformed figure of the captain.' For the *Time Out Film Guide* the film isn't as great as others suggest, saying, 'Staged with what passed at the time for honest understatement, it now looks impossibly patronising . . . a reminder of the structures of snobbery and privilege in the services which were largely responsible for Labour's post-war election victory.' The film recovers its reputation in *Leonard Maltin's Movie and Video Guide*: 'Unlike many World War Two films, this masterpiece doesn't date one bit.'

MEDALS OF HONOUR: At the 1942 New York Film Critics Circle Awards the film won Best Picture. It was nominated for an Oscar in 1944 in the categories of Best Picture and Best Original Screenplay.

OTHER BATTLEFRONTS: *The Cruel Sea* (Charles Frend, 1953) explores the British naval experience in World War Two in which the resolve and endurance of the British Navy are dramatised and celebrated. Then there is the lesser-known *Convoy* (Penn Tennyson, 1940), a film that predates *In Which We Serve* and which adopted a documentary style. In the 1920s Russian filmmaker Sergei Eisenstein fashioned the near immortal film *Battleship Potemkin*.

The Life and Death Of Colonel Blimp (Michael Powell, 1943), a chronicle of a British military man, is a decades-spanning story about a career soldier having to acknowledge that life is change. The film features a stunning monologue in which one character talks about the rise of fascism in Germany. This expansive film has an autumnal sense of fading glory, encapsulated in a shot of a fallen leaf close to the end of the film.

THE HOMEFRONT: *In Which We Serve* is available on DVD with a 25-minute documentary included plus the theatrical trailer.

FINAL BRIEFING: *In Which We Serve* is a film as 'classic' as its reputation suggests. Even though elements may appear dated, there is an emotional truth and the recreation of combat successfully captures its intensity. The film's range of emotions and tones are highly satisfying. The action sequences are unfussy and not dated. The film's emotional understatement is all the more affecting, such as when Hardy, on being given news of his wife's death, simply throws the letter he was writing to her into the sea. The film is marked by small but powerful gestures, such as when Kinross has to release the grip of a dead man's hand on his arm, or when Attenborough's eyes well with tears when Kinross refers to him anonymously for failing in his duty during battle for deserting his post. The film is also something of a social document of how families lived and related to one another.

FINAL SALUTE: Of the premiere, Coward commented, 'Toward the end there was a great deal of gratifying nose-blowing and one stern-faced Admiral in the row behind me was unashamedly in tears.'

The Dam Busters (1955)

102 minutes

Associated British Motion Picture Corporation
Director: Michael Anderson

Screenplay: RC Sherriff, based on the books by Paul Brickhill, and *Enemy Coast Ahead* **by Guy Gibson**
Cinematographer: Erwin Hillier
Editor: Richard Best
Music: Eric Coates (additional music Leighton Lucas)
Art Direction: Robert Jones
Visual Effects: George Blackwell and Gilbert Taylor

CAST: Michael Redgrave (*Barnes Wallis*), Richard Todd (*Wing Commander Guy Gibson*), Ursula Jeans (*Mrs Wallis*), Charles Carson (*Doctor*) Stanley Van Beers (*Sir David Pye, CB, FRS*), Colin Tapley (*Dr Glanville*) Raymond Huntley (*Official*), Hugh Manning (*Official*), Patrick Barr (*Captain Joseph 'Mutt' Summers*), Basil Sydney (*Sir Arthur 'Bomber' Harris*), Derek Farr (*Group Captain JNH Wentworth*), Harold Siddons (*Group Signals Officer*), Brewster Mason (*Flight Lieutenant RD Trevor-Roper*), Anthony Doonan (*Flight Lieutenant REG Hutchinson*), Nigel Stock (*Flying Officer FM Spafford*)

RATING: U

WAR STORY: *The Dam Busters* begins in the spring of 1942. Barnes Wallis is experimenting with ways to fire bombs across water. Wallis is working long hours, to the concern of his wife, for both Vickers the arms company and on his own bouncing-bomb project. Wallis explains his concept to his doctor in an informal chalk-and-talk session when the GP comes to visit.

In London, Wallis asks the Ministry of Defence to allow him more time to refine his concept. As a series of tests continue, from a miniature simulation of a dam being smashed at Harmondsworth to a series of bouncing-ball tests at a huge water tank in Teddington, Wallis finds that the RAF are uneasy about loaning a Wellington bomber for the major trials of the concept. Wallis even goes to Bomber Harris to pitch the idea in the hope of securing his support. Thankfully, Harris can see the potential for the concept. The RAF, though, are also financially restrained. Learning through the grapevine that the idea has been dropped by the Ministry and RAF, Wallis resigns from Vickers, only to then be invited to London the following day to be officially told by the Ministry of Aircraft Production that the project has in fact been given the go-ahead by the government.

Time is short. Wallis has two months in which to prepare for a May attack on the dams. The chosen unit, 617 Squadron, is comprised of the most experienced crew personally selected by Wing Commander Guy Gibson, who is appointed squadron leader just when he thought he was due a holiday after running a number of successful bombing raids. Gibson quietly and dutifully accepts the top-secret mission, unable even to tell his men what their target is until very late in the training process. They have to put up with the taunts of their fellow pilots for being the only squadron that never goes into action.

Low-level flying practice begins over British lakes. Gibson, still ignorant himself of the final targets, is introduced to Wallis, who screens test footage for him. Gibson is finally and officially informed of the mission: to ensure the bombs are dropped and land right at the wall of the German dams, where they then drop below the surface and explode. In Kent, where Barnes Wallis is running more bombing tests, the bombs are found to disintegrate on impact. The bureaucrats look uneasy and the pressure mounts on the inventor, who insists that he will find a way to make the bombs more robust.

Gibson goes to London for some rest and relaxation after the south-coast tests. At the theatre, Gibson is struck by inspiration and realises how they can ensure precision dropping of the bombs: by aligning two spotlights on the water.

More bomb-drop trials ensue, with Gibson watching and talking with Wallis. Wallis asks if Gibson and his crew would be prepared to fly just sixty feet above the water to ensure the correct trajectory for the bomb deployment. Gibson says that would not be a problem. Finally, the bomb-drop trial is a success and the bureaucrats are satisfied. Gibson has just a week to go until the raid is to take place. At Derwent Water a series of tests are undertaken to practise and perfect an alignment device of striking, beguiling simplicity. The targeting practice is successful, and Gibson is informed that the raid will take place a little sooner than a week hence.

The night of the bomb attack comes and 617 Squadron are briefed, and are finally informed of their targets. Gibson's dog, and lucky charm, has been hit by a car and killed. Gibson asks for the dog to be buried to coincide with the time the bombers will go in on the dams.

The squadron take off from England towards the heavily defended Dutch coastline, where one of the planes is struck down by German gunfire. The Dam Busters raid proves tense and dangerous. Gibson's run on the Möhne Dam is ultimately victorious. The Eder Dam is the next target and Gibson's plane is caught up in one of the bomb blasts, whilst a second bomb does not prove effective. There is only one bomb remaining, which does its job perfectly. The mission has succeeded, but eight of the fourteen bomber planes have been lost.

CONCEPT/THE MISSION: *The Dam Busters* was adapted from Guy Gibson's book *Enemy Coast Ahead* and the film is ultimately partly a documentary about the project to destroy the German dams and flood the region's industrial complex. Michael Anderson, the director of the film, had followed a 'traditional' British film industry career path, joining Elstree Studios as a runner and becoming an assistant director in 1938. *The Dam Busters* would prove to be Anderson's finest moviemaking hour. After the success of *The Dam Busters* Anderson would go on to direct *Around the World in Eighty Days* (1956) and *Logan's Run* (1971).

Anderson also directed another story of international conflict, namely *Yangtse Incident* (1957) which dramatised the capture of British frigate the *Amethyst* by Chinese Communists in 1949. Anderson's notable skill was in developing suspense and he went on to direct *The Wreck of the Mary Deare* (1959) after Alfred Hitchcock, the widely accepted master of suspense, dropped out of the film. Anderson's other wartime film was *Operation Crossbow* (1965), which dramatised the creation of a new bomb. Anderson also directed *The Quiller Memorandum* (1966) about a neo-Nazi gang in Berlin. Anderson had also worked in his early years as an assistant director on *In Which We Serve.*

Given the heroic and dynamic presentation of the bombers in the film it is worth contrasting cinema's portrayal of aerial combat and war with fairly contemporary paintings of the time by Paul Nash, famous for his *Battle of Britain* painting. Nash's work had an anti-heroic quality to it. The painter had longed to fly himself but chronic asthma ended that dream. Nash also painted the wreckage of fighter planes downed in the English countryside and he painted the *Totes Meer*, which is German for *The Dead Sea.*

The first part of the film dramatises the development of the bouncing bomb concept, whilst the second part functions far more as combat adventure and the cost of war. Anderson spent two years researching the film, especially the 'battle' that Barnes Wallis had to fight to get his idea accepted. Condensing any real-life event into a film is always a challenge, and to some degree historical accuracy will be compromised. The producer of the film wrote to Barnes Wallis with the observation that the film would offer a 'somewhat simplified treatment of highly complicated issues'.

In his detailed account, *The Dam Busters Raid*, writer John Sweetman writes, 'The Dam Busters raid, visually so dramatic in its execution and achievement, is possibly the best known single operation in the history of aerial warfare.'

CASTING/RECRUITMENT: Michael Redgrave, who was cast as Wallis, was an accomplished and popular film actor who had also appeared in *Kipps* (Carol Reed, 1941), *The Way to the Stars* (Anthony Asquith, 1945), *The Browning Version* (Anthony Asquith, 1951), *The Importance of Being Earnest* (Anthony Asquith, 1952), *The Sea Shall Not Have Them* (Lewis Gilbert, 1954), *The Hill, The Heroes of Telemark* and *Oh! What a Lovely War*.

Richard Todd, a sort of British George Clooney of the time, was a major star and his credits include *The Hasty Heart* (Vincent Sherman, 1949), *The Story of Robin Hood and His Merrie Men* (Ken Annakin, 1951), *Yangtse Incident, The Longest Day* (Ken Annakin, 1962) and *Operation Crossbow*.

For Todd, his favourite scene in the film was the last he shares with Redgrave after returning from the raid and coming to terms with the losses. Todd, rightly so, responded to the understated heroics of him simply walking off into the distance to write letters home to the families of those pilots who died.

BACKUP: Anderson's key collaborator was cinematographer Erwin Hillier, with whom Anderson ultimately made ten films. Hillier's other credits as cinematographer included *I Know Where I'm Going* (Michael Powell, 1945), *Operation Crossbow, The Quiller Memorandum* and *The Valley of Gwangi* (Jim O'Connolly, 1969).

The film's screenwriter had also written the scripts for *The Four Feathers* (Zoltan Korda, 1939) and *Goodbye, Mr Chips* (Sam Wood, 1939). Supervising the extensive special-effects sequences that played their part most prominently in the latter half of the film was Gil Taylor, who went on to become a fully fledged cinematographer.

The film's editor, Richard Best, went on to edit *Ice Cold in Alex* (J Lee Thompson, 1958) and also many episodes of the cult TV series *The Avengers*.

PRODUCTION/IN THE TRENCHES: Before filming began the film's miniature work was completed. Five Lancaster bombers were rebuilt for the film and a studio aircraft was mounted on a 'gimbal' that allowed it to bank and tilt.

At Elstree Studios three immense models were made of the three dams that were to be hit in the raid. The models were not only of the dam structures, but also of the countryside around them.

For shots of the pilots in the cockpits during the raid, six separate optical elements were composited to create the illusion of them flying above the landscape.

MARTIAL MUSIC: Numerous film scores have worked their way into the popular imagination, taking on a life of their own beyond the screen, and standing as complete and valid pieces of musical expression in their own right. The theme music for *The Dam Busters* is one such piece. Composed by Eric Coates, the music is as recognisable and identifiable with its source film and also a certain image of movie heroism as Elmer Bernstein's theme for *The Great Escape* and, more recently, John Williams' piece *Hymn for the Fallen*, composed for *Saving Private Ryan*. Coates' music has also been played at numerous memorial and commemorative war tributes, a truly legitimate piece of popular music that defines an era. Coates had composed what became the theme for the film about ten years before, when he had written a piece of music to celebrate a World War Two victory. Coates's theme for *The Dam Busters* became a Top Ten hit in 1955.

REIMAGINING REALITY: Most of the film concerns itself with Barnes Wallis's development of his idea and the battle to see it supported by the Ministry of Defence.

The actual Dam Busters raid went under the code name Operation Chastise, in which nineteen Lancaster bombers attacked a number of dams, which when destroyed would flood German industrial regions. The attack took place on 16 May 1943 and was considered such a success that Joseph Stalin contacted Churchill to congratulate him on the effectiveness of the raid. The media were quick to cover this moment of the war, developing ever more the relationship between combat and representations of it. Sweetman has commented that 'inaccuracies and embellishments gradually became an integral part of the legend'.

Official records about the operation were closed to the public until the 1970s and Guy Gibson's own published account in 1950 was unable to go into many details of the mission. Indeed, Gibson's book could not even mention the name of Barnes Neville Wallis.

In order to give the audience a focus and figure of empathy and heroism, the efforts and accomplishments of Barnes Wallis were slightly embellished. The film suggests that Wallis virtually single-handedly devised the concept of the inaccurately labelled 'bouncing bomb' (more accurately, a back-spinning depth charge) from scratch. Official records show that Barnes Wallis was building on the work and developments of others. For example Wing Commander CR Finch Noyes had already worked on a concept that Wallis was able to refine.

From mid-1940 onwards Wallis had access to government development plans to aid him in his work. Prior to the efforts of Wallis the Special Operations Executive and Combined Operations had considered rockets, pilotless aircraft and even a boat filled with explosives as a way to destroy the dams.

Wallis received the go-ahead for his proposal on 26 February 1943, giving him and the RAF just under three months to prepare the mission. There were not even any full-scale drawings of the weapon and the only test run took place on 13 May 1943. Barnes Wallis called the mission 'a beloved child'.

The night of the Dam Busters raid was hampered by navigational errors, bad weather and mechanical failure. The mission had a very short turnaround time. One aircraft even attacked the wrong dam, and flying at just 100 feet above the water the Lancasters were vulnerable without a mid-upper-gunner facility. Flying Officer EC Johnson said of the raid on the Eder dam, 'The recovery from low level as the bomb was released . . . was quite hair-raising and required . . . a climbing attitude not approved in any flying manuals and a period of nail-biting from the rest of us.'

Though significant British casualties were incurred, the raid did much to boost the Allied forces' morale and commitment to defeating Germany. Certainly the raid captured the imagination of the public and continues to do so today. The film can be readily considered a piece of romantic filmmaking for the most part that both valorises and personalises the RAF. The film is admirable for the clarity with which it explains the scientific and military principles at work without ever becoming staid.

In 2002 the film and the real event was given a very fitting and poetic coda. Many years after the film's original release, and as a sign of how firmly lodged *The Dam Busters* is in British popular culture, Richard Todd flew with the real pilots of the raid in a commemorative flight to mark its 59th anniversary. Todd was aged 82 as he sat with 617-squadron members George Chalmers, Ron Burton and Jack Gagg to fly over Ladybower Reservoir in the Derwent Valley, Derbyshire. After the flypast the men laid a wreath at a memorial stone at Derwent Dam and then scattered poppies on the water as a sign of remembrance of the men who died in the raid.

HEART OF BATTLE: We often talk about the American can-do spirit but *The Dam Busters* unreservedly celebrates the same strain in the British. *The Dam Busters* is very much an action adventure in its last half-hour, and when the bombers do move in on their targets it is hard to resist some sense of excitement to finally see Wallis's concept and the pilots' training put into practice. The film celebrates the RAF as being without fault, though the film's final scene quietly testifies to lost lives.

During the first part of the film bureaucracy and politics are represented as being far from heroic or visionary. In contrast the RAF pilots are quick to take on board the needs of the mission. The unity and courage of the pilots are paramount.

There is a boyish energy to the film, even in its coda of mature respect. The emphasis on models, plans and the romanticism of adventure are sure-fire ways to many men's hearts.

CHARACTER: The character of Barnes Wallis is a slightly eccentric but very lovable figure, whose family-man credentials are made clear from the start. Indeed, the film portrays Wallis as something of a father to 617 Squadron, and particularly to Gibson. Wallis is the intellectual hero, the inventor whose commitment sees him through. Gibson's courage and team spirit is his contribution to the mission. Wallis is committed and decent, and also a dreamer. Against the tide of resistance he comments that 'Somehow or other I must keep it alive until I'm ready.' There is a charming moment of detail as Wallis's eyes dart with anticipation back and forth around the table at a ministry meeting. He is ultimately a boyish figure, wading off into the water to gather up pieces of broken bomb after everyone else has gone home, and a picturesque wide shot emphasises his loneliness. A similar isolation accompanies the different heroism of Guy Gibson, who walks off alone to finish his work at the end of the film.

Where Wallis expresses his anxieties easily, Gibson is characterised by an unflappable and quiet confidence. He is initially pictured in heroic terms as he emerges from the Lancaster after a bombing raid, framed against the sky, an image that might be a recruitment poster for the RAF. The same image is repeated later in the film. Gibson, too, is very boyish in his energy and love for his dog. He is also capable not only of great heroism and certainty in combat, but also of a more down-to-earth heroism and responsibility at the film's quietly powerful climax. Gibson is a class act under pressure, always ready with an understated quip to ease the tension. 'Everything depends on secrecy in a show like this,' he tells his men, and during the raid he tells his crew, 'They know we're here now, so keep your eyes open.'

The other pilots of 617 Squadron are upbeat and boisterous. When one of them is asked by a fellow airman why he is having a shave before they head out he replies, 'If we have to bail out you never know who we might meet.' The film is most affecting, though, in its portrayal of the airmen when we see several of them anticipating the raid as they lie on their beds or sit writing letters to loved ones should they not return from their mission.

STYLE: Being in black-and-white, the film is able to enhance the romanticism it treats its subject with. The monochrome images bring a quality of 'fantasy' to the film whilst shooting in black-and-white also allowed the integration of production footage with archive material of the bomb trials.

With its unsurprising fidelity to realism, the film displays welcome flourishes of something more expressive and transformative. There are several loving shots of the Lancasters parked up and ready to go, and also a number of romantic wide-screen shots of the planes in formation and silhouette riding towards sunset skies. Perhaps the most affecting visuals, though, are found in the sequence of silent shots that indicate absence through death, as the camera quietly pushes in on the belongings and letters of those airmen who do not return from combat.

For the raid, Anderson's film builds suspense and the point-of-view shots enhance the sense of immediacy. The most thrilling moment is when, as the planes charge along the runway to take off, the camera races alongside them, investing the departure with added energy and excitement. The intercutting between the energy and noise of the raid and the pensive silence of mission control is affecting as Wallis sits hunched and silent awaiting news, everything resting on his shoulders. For all of the hardware and technical talk in the film, the human response to the events always remains central.

CRITICAL CROSSFIRE: When the film was released the *Monthly Film Bulletin* wrote that the film was '. . . an attempt to express a more deeply felt emotion than one has come to expect in recent times . . . The film is over long and the music score is, regrettably, very blatant; but despite these drawbacks, a mood of sober respect is maintained.' For the *Time Out Film Guide* the film '. . . slips some thoughtful reservations and some gross sentimentality into its bouncing bombast'.

MEDALS OF HONOUR: The film was nominated at the 1956 Oscars for Best Special Effects, and in the same year was BAFTA nominated in the categories of Best British Film, Best British Screenplay and Best Film.

OTHER BATTLEFRONTS: *The Dam Busters* now stands as one of the most well-remembered, accomplished and enjoyed British war films. Others to view would be the realist films produced by the Crown Film Unit such as *Target for Tonight* (1941) and *One of Our Aircraft is Missing*, both of which dealt with aerial combat. Ealing's *San Demetrio London* (Charles Frend, 1943) and Two Cities' *The Way to the Stars* were also significant.

For the most part, though, British war films made immediately after the war were not especially popular, with the exception of the film *Against The Wind* (Charles Crichton, 1948) which was about undercover work in Belgium. Interestingly, combat is less central to those initial attempts. Instead, the focus of several key films was on veteran experience in films such as *Good Time Girl* (David McDonald, 1948), *Man on the Run* (Lawrence Huntington, 1948) and *They Made Me a Fugitive* (Alberto Cavalcanti, 1947). The 1950s saw 'veteran' dramas with *The Intruder* (1953), *The Ship that Died of Shame* (Basil Dearden and Michael Relph, 1955) and *Tiger in the Smoke* (Roy Ward Baker, 1956).

Indeed it was not until the 1950s that more combat-based films were made, and throughout the decade the British film industry was built very much around films set during the Second World War. *The Dam Busters*, to some quiet degree, still functions as propaganda. Britain's first propaganda film had been *The Lion has Wings* (Michael Powell, Brian Desmond Hurst, Adrian Brunel, 1939), which celebrates the Royal Air Force. Producer Alexander Korda had for a period in the 1930s employed Winston Churchill as a scriptwriter, and Korda promised Churchill that if war did arise then he would produce the ultimate British propaganda film. The film was popular but has not had longevity. For a very different take to *The Dam Busters* on the experiences of a World War Two pilot, watch *A Matter of Life and Death* (Michael Powell, 1943).

THE HOMEFRONT: *The Dam Busters* is available on DVD and includes the trailer but no more than that.

FINAL BRIEFING: Anderson's film is so effective because of its combination of the personal story of Wallis's battle to get his concept approved and the subsequent action-adventure qualities of the late part of the story. Yes, the film glamorises the RAF, but its patriotic fervour is balanced with quieter moments towards the end of the film that remind us of lives lost for ever. Certainly the film creates genuine excitement and tension during the attack scenes, and the visual-effects work for these latter stages of the film is terrific. The film's most enduring scene is the sequence that shows the men getting ready to leave for their mission. Courage and a hint of anxiety fuels the moment and encapsulates the war film at its best.

FINAL SALUTE: 'We had this massive library of old war movies – *The Dam Busters*, *The Battle of Britain* . . . and about forty-five other movies. We . . . picked out scenes to transfer to film to use as guidelines in the battle.' Gary Kurtz, producer of *Star Wars*, explaining the influence of *The Dam Busters* on the space dogfight that concludes the space adventure.

The Bridge on the River Kwai (1957)

161 minutes

Columbia Pictures
Producer: Sam Spiegel
Director: David Lean
Screenplay: Michael Wilson (uncredited), Carl Foreman
(uncredited) based on the novel by Pierre Boulle
Cinematographer: Jack Hildyard
Editor: Peter Taylor
Music: Malcolm Arnold
Art Direction: Donald M Ashton

CAST: William Holden (*Shears*), Alex Guinness (*Colonel Nicholson*), Jack Hawkins (*Major Warden*), Sessue Hayakawa (*Colonel Saito*), James

Donald (*Major Clipton*), Geoffrey Horne (*Lieutenant Joyce*), André Morrell (*Colonel Green*), Peter Williams (*Captain Reeves*), John Boxer (*Major Hughes*), Percy Herbert (*Grogan*)

RATING: PG

TAGLINE: It spans a whole new world of entertainment.

WAR STORY: A vulture circles the sky above the jungles of Thailand. At ground level many graves line the side of a railway under construction by the Japanese to reach from Bangkok to Rangoon. The route they are making will allow Japanese forces to move on into India as part of their campaign. The Allied forces need to stop the bridge being constructed across the River Kwai that will allow the railroad to continue its progress.

Into a Japanese prisoner-of-war camp march a large number of captured British soldiers under the leadership of Colonel Nicholson. As they march in whistling, an American POW named Shears watches with interest. Lieutenant Jennings says they should plan an escape, but Nicholson replies that they will do no such thing. Colonel Saito, the commandant of the camp, addresses the soldiers and states that all British soldiers will now set to work on the bridge. Nicholson objects, stating that under the Geneva Convention officers are not supposed to labour, they can only supervise and administrate, and he orders his officers not to work. Saito is about to have the officers shot when the British doctor at the camp rushes out and tells Saito that there are witnesses in the camp hospital of his plan to murder the men. He backs down, but the officers are left standing without food or water in the heat.

The officers are finally put into a detention area and Nicholson is taken to Saito's quarters, where he is beaten up and then dragged back outside and placed in solitary confinement in the 'Oven'. Over a period of a month, Nicholson continues to resist the order to work, to the mounting frustration of Saito. Shears watches the situation unfold, unconvinced by Nicholson's idealism. He is determined to escape the camp when the moment presents itself, even though Saito has warned that nobody will survive the jungle. One night, two prisoners try to escape but are shot dead. The third, Shears, gets away.

Nicholson is visited in the Oven by Dr Clipton, who tells him of the escape. Work has begun by the British soldiers on the construction of the bridge, and the doctor asks Nicholson to consider relenting and committing to labour. Nicholson will not yield. Clipton informs Saito that Nicholson will not allow his officers to perform manual work.

In the jungle, a ragged and exhausted Shears reaches a village, where he is taken in and then given a boat with which to continue on his journey. Shears collapses in the boat as it drifts out to sea.

At the camp, Saito is aware that bridge construction is falling behind schedule. He addresses the soldiers once again and informs them that he will now personally supervise construction of the bridge. The first thing to happen on Saito's watch is that a huge portion of the bridge collapses.

In the camp, Nicholson is taken from the Oven to see Saito. Nicholson suggests that his officers could supervise the building of the bridge. Saito has no answer; Nicholson is freed from the Oven and the officers are released from detention. Nicholson is carried like a hero on the shoulders of the soldiers.

The Englishman gathers his officers together and they discuss how best to construct the bridge. They take their thoroughly considered plans to Saito, who agrees to the idea of starting the bridge again from scratch.

In Ceylon, Shears recuperates at Mount Lavinia Hospital when he is called to a meeting with a Major Warden, who wants to find out what Shears knows about the building of the bridge on the River Kwai. Before he knows it, Shears finds himself recruited as part of a four-man team to navigate through the jungle he has just escaped from. The unit will take explosives with them in order to blow up the bridge and prevent further Japanese progress. Shears hates the idea of going back into the jungle.

Shears, Warden and Chapman are joined by a young Canadian named Joyce. They parachute into the jungle and Chapman dies when he lands in a tree. Warden is injured and has great difficulty walking, but they solider on. Warden saves Joyce from a Japanese bullet when several Japanese soldiers discover the riverside camp of the team.

The bridge is finally completed under Nicholson's supervision and Saito is pleased with it. There will be a grand opening with a train crossing.

Shears, Warden and Joyce reach a promontory overlooking the river. By night Shears and Joyce rig their explosives and wire. In the camp, the soldiers, Nicholson included, finally relax.

The following morning disaster strikes. The river has dropped, revealing the explosive wiring under the bridge. Nicholson spots it and takes Saito to investigate, and they follow the wire all the way to the detonator. As the train approaches the bridge, Shears realises the plan to blow up the bridge is in jeopardy. Joyce kills Saito and Nicholson takes a bullet, stumbles and collapses onto the detonator just as the train crosses the bridge. The bridge explodes, taking the train with it.

The doctor, looking on, describes the situation as 'madness'. The vulture circles the skies above the devastation of man.

CONCEPT/THE MISSION: *The Bridge on the River Kwai* is often cited as David Lean's first true epic. It is one of a cluster of films that effectively comprised the second half of his career and for which he is best known. Lean had made a series of successful 'small' films, the first of which was the British wartime classic *In Which We Serve*, which he co-directed with Noel Coward. *The Bridge on the River Kwai* gave Lean the opportunity to display his finesse and skill at fusing personal stories against epic-scale events without compromising the pleasures of either approach. Intriguingly, one of Lean's favourite films had been the phenomenal French prisoner-of-war film *La Grande Illusion* and what Lean especially warmed to was its delicate and considerate portrayal of the relationship between the camp commandant and the prisoners.

For all his exotic filmmaking adventures, David Lean had been born and raised in glamorous Croydon, and had begun working in the film industry at Lime Grove Studios. By 1930 he had become an editor with Gaumont Sound News. He had even been screen-tested as a potential actor.

He started out as an editor of low-budget British features such as *Money for Speed* (Bernard Vorhaus, 1933) and *The Ghost Camera* (Bernard Vorhaus, 1933). From these films Lean moved on to edit large-budget feature films *As You Like It* (Paul Czinner, 1936), *Pygmalion* (Anthony Asquith, 1938) and *Major Barbara* (Gabriel Pascal, 1940). Then after his directing debut with *In Which We Serve*, he followed it with his first solo effort, *This Happy Breed*, notable for its opening shot that moves from an overhead shot of the River Thames to the front door of the Gibbons' south London terrace. Lean also directed *Blithe Spirit* and then had his artistic breakthrough with *Brief Encounter*.

Lean then directed two adaptations of Charles Dickens' work: *Great Expectations* (1946) and *Oliver Twist* (1948). Lean was known to be obsessive about filmmaking. His early collaborator Anthony Havelock-Allan commented about Lean: 'He thought about film as a Jesuit thinks about his vocation.'

The Sound Barrier (1952) and *Hobson's Choice* (1954) were notable efforts. By the mid-1950s, though, Lean stood at a creative and a career crossroads. Would he remain a master of the small-scale, well-crafted film or would he shift into directing larger films with more international (and certainly American) appeal. Lean had been due to direct an adaptation of *The Wind Cannot Read*, but disagreements with producer Alexander Korda resulted in Lean not moving forwards with the script, and he was without a film to make. Lean was contacted by producer Sam Spiegel, who was searching for a director for a new project. Thus began a powerful and productive collaboration with Spiegel, who hired Lean to make *Bridge on the River Kwai*. It was to be an exhausting process and one that began with the arduous task of getting the screenplay to a point where it met with Lean's approval.

Producer Sam Spiegel had read Boulle's novel on a plane journey and was so excited by its cinematic potential that he immediately investigated who, if anyone, owned the rights to the novel. The first to option the novel had been Henri George Clouzot, and British producer Alexander Korda had also considered adapting the story. Filled with enthusiasm, Spiegel initially approached a range of major Hollywood directors, namely John Ford, Elia Kazan, Nicholas Ray, Carol Reed, William Wyler, Fred Zinneman and Howard Hawks. Only Hawks expressed significant interest, but then became concerned about its commercial potential and suggested it be made on a low budget with a British cast and crew. Hawks had also wanted to significantly revise the ending of the novel. With the project seemingly stalling it was at this point that Spiegel approached Lean.

Pierre Boulle's novel had been published in 1952 in France and then in 1954 in Britain. In the novel the bridge is not actually destroyed, and when Lean broached the subject of how to resolve the film narrative, Boulle explained that he had wanted the bridge to be destroyed in the novel but had not been able to do so narratively to his satisfaction. Lean's main concern initially was in toning down the novel's anti-British stance.

Prior to Lean agreeing to direct the film, Sam Spiegel had hired screenwriter Carl Foreman, who had written *High Noon*, to adapt Boulle's novel. However, Lean did not respond to Foreman's draft at all, considering it stereotypical and lacking any sense of human warmth in its portrayal of the Japanese. Lean also had reservations about the structure of the screenplay. Foreman had elected to have the central story framed by Shears and Warden on a British submarine, recounting their experiences.

Lean voiced his frustration to Spiegel about the first draft, and invited his writer friend Norman Spencer to New York, where Lean was at the time, so they could fully rewrite the treatment for the film. Lean and Spencer worked on a new version of the story outline over a six-week period, with Spiegel regularly contributing to this process. Still, though, the fate of the bridge at the end of the film had not been resolved.

Even though Lean had been unhappy with Foreman's draft, Spiegel insisted on Foreman remaining involved in the project. In the immediate period after Lean's downbeat reaction to Foreman's draft, Lean briefly worked with Calder Willingham, who had co-scripted *Paths of Glory*, but Lean was unhappy with his contribution to the development of the *Kwai* script. (Wilingham's notable contribution was in defining the Shears character more fully and introducing the studio's wished-for love interest.) To replace Willingham, Lean suggested British writer HE Bates, who had written Lean's film *Summertime* (1955). This did not come to pass, and finally Spiegel brought in a writer called Michael Wilson. Lean had found his creative soul mate. Wilson joined Lean on location in Ceylon (now Sri Lanka) in September 1956 in the months leading up to the beginning of production.

For Lean, the bridge was a metaphor for the bizarre twists of thought war and combat can create. Lean's original concept for the ending was that Colonel Nicholson intentionally chooses not to expose the commandos and therefore must destroy the bridge himself. At Spiegel's suggestion, the ending where Nicholson is hit and falls onto the plunger, thereby detonating the bridge, was adopted.

The film's screenwriters Michael Wilson and Carl Foreman were both blacklisted screenwriters because of their left-wing political sympathies, so were not acknowledged in the credits when the film was originally released. Only in 1984 did they receive posthumous Oscars for their work on the film. Consequently, the only writer credited with the script, rather bizarrely as he did not work on it at any stage, was Pierre Boulle. At the time of the film's original release the film industry were aware of who had really written the screenplay.

It could be said that 1957 was a banner year for war films of very differing tones and styles. Not only was *The Bridge on the River Kwai* released, but also two astonishing smaller-scale black-and-white films. One was *Paths of Glory* and the other was *Kanal*.

Lean's subsequent, post-*Kwai* films have been noted for their combination of spectacle and adventure alongside a focus on characterisation and Lean's great 'student', Steven Spielberg, has made films that abide richly by this principle. In the late 1980s, Spielberg and Lean had considered collaborating on an adaptation of Jospeh Conrad's densely written novel *Nostromo*, with Spielberg producing and Lean directing. For an account of their work on the project read Kevin Brownlow's immense biography of David Lean.

CASTING/RECRUITMENT: Columbia Pictures, the studio who were financing and would distribute the film, were keen for a major star to draw in the audience. Historically, Americans had been prisoners of war alongside British soldiers, so at least commercial imperatives were consistent with history.

Originally, Humphrey Bogart and Cary Grant had been considered for the role of Shears before William Holden was cast (Grant, apparently, was particularly frustrated to have missed out on the part). Holden also starred in *Stalag 17* (Billy Wilder, 1953). At the time of *Kwai's* production, he was a major Hollywood star and his fee for the film made him the most highly paid actor at that time, earning $300,000 and a ten-per-cent share of the profits.

Casting for the role of Nicholson proved particularly tortuous because of Lean's intense sense of the character. Whilst Spiegel had felt Alec Guinness would be appropriate, Lean felt other actors were worth considering first. Those in contention included Spencer Tracy, Tyrone Power, Laurence Olivier, Ralph Richardson and John Gielgud. Olivier was busy, as was Richardson, and Gielgud turned the role down flat. James Mason, Douglas Fairbanks Jr, Ray Milland and Anthony Quayle were all considered, too. Lean had thought Eric Portman or a thinned down Charles Laughton might be more viable, but continually resisted considering Guinness. Guinness only finally accepted the part a matter of weeks before filming began. It was producer Sam Spiegel who perhaps prevailed most on Guinness to take the role of Nicholson even though Lean had expressed reservations about the actor for this particular role.

Alex Guinness had previously collaborated with Lean on both *Oliver Twist* and *Great Expectations*, playing Fagin and Herbert Pocket respectively. Guinness had also been synonymous with a run of Ealing comedies, starring in *The Lavender Hill Mob* (Charles Crichton, 1951), *The Man in the White Suit* (Alexander Mackendrick, 1951) and taking on eight roles in *Kind Hearts and Coronets* (Robert Hamer, 1949). Despite the fraught creative work between the director and the actor, they went on to collaborate again on *Lawrence of Arabia* (1962), then *Dr Zhivago* (1965) and finally in *A Passage To India*. He was to impact on a generation of young cinemagoers when he appeared in *Star Wars*

(George Lucas, 1977) and was the spy George Smiley in television's *Tinker, Tailor, Soldier, Spy*.

For the role of Joyce, Shears' sidekick, Spiegel and Lean had also considered the great Montgomery Clift but they felt Clift lacked focus.

Actor Sessue Hayawaka, who portrayed Saito, was a notable Japanese actor who had been a star of Japanese silent cinema. In keeping with his usual way of working, when Hayawaka was given the script he tore out all the pages on which his character did not appear and threw them away. Subsequently, he never knew how his role formed a part of the bigger picture.

BACKUP: Sam Spiegel had produced *The African Queen* (John Huston, 1951), amongst other titles. Don Ashton, the production designer, was to perform the same role for *Billy Budd* (Richard Brooks, 1962) and *Oh! What a Lovely War*.

Carl Foreman's most notable writing credit had been for *High Noon* and he went on to write and produce *The Guns of Navarone* (J Lee Thompson, 1962) and *McKenna's Gold* (J Lee Thompson, 1969). Michael Wilson's previous writing credits had included co-writing the Oscar winning *A Place in the Sun* (George Stevens, 1951) and uncredited work on the Oscar nominated *Friendly Persuasion* (William Wyler, 1956). He went on to work with Lean as an uncredited writer on *Lawrence of Arabia* and also scripted *Planet of the Apes* (Franklin J Schaffner, 1968), which was also adapted from a Pierre Boulle novel.

Make-up duties on the film were supervised by Stuart Freeborn, who would go on to contribute make-up effects for *2001: A Space Odyssey* (Stanley Kubrick, 1969) and *Star Wars: The Empire Strikes Back* (Irvin Kershner, 1980) for which he supervised the creation of Jedi Master Yoda.

PRODUCTION/IN THE TRENCHES: Like so many great, enduring, creatively rich films, the challenge and trials in the creation of the work are all ultimately for the good. *The Bridge on the River Kwai* was an arduous project, conceptually and logistically, with relations between the director and the crew understandably tense.

Throughout the process, Lean and Spiegel worked with tension and conflict, yet it is often in having creative choices challenged that the strongest ideas come to develop. Spiegel had not wanted the expense of filming in Asia but Lean insisted. Alarming and wrongheaded though it may seem now, Spiegel had hoped to film in Eastern Europe, where they could matte in establishing shots of the jungle. A matte painting tends to be of an environment that might otherwise be too costly or impossible to construct or travel to. This image, usually painted on glass, though now often rendered on a computer, is then combined with the existing images of actors performing a scene or of an establishing shot. For a dazzling survey of this very beautiful aspect of filmmaking check out the book *The Invisible Art* by Mark Cotta Vaz.

The art director Don Ashton took a location scout to Ceylon – he had been there during World War Two, and remembered the terrain and how viable it would be for the film. Thailand, home of the actual River Kwai (where portions of *The Deer Hunter* were filmed) was not considered wild enough to be used as the location for filming. The heat and relative remoteness of the location were inherently problematic, and for Lean it was a long way from Croydon.

The filming of the bridge explosion was a tense and initially fraught situation, with one of the multiple cameras used to capture the action not being turned on by its operator. Lean realised this and called for the shot to be abandoned, but the train was already heading towards the sand break, where it slammed to a halt.

Rather comically, and in the spirit of the grand producer that fuels so many stereotypes, Spiegel would tell whoever asked that the bridge had cost a quarter of a million dollars to construct, when in fact it had cost around forty thousand. In an age when quality was equated with quantity and expense, it was a comforting exaggeration of the truth in true showman style.

The film eventually went $200,000 over budget, with the edit being done in Paris, as Lean was unable to set foot in England because of his complicated tax situation.

MARTIAL MUSIC: The score for the film was written in three weeks by Malcolm Arnold, with whom Lean favoured collaborating. The famous whistling sound was achieved by a fusion of a piccolo and seventeen men of the Irish Guards whistling (the words of the song were considered too impolite to include). The theme music 'Colonel Bogey's March' was played at Lean's funeral at St Paul's Cathedral.

Malcolm Arnold's other film credits numbered over a hundred, but included music for the films *The Sea Shall not Have Them*, *Hobson's Choice*, *Whistle Down the Wind* (Bryan Forbes, 1961) and *The Heroes of Telemark*. Arnold has also composed numerous symphonies and concerti.

REIMAGINING REALITY: The film dwells very powerfully on the life of the prison camp and the construction of the bridge. However, the harder, historical truth is that the several bridges built on the River Kwai during the war were not comparable with the scale and grandeur of the film version. This particular film is a spectacle amongst other things.

Those bridges that were constructed were mainly built by the many American POWs who had been captured in the Phillippines, some of whom had endured the Bataan death march, and others whose ships had been sunk. There were many deaths building the bridges, but there was certainly nothing as heroic and crazed as the efforts of Nicholson, Shears and Warden.

HEART OF BATTLE: For producer Sam Spiegel the bridge was where the central meaning of the film resided, with the construction of the bridge as a metaphor for obsessive behaviour. As such it embodies the characteristics of the duelling protagonists, who take the admirable qualities of professionalism and integrity to useless extremes. The context of war allows a story to develop of physical and emotional endurance. Like *La Grande Illusion*, the film dramatises the concept of respect during war across warring sides, and certainly presents the human dynamics revealed by combat and conflict.

CHARACTER: Of the characters in this film, and indeed in several of his other, later pictures at least, David Lean commented: 'I'm fascinated by these nuts . . . Nicholson was certainly a nut, so was Lawrence [of Arabia], in a wonderful way.' Perhaps Lean saw something of himself in these obsessed, singular characters. In his phenomenally expansive biography of David Lean, Kevin Brownlow comments that 'Colonel Nicholson, David felt, was a magnificent tragic-comic figure well out of the usual run of film characters.'

Against the jungle setting and action set pieces is the story of the conflict between Nicholson and Saito. The Shears adventure story plays out alongside it. Saito says to Nicholson, 'You speak to me of code. What code? The coward's code. What do you know of the soldier's code? Of *bushido*.'

Nicholson resists having his officers work (again like *Paths of Glory* and *In Which We Serve*, the social hierarchy and class delineations of the military are foregrounded) and he willingly accepts the punishment, saying to the doctor, 'This is where we must win through.' He is admirable rather than lovable, but certainly by the close of the film we feel for Nicholson as he watches his beloved bridge about to perish. It seems impossible to think he falls on the detonator intentionally. Nicholson's wild-eyed stare through much of the film registers a man gradually losing his sanity in the wilderness.

Saito begins the film as a strong commander but, like von Rauffenstein in *La Grande Illusion*, he shows concern and consideration for the men. Indeed, the first image we are given of Saito places a white orchid in the same frame, as an indicator of his more gentle, nurturing side. Midway through the film his conversation with Nicholson reveals that where Nicholson is a career soldier, Saito had begun his life as an artist. Saito, for all his professionalism, ultimately concedes to Nicholson that he hates the British, saying, 'You endure, but you have no courage.'

The audience feels Saito's shame at having the British troops take command of the bridge construction in that very affecting moment when, from a respectful distance, the camera watches Saito break down and cry. Nicholson and Saito break one another emotionally as they become increasingly mad. Saito also talks about how any attempt to escape the camp is ultimately 'an escape from reality' and comments that the war 'is not a game of cricket'.

Dr Compton and Shears function in part as commentators on the action as it spirals out of reasonable behaviour. In the latter part of the film, Shears angrily says to Warden, 'This is just a game, this war . . . you're crazy with courage. The only important thing is to live as a human being.'

This 'superman' approach to the war that Nicholson and Saito have thankfully finally falls away upon completion of the bridge, with Nicholson reflecting aloud on his career as Saito listens. The scene is gentle, reflective and lyrical, and indicates the deep insecurity at the heart of Nicholson. At this point he becomes a sympathetic character, unsure of whether he has made a useful difference to people's lives. With the bridge he feels he has, and he takes great pride in nailing up the plaque upon its completion. It is a sad moment when later the same plaque floats in the river, just another piece of debris after the explosion. This characterisation of 'supermen' in the jungle is echoed in *Apocalypse Now*. The screenwriter of that film, John Milius, considers *The Bridge on the River Kwai* one of the great adventure films set against the backdrop of war. Like Nicholson, Warden is equally single-minded in seeing through his mission to blow up the bridge.

Shears is the everyman with whom the audience identifies. The other soldiers' professionalism perhaps obscures their sense at times. When

Shears comments on the madness of Warden and also of Nicholson, the viewer is inclined to agree.

STYLE: The tracking shot that glides through the jungle in the opening credits immerses us in an environment where nature is all encompassing. Lean's shot designs alternate between the expansive and energetic to the small and quiet. When Saito steps out to view the newly arrived prisoners, Nicholson is framed by the legs of Saito in the foreground. Saito stands over Nicholson like a giant.

Late in the film, when Nicholson reflects with some melancholy on his career, his back is to us as Saito listens. The setting sun symbolises the close of Nicholson's career.

As the soldiers march into the camp whistling 'Colonel Bogey's March' the camera tracks with them, so that the audience is drawn into the group, tied in so thoroughly to place and atmosphere.

The image of the vulture book-ends the film, crystallising the sense that nature endures over petty human endeavours and conflicts.

Whilst Lean's visuals do suggest the harshness of the jungle the film also revels in its beauty: the moonlight dancing off the water in the blueness of night, the early morning mist in the valley, and the sunlight through the canopy.

CRITICAL CROSSFIRE: From the *New Statesman*, '*Bridge on the River Kwai* is a huge, expensive chocolate box of a war picture. Inside it is perhaps a better and ironic idea . . .'

The *Time Out Film Guide* felt the film was ultimately 'A classic example of a film that fudges the issues it raises', whilst *Leonard Maltin's Movie and Video Guide* sticks to the familiar great praise for the film as a 'psychological battle of wills combined with high-powered action sequences'.

MEDALS OF HONOUR: *The Bridge on the River Kwai* won the Academy Award in 1958 for Best Actor (Alec Guinness), Best Cinematography (Jack Hildyard), Best Director (David Lean), Best Film Editing (Peter Taylor), Best Music (Malcolm Arnold), Best Picture (Sam Spiegel), Best Writing based on Material from Another Medium (Pierre Boulle – and later Michael Wilson and Carl Foreman). Nominated for an Academy Award was Sessue Hayakawa for Best Actor in a Supporting Role. At the BAFTA Awards the film won Best British Actor, Best British Film, Best British Screenplay and Best Film. At the awards of the British

Society of Cinematographers the film won Best Cinematography, and it won Best Foreign Production at the David di Donatello Awards in Italy in 1958. David Lean won the DGA award in 1958 for Best Directorial Achievement and at the Golden Globes the film won Best Motion Picture, Best Motion Picture Actor (Alec Guinness), and Best Motion Picture Director. Again Sessue Hayakawa was nominated in the Best Supporting Actor category.

In 1997, the film was entered into America's National Film Registry as a film deserving of preservation.

OTHER BATTLEFRONTS: Viewers compelled by the exotic adventure and combat of *The Bridge on the River Kwai* should consider viewing David Lean's next film, *Lawrence of Arabia*. The film dramatises the life of TE Lawrence and his book *The Seven Pillars of Wisdom*. Lawrence was the son of an English peer, and something of a self-made hero who became involved with the Arab–English challenge to Axis Turkey. In real life he was a short man, but the film casts tall Peter O'Toole, with his otherworldly, godly countenance, in the role. Lean collaborated with British playwright Robert Bolt on the project and emphasised the sense of Lawrence's journey. The film took three years to write, film and post-produce, and employed the services of the Moroccan Army as well as reconstructing sections of Damascus, Cairo and Akaba.

In 1963 *The Great Escape* was released, another action adventure based around prison-camp experience. In 1987 Steven Spielberg made the wonderful *Empire of the Sun*, one of his best films ever, and based on the novel of the same name by JG Ballard. It is Jean Renoir's POW drama *La Grande Illusion* that perhaps supersedes them all in its exploration of the relationships and bonds that flourish in desperate times. That said, the first half of Lean's film bears out quite clearly the impact of Renoir's film on the relationships between Nicholson, Saito and the soldiers.

THE HOMEFRONT: *The Bridge on the River Kwai* is available on a special edition DVD that features a behind the scenes, retrospective documentary and also an appreciative commentary from writer/director John Milius. It was Milius who wrote *Apocalypse Now*, some of that film inspired by *The Bridge on the River Kwai*, and who also directed the war-themed pictures *Red Dawn* (1984), *Farewell to the King* (1989) and *Flight of the Intruder* (1991).

FINAL BRIEFING: *The Bridge on the River Kwai* is an astonishing adventure film that achieves what so few such films of the genre do, namely the integration of strong characterisation (which means that all aspects of human feeling are shown and not just tough heroics) with a tense storyline in which the classic adventure question, 'Are you good enough to meet the challenge?' is posed.

Certainly the first part of the film is the most compelling, with the battle of wills between Nicholson and Saito forming the basis of the drama.

Lean's film satisfies on all counts. It is expansive, tense and lyrical at moments. It is also a very funny film in many ways, and in the camp-centred first half of the film one can readily see the influence of *La Grande Illusion*.

The Bridge on the River Kwai is as entertaining and compelling as its reputation suggests.

FINAL SALUTE: One of the most famous filmmaker fans of *The Bridge on the River Kwai* is the writer–director John Milius. His credits include *Dillinger* (1972), *The Wind and the Lion* (1974) and the little-seen *Farewell To The King*. Of *Kwai*, Milius said, 'It has incredible tension . . . a perfect example of an action film.'

Kanal (1957)

96 minutes

Film Polski
Producer: Stansilaw Adler
Director: Andrzej Wajda
Screenplay: Jerzy Stefan Stawinski (based on his short story)
Cinematographer: Jerzy Lipman
Editor: Halina Nawrocka
Music: Jan Krenz
Art Direction: Roman Mann
Costume Design: Jerzy Szeski

CAST: Teresa Izewksa (*Daisy Stokrotka*), Tadeusz Janczar (*Corporal Korab*), Wienczyslaw Glinski (*Lieutenant Zadra*), Tadeusz Gwiazdowski

(*Sergeant Kula*), Stanislaw Mikulski (*The Slim*), Vladek Sheybal (*Composer*), Zofia Lindorf (Old Woman)

RATING: X

WAR STORY: Warsaw, September 1944. In a city under siege and utterly reduced to rubble, the unit of men and women resistance fighters are one of the few remaining pockets continuing to fight back as the German troops take control of the city.

The rebel unit march through the rubble, led by Lieutenant Zadra. Injured people lie in the rubble and some are carried off on stretchers. The unit make a camp in the remains of a house and here the dynamics amongst the small group of freedom fighters are established. There is warmth and tension amongst the soldiers, who have a young teenager to run messages for them. A composer named Michael calls home and momentarily speaks to his daughter and wife. Smulky and his lover Halinka make love. Zadra knows the German forces will soon attack them.

Young soldier Jacek is reunited with his girlfriend Daisy when she rejoins the unit. The ruined house comes under attack from the Germans. A Goliath tank approaches and Jacek disarms it. His bravery is not rewarded and he is shot in the chest, before being rescued by Smulky. The unit go into hiding after the skirmish, awaiting the next bombardment.

Zabawa, the commandant of the unit, arrives and orders that the rebels are now to protect themselves and head into the city's sewers (the *kanal*) and make their way to the centre of Warsaw. Zadra is uneasy about this order but Zabawa, his superior, tells him to keep his act together. At nightfall the unit commence their journey towards the world beneath the streets, as the German forces sweep the rubble with spotlights and foot soldiers. In the streets chaos reigns, with the soldiers controlling the crowds.

In the sewers Jacek's chest wound worsens and his energy depletes and Daisy does all she can to maintain his focus and energy and reason. Michael splits from the group, the tension proving too much for him. Smulky and Halinka make slow progress, but Jacek and Daisy weaken. When Daisy begins climbing towards an exit Jacek follows, but then falls back down the sewer. Daisy goes back to help him but time is running out. When they see someone approach they are scared, but it is only the musician Michael, who walks along playing his flute.

Smulky and Halinka are finding it difficult to find a route out and their mood becomes desperate and ever more hopeless. He then confesses to her that he is married. Halinka kills herself and Smulky goes on, leaving her body where it is as he continues to try to find the sewer that leads to their goal, Wilcza Street.

Eventually Jacek and Daisy appear to be safe, but find that though they can see daylight and taste the air, a grille they cannot break blocks their exit. They collapse in the sunlight that fills the sewer, but do not taste freedom. They hold on to one another, their journey at an end.

Smulky finds an exit and begins climbing towards the sunlight. He hauls himself out towards freedom, only to find a Nazi officer standing over the hole that he emerges from. He stands up and turns to see dozens of others who were using the sewers as an escape. Smulky, in exhausted despair, walks over to a heap of dead bodies and collapses to his knees.

In another part of town Lieutenant Zadra continues on through the sewer. One of the men he is with sights an exit but finds it booby-trapped with small grenades strung across the opening. The man begins defusing the grenades, but is finally blown up when his foot slips as he precariously balances to reach them.

Lieutenant Zadra emerges into the sunlight to find himself alone. He climbs back down into the sewers.

CONCEPT/THE MISSION: *Kanal* is one of several films from one of Europe's most celebrated directors, Polish filmmaker Andrzej Wajda, who has worked in both theatre and film. Wajda attended the Fine Arts Academy of Poland in 1946 and studied painting, but began to feel that it was not powerful enough as a means of expression.

Wajda had witnessed death camps, arrests and the Warsaw Uprising. By 1948 the spirit of social realism in art and creative work in Poland was beginning to take its hold, and painting was needed as a medium of reflecting the new emerging Polish post-war identity as it became 'sovietised'. It was then that Wajda and his classmates decided the Academy was no longer the place to develop their creative work. Wajda had grown up in a climate where the artistic movements Constructivism and Futurism prevailed, and where the spirit of the avant-garde, such as Rhythm and Blok, were a major part of cultural life. Fascism threatened such ways of expression. Wajda's interest in film was spurred when he saw an advert for the Krakow Film School, who were looking to recruit.

His first film-school project was a feature-length piece about the first socialist city in Poland. Of his film-school experience Wajda commented that 'On the one hand our professors at the school wanted us . . . to make all these social realist movies, and, on the other, they brought us closer to real art.'

After leaving film school, Wajda pursued his independence as a filmmaker so as not to become embroiled in being politically controlled. The first film he made was *A Generation* (1955). The second film was *Kanal* and it stood as part of the newly defined filmmaking spirit in Poland. There was the sense of a new Poland being born from the rubble of World War Two. As a sixteen-year-old, Wajda had experienced contact with the resistance and so had some developed political awareness.

Poland had operated with a very low level of film production, not even producing films in double figures by 1954. The first Polish post-war film was *Forbidden Songs (Zakazna piosenki)*, directed by a popular prewar director called Leonard Buczkowski in 1947. There was also *The Last Stage (Ostatni etap)* directed by Wanda Jakubowska in 1948. The post-war cinema of Wajda and his contemporaries was committed to avoiding stereotypes of Poland. There was an effort to create subtle emotional and intellectual effects stemming from the new filmmakers' engagement to realism. Widely considered the most significant post-war film to begin advancing this realist effort was Aleksander Ford's *Five Boys from Barska Street* (1954), a breakthrough in that it dealt with protagonists who were not idealised characters but rather juvenile delinquents.

In the late 1950s Poland pulled its film production into shape, allocating film units headed up by established filmmakers of the time, and Wajda benefited from this more organised, productive structure.

Kanal was Wajda's career tipping point, the film that placed his work on the international cinema scene. The story for the film came from Jerzy Stawinski, the literary editor of the Kadr studio, who had written the short story. It was Stawinski too who ensured the screenplay for the film was given the go-ahead by the Assessment Commission for Films and Screenplays.

Wajda had a desire to showing 'the truth' of the Warsaw Uprising against the fascist forces, and was committed to his sewer-set story, even though he knew this may not make the film especially commercial or 'entertaining'. To Wajda's surprise, and no doubt the surprise of the Polish film industry at the time, the film was screened at the Cannes Film Festival, where it won the Silver Palm, the Jury Award.

For Wajda, a key influence and inspiration for the film was Dante's *Inferno*, which the filmmaker overtly applied as a metaphor to the plight of the resistance force. Wajda was also inspired by the pace at which Western cinema, particularly popular American cinema, moved. He elected not to investigate the political context (a choice that many writer–directors of war films make, it seems) of the film's subject, though originally there was to have been a pre-credit sequence of *Uhlans* galloping to attack. These cavalry charges were all military disasters. Wajda abandoned this concept to the delight of his contemporaries and colleagues, who regarded this edit of the material judicious. The underground left played a significant role in indicating the future for Poland.

In his preface to a collection of Wajda's scripts, Boleslaw Sulik writes that Wajda 'was largely concerned with the sheer size and intensity of the catastrophe, and not content with what could be achieved by direct description, he was searching for a suitably grand parallel, something that would make images transcend the limiting subject matter'.

In more recent years, Wajda has been a member of the Polish parliament and was an active member of the Solidarity movement.

Looking back on *Kanal* from the vantage point of almost fifty years, Wajda recently wrote, 'We chose to create cinema from scratch . . . We watched the films of Italian Neorealism and were inspired by them.'

Many years after *Kanal's* production Wajda visited the set of Steven Spielberg's *Schindler's List* while it was filming in Poland, and wrote Spielberg a letter wishing him well for the project. There is a sequence midway through *Kanal* showing the Nazis on the streets of Warsaw with people running and screaming. *Schindler's List* echoes these images and in a sense complements Wajda's astonishing film well.

CASTING/RECRUITMENT: Wajda was not the only new, emerging talent on the film. *Kanal* stands as a film that features many Polish actors who were beginning in film, several of whom went on to long-lasting careers, notably Wienczyslaw Glinski and Stanislaw Mikulski. The actor Vladek Sheybal, who portrays Michael, went on to appear in *Casino Royale* (John Huston, 1967), *The Wind and the Lion* (John Milius, 1975), the TV mini series *Shogun* (Jerry London, 1980) and *Red Dawn* (John Milius, 1984).

BACKUP: *Kanal's* crew, like its actors, were largely newcomers to the reviving Polish film industry of the time.

PRODUCTION/IN THE TRENCHES: The film was shot on location in Warsaw. Wajda's film gains its immediacy from being a film shot so clearly in the actual rubble and ruin of post-war Warsaw and certainly the production's very physical dynamic was made all the more so by the terrain being worked in.

MARTIAL MUSIC: The music is brash and shrill and dark. Essentially, it is desperate and contains none of the nobility or melancholy that some war-film scores do. Instead it only matches the rough, brutal landscape we can see. The military drums fuse with something more discordant.

REIMAGINING REALITY: The Polish Home Army's grand plan in starting the Uprising had been to liberate Warsaw from the Germans in time for the arrival of the Red Army from Russia seen as allies. However, Stalin considered the Polish resistance an obstruction to his own plans for Poland. It is widely agreed that when Daisy, at the end of *Kanal*, gazes out to something offscreen, what she is looking out at is the ineffectual Russian army who had paused in moving into Poland, allowing the German soldiers to eliminate the Poles and in effect doing the job on Stalin's behalf.

Kanal does its best not to romanticise the insurgents, and ultimately testifies to the tragedy of the brave effort to liberate Warsaw from German occupation. The outbreak of the uprising on 1 August 1944 was ordered by the Home Army in agreement with the Polish government in exile. Unfortunately, a line of communication with approaching Soviet armies east of Warsaw was not effective, and the Germans had the advantage. The Nazis overwhelmed the insurgents, and whilst the uprising challenged the Germans for two months, it was ultimately suppressed. Warsaw was evacuated and much of it demolished.

The film opens with a voice-over comment that invites the audience to 'Watch them as they live their last hours.' The film isn't interested in creating suspense – we know the outcome from the start. For Wajda the compulsion was to explore the toll that combat took on the sanity of the fighters. Subsequently, there was a difference in the official version of the uprising and the popular, folk memory of events. Wajda was seen to have overamplified the sense of tragedy. Amusingly, but tellingly, the day after the film was premiered on 20 April 1957 at the Cannes Film Festival, the *Nice Matin* newspaper complained that films such as *Kanal* were not fit for the wealthy people watching the films there.

HEART OF BATTLE: The film seeks to honour the truth of feeling around the Warsaw Uprising. An officer cadet during the uprising, named Jozef Szczepanski, wrote a poem, part of which reads, 'But know this: from our tombstones/A victorious new Poland will be born/And you will not walk this land/You red ruler of bestial forces!'

From the beginning of the film we are given a clear indication that we are watching a tragic story unfold. The film celebrates the community of oppressed people, rather like the war film *Land and Freedom* (Ken Loach, 1995), and takes time to let the audience understand the frailties and moments of aliveness the fighters experience before their literal and symbolic descent.

The sewers serve as a crucible in which despair causes some alliances to fracture and others to strengthen. There is a sense of hysteria and certainly of nightmare.

One soldier early on asks another, 'Future generations will honour us, won't they?'

CHARACTER: *Kanal* is very much an ensemble piece, especially in its first half. As the film progresses its focus narrows. One of the most striking characters, and the least gung ho of all the fighters, is Michael. He has a haunting and gaunt face and his incongruous character continues through the film to the point where he breaks away from the group as they push through the sewers. Michael is too fragile to endure the journey. Early in the film, Michael serves as something of a chorus for the action, an artist able to comment on the trauma when he says, 'Everything is so empty, so hollow. I'm impotent. I'm just a shell.' What Michael is saying is surely common to any war zone.

The desensitising effect that Michael acknowledges is common to several other critical war films, for instance in *Paths of* **Glory**, when one of the soldiers about to be shot explains how he has not had a sexual thought since he was court-martialled. *The Deer Hunter*, *Born on the Fourth of July* and *Saving Private Ryan* all invoke that same sense of distance and numbness.

Into the predominantly male world of *Kanal* comes the strong-willed and very beautiful Daisy. Her boyfriend and fellow freedom fighter Jacek commends her realistic outlook. Daisy is surely the most beautiful realist in all of cinema, and she is as wonderful to behold as Natalie Wood or Anita Ekberg. She is determined, and as she pushes through the sewer carrying a gun, her appearance and character anticipate the far more widely known image of Ripley in the films *Alien* (Ridley Scott, 1979) and *Aliens* (James Cameron, 1986), or even Sarah Connor in *Terminator 2: Judgement Day* (James Cameron, 1991). Daisy is focused and committed and her back-story clarifies her familiarity with the sewers and how in her youth they were 'an escape from fear'. When Daisy says to Jacek, 'We must live,' it is as if she is addressing the audience. She is the most heroic character in the film.

Daisy's boyfriend Jacek is a handsome, competent and courageous soldier who pays the price for his conviction, yet dies as a hero.

STYLE: Wajda's first film, *A Generation*, had indicated a commitment to social realism and positive portrayal of working-class heroes. *Kanal* continued this approach. In his notes prior to beginning filming, Wajda wrote: 'The picture must swell in time with the action of the story, and so the whole of the first part . . . ought to be kept in as documentary a style as possible: long takes, travelling shots, long shots, no close-ups.'

During the first part of the film the rubble is very much a graveyard, the wilderness of war marked with makeshift crosses on burial sites. This sense of death will continue throughout the film, becoming ever more stark.

An apocalyptic tone is present from the first image (a dazzling long take and tracking shot), which not only introduces us to the protagonists as they march through the rubble but which also emphatically shows the burned-out world that Warsaw has become. The film's opening shots of war-torn Warsaw establish a documentary feel, and the voice-over informing the audience that they are about to watch a scenario as it 'draws to its tragic close' adds to this effect. The long takes unfold in real time and immerse the audience in the action.

In the night sequence when the freedom fighters race to the sewers, the smoke is backlit across the rubble, creating an eerie, unearthly environment, similar to the unworldly way in which war zones are depicted in films like **Paths of Glory** and **Apocalypse Now**. Once the action enters the sewers, *Kanal* becomes something of a horror film as the characters move through this 'haunted' environment. A strange wailing sound turns out to be an old colonel lying in the muck of the sewer, crying out as though he has lost his mind. The freedom fighters have no time to help him and just keep pushing on. One of the eeriest images, though, is of the musician Michael walking through the mist and darkness playing his flute. The sound is both unsettling and playful, and Michael's ghostly countenance is fully realised.

Such supernatural moments contrast with more blatant shocks, such as a close-up of Halinka after she has shot herself, her eyes still open in the half light. Equally horrific, and symbolising the primal impulse to survive, is the moment when the unit haul a Nazi from the ledge above where they are hiding and beat him to death with rocks. Another surprisingly graphic instance occurs early in the film when a blanket falls away from a young woman on a stretcher to reveal she has lost a leg.

Moments of grace and humanity are accompanied by the playing of music. When the Warsaw rebels occupy a bombed-out house as a makeshift camp, Michael sits playing the piano as the soldiers rest and plan their next move. In *Saving Private Ryan* it's Edith Piaf playing on a gramophone who accompanies the anticipation of battle. In the American Civil War film *Glory* (Ed Zwick, 1989), the soldiers gather and sing the night before they go into battle.

CRITICAL CROSSFIRE: Writing in the newspaper *Zycie Warszawy* in the month the film was released, Stanislaw Grzelecki wrote that '*Kanal* can be viewed in two ways: either as an artistic, dramatised relation of events, or as an attempt to create a universal human drama. In both cases, part of the audience was unable to liberate themselves from the pressures of their own personal memories.' For *Le Monde*, 'Wajda is unable to resist a certain romanticising of horror.' For the *Time Out Film Guide* 'it certainly has a unique intensity and gloom', and *Leonard Maltin's Movie and Video Guide* is of the same opinion, saying the film is 'intense' and 'almost unrelentingly graphic'.

MEDALS OF HONOUR: In 1957 the film won the Special Jury Prize at the Cannes Film Festival. At the 1959 BAFTA awards the film was nominated in the Most Promising Newcomer category for the actress Teresa Izewska.

OTHER BATTLEFRONTS: *Kanal* forms the middle chapter of Wajda's celebrated trilogy that is book-ended by *A Generation* and *Ashes and Diamonds* (1958). Together the films form an informal trilogy that explores the life of Poland in the post-war years.

During the war a British film had been made called *Dangerous Moonlight* (Brian Desmond Hurst, 1941) which was a wartime romance set in Poland at the time of the uprising. For the film a piece of music was composed by Richard Addinsell that went on to become a popular hit, namely his *Warsaw Concerto*, which pastiched the style of the composer Rachmaninoff.

The Pianist (Roman Polanski, 2003) has a number of similarities with *Kanal*, especially its final phase in which the protagonist wandering through the apocalyptic rubble of Warsaw finally comes across a piano and is able to play it, thereby sustaining him emotionally in his Robinson Crusoe-like existence.

THE HOMEFRONT: *Kanal* is available as a Region 1 DVD.

FINAL BRIEFING: *Kanal* is a stunning film, one of the greatest war films ever made, and yet so rarely seen (or even known, it would appear). The film proved unpopular with Polish audiences whose parents had taken part in the uprising, probably because it did not portray an uplifting kind of story.

Kanal is relentlessly bleak but also very dynamic, and is as compelling, intense and moving as anything by Kubrick, Spielberg or Weir. It is about a desperate moment in time, and is not an exhilarating war film but a meditation on fear and the fracturing of hope. Had the film ended with Jacek and Daisy collapsed and gazing out at the water through the grille then maybe we could imagine some sense of promise, but ending as it does with a man, battered and broken, choosing to descend back into 'hell' like an animal is powerfully and uncompromisingly hopeless.

Given how used we have become to a certain brand of movie heroism and war film bravery, perhaps *Kanal* offers a more definitive and honest sense of how people behave under intense pressure and the threat of imminent death. As the war film has evolved over the twentiety century, and now into the twenty-first, the genre must confront the rawness of anxiety, mass panic and despair with increasing accuracy and honesty.

FINAL SALUTE: In 1999 Steven Spielberg wrote to the Academy of Motion Picture Arts and Sciences to recommend Andrzej Wajda for an Honorary Academy Award for his career. Part of Spielberg's letter read: '. . . he has inspired all of us to re-examine the strength of our common humanity'.

The Great Escape (1963)

169 minutes

United Artists
Producer: John Sturges
Director: John Sturges

Screenplay: James Clavell, WR Burnett (based on the book
The Great Escape by Paul Brickhill)
Cinematographer: Daniel Fapp
Editor: Ferris Webster
Music: Elmer Bernstein
Production Design: Fernando Carrere
Art Direction: Fernando Carrere
Costume Design: Bert Henrikson

CAST: Steve McQueen *('Cooler King' Hilts)*, James Garner (*'The Scrounger' Hendley*), Richard Attenborough *('Big X' Bartlett)*, James Donald (*Senior Officer Ramsey*), Charles Bronson (*Danny Velinski*), Donald Pleasence (*'The Forger' Blythe*), James Coburn (*'The Manufacturer' Sedgwick*), David McCallum (*Ashley-Pitt*), Gordon Jackson (*MacDonald*), John Leyton (*Willie*)

RATING: PG

TAGLINE: The great adventure! The great entertainment!

WAR STORY: A line of trucks brings British and American prisoners of war to a new camp in rural Germany. When the men are let down from the trucks we follow several of them as they immediately set about getting a sense of how secure the camp is. This is a prison camp for all those who have tried to escape prison camps before. As the camp commandant says, he has all the rotten eggs in one basket. Captain Ramsey, the British Air Force captain, is made the liaison between prisoners and the Germans, and says the duty of the prisoners is to try and escape.

Several early escape attempts, all unsuccessful, are made by various POWs. The most notable of these is American Virgil Hilts, who is repeatedly put in the cooler (solitary confinement) for a number of days. A new prisoner arrives at the camp, a Briton named Bartlett who is considered to be the most dangerous of all hard-core escapees. Bartlett immediately calls a meeting with those men he has known before and maps out his general plan to create an escape for two hundred and fifty men using three tunnels. Each man is charged with a particular responsibility, and a number of very inventive solutions are found to the problems of building the tunnels and sourcing equipment for the job. Hilts agrees to break out of the camp and be recaptured just in order to recce the woods and local area beyond the camp.

Sure enough, he gives himself up and is put in the cooler again. Forged documents and clothes are created for the men to carry and wear when they escape. Only one of the three tunnels is ultimately to be used. One POW, Ives, is shot dead when he attempts to climb the wire fence, his resolve and nerve finally shattered by so many escape attempts that have been foiled. Danny the tunnel digger becomes anxious and unsure he can handle the digging any more. Bartlett then informs Blythe, who has forged all the papers for the escape, that he cannot be allowed to be part of the escape. Blythe is losing his eyesight and would be a hindrance and danger to the other men. The Scrounger says he will 'look after' Blythe and ensure he is not a hindrance in the escape.

The time to break out comes and the tunnel is found to be twenty feet short of where it should be. The men risk the danger and a number of them get free. Others do not and return to camp at gunpoint. The men who have escaped split up. Bartlett and Sandy MacDonald travel by train. Sedgwick heads off alone and escapes, while Danny and his pal row a boat to freedom. Bartlett and Mac are caught, and Bartlett is shot en route back to the prison camp. Hilts steals a German motorbike and is chased across the German countryside before finally being caught. Blythe is killed and the Scrounger is rounded up and returned to the camp. Fifty escapees in all are killed. Hilts returns to the POW camp.

CONCEPT/THE MISSION: John Sturges had previously directed *The Magnificent Seven*, which, like *The Great Escape*, was about a team of men united in a common goal. Sturges had made a notable career as a director of action movies. John Sturges had also directed *Gunfight at the O.K. Corral* starring Burt Lancaster and Kirk Douglas.

Famously, Paul Brickhill's novel/memoir *The Great Escape*, first published in 1950, does not feature the character Virgil Hilts. The character was instead based on General David Jones of the US Air Force, who had been involved in America's Dolittle Raids on the Japanese in the wake of the bombing of Pearl Harbour on 7 December 1941. Jones was also imprisoned in a German POW camp.

Brickhill had been head of a team whose job in the camp was to protect forgers, who were especially open to being found out as they had to do their work by the windows of the barracks for light. Brickhill writes of himself, 'I am sort of Boswell, not a hero.' Brickhill also wrote the novel *Reach for the Sky*, which became a film of the same name charting the experiences of RAF pilot Douglas Bader, famous for losing his legs in a flying accident and learning to walk (and fly) again with the use of artificial limbs.

In Brickhill's book the deaths of the fifty men shot dead is marked by the commandant permitting the men to build a vault to house the ashes, with each man's ashes in an urn engraved with their names. The fifty were cremated to cover the means by which they all died. Brickhill's book is dedicated 'To the Fifty' and he comments: 'It was pretty clear they'd just taken fifty and shot them as an example. God knows that was logical enough under Hitler.' In a neat turn of film fate, the other source for *The Great Escape* was a film entitled *Danger Within* (Don Chaffey, 1959) that had starred Richard Attenborough.

CASTING/RECRUITMENT: Steve McQueen stars as Virgil Hilts and was coming off the back of his star turn in *The Magnificent Seven*. McQueen's career had begun in television, perhaps most notably in the western series *Wanted: Dead or Alive*. McQueen had also featured in *The Blob* (Irvin S Yeaworth Jr, 1958). He went on to make films such as *Baby, the Rain Must Fall* (Robert Mulligan, 1965), *The Cincinnati Kid* (Norman Jewison, 1966), *Nevada Smith* (Henry Hathaway, 1966), *The Sand Pebbles* (Robert Wise, 1966), and became a major star of the 1960s and 1970s with roles in *Bullitt* (Peter Yates, 1968), *The Thomas Crown Affair* (Norman Jewison, 1968), *The Reivers* (Mark Rydell, 1969), *The Getaway* (Sam Peckinpah, 1972) and the brilliant *Junior Bonner* (Sam Peckinpah, 1972). McQueen also starred alongside Dustin Hoffman in *Papillon* (Franklin J Schaffner, 1973). McQueen's last film, made as he was living with cancer, was *Tom Horn* (William Wiard, 1980).

Charles Bronson has had an enduring Hollywood career appearing in *House of Wax* (Andre de Toth, 1953), *Vera Cruz* (Robert Aldrich, 1954), *Run of the Arrow* (Samuel Fuller, 1959), *The Magnificent Seven*, and more recently *The Indian Runner* (Sean Penn, 1991).

Richard Attenborough had appeared as the hapless and cowardly young seaman in *In Which We Serve*, was in *A Matter of Life and Death*, and took a starring role as Pinky in *Brighton Rock* (Carol Reed, 1947). Other films for Attenborough as an actor included *The Ship That Died of Shame*, *The Flight of the Phoenix* (Robert Aldrich, 1965), *The Sand Pebbles*, *10 Rillington Place* (Richard Fleischer, 1971), *Brannigan* (Douglas Hickox, 1975), *Jurassic Park* (Steven Spielberg, 1993) and *Miracle on 34th Street* (Les Mayfield, 1994). Attenborough moved into a highly successful directing career with *Oh! What A Lovely War* (1969), *Young Winston* (1972), *Ghandi* (1982), *A Chorus Line* (1985), *Cry*

Freedom (1987), *Chaplin* (1992) and perhaps his most powerful and affecting film *Shadowlands* (1993), which charted the romantic life of writer CS Lewis and his love for American Joy Gresham.

James Coburn had starred in *The Magnificent Seven* and had also appeared in *Ride Lonesome* (Budd Boetticher, 1959). He went on to appear in *The Americanization of Emily* (Arthur Hiller, 1964), *Midway* (Jack Smight, 1976), *Cross of Iron* (Sam Peckinpah, 1977) and *The Player* (Robert Altman, 1991).

James Garner had, like McQueen, starred in a western TV series, *Maverick*. Garner went on to appear in the films *Grand Prix* (John Frankenheimer, 1966) and *Space Cowboys* (Clint Eastwood, 2000), and also starred in the 1970s TV detective series *The Rockford Files*.

Donald Pleasence's film roles include *Look Back in Anger* (Tony Richardson, 1958), *The Greatest Story Ever Told* (George Stevens, 1965), *Fantastic Voyage* (Richard Fleischer, 1965), *THX 1138* (George Lucas, 1971), *The Last Tycoon* (Elia Kazan, 1976) and *The Eagle has Landed* (John Sturges, 1976).

BACKUP: Cinematographer Daniel Fapp had also worked in this capacity on *West Side Story* (Robert Wise, 1961) and was to work on *Ice Station Zebra* (John Sturges, 1968).

The screenplay was by James Clavell, a novelist and screenwriter who began his career as a scriptwriter before moving into writing prose. Clavell's credits include the screenplay for the cult horror film *The Fly* (Kurt Neumann, 1958). He also wrote *Watusi* (Kurt Neumann, 1959) a film that dramatised the conflict between the Watusi tribe in Africa with British imperialist forces. Clavell went on to write and direct a film called *The Bitter and the Sweet* (1967) charting the relationship between Canadians and Japanese in the years after the Second World War. In 1962, Clavell wrote his first novel, *King Rat* (1965), about a prisoner of war and his efforts to survive. The book soon became a film directed by Bryan Forbes and starring George Segal. Clavell was an uncredited producer on *The Great Esape*. Later in his career Clavell wrote the novel *Shogun* and in 1971 he wrote and directed the film *The Last Valley*.

PRODUCTION/IN THE TRENCHES: *The Great Escape* was filmed in Germany and the set was based particularly on Stalag Luft III near Zagan in Poland. During production McQueen was apparently nervy about James Garner overshadowing him and it got to the point where director Sturges threatened to fire McQueen if he did not cool down.

The bike-chase scene that concludes the film and offers up its most famous images was incorporated by director Sturges in response to McQueen's enthusiasm for riding motorcycles. The biggest jump Hilts performs on the bike was done not by McQueen but by stuntman Bud Ekins, with McQueen at one point playing one of the German soldiers pursuing Hilts.

MARTIAL MUSIC: The now world-famous, whistle-friendly march that is the theme for the film was composed by Elmer Bernstein. Bernstein had come to the fore as a Hollywood film composer in the early 1950s and his career lasted until 2002 when he composed the gorgeous score for *Far From Heaven* (Todd Haynes, 2002) – this was to be his last, exquisite soundtrack. Bernstein's other film credits include *To Kill A Mockingbird* (Robert Mulligan, 1962), *The Man with the Golden Arm* (Otto Preminger, 1955), *The Magnificent Seven* and the brilliant accompaniment to *The Age of Innocence* (Martin Scorsese, 1993).

REIMAGINING REALITY: *The Great Escape* is inspired by the reality that many downed Allied aircrew were kept in Air Force POW camps called Stalag Luft, which is an abbreviation of Stammlager Luft (Permanent Camps for Airmen). Stalag Luft III held 10,000 POWs, was 59 acres in size and was bound by five miles of perimeter fencing. The tendency was for treatment of air force POWs to be markedly more tolerable than the treatment meted out in other camps by the SS or Gestapo. Most chose not to attempt escape, with only around five per cent being hard-core escape attempters. In his book *The Great Escape*, Paul Brickhill writes, 'You learn to escape the hard way. It took us three years to become proficient.'

HEART OF BATTLE: *The Great Escape* is not especially interested in exploring the subtleties of oppression or even the emotional dynamic of prison-camp life. Instead the historical situation provides the opportunity for traditional, old-fashioned male movie heroics. The most moving moment is when the Forger realises he is losing his sight. However, *The Great Escape* lacks the emotional and psychological depth of Renoir's **La Grande Illusion**.

CHARACTER: Virgil Hilts is the film's most memorable character, forever challenging authority with his escape attempts and every time being thrown back into the cooler.

Bartlett is the real hero of the film, a steely, determined British officer who is singular and serious. He will not yield to the POW life and as such he is a dreamer and schemer. Towards the end of the film Bartlett tells Mac that 'I've never been happier.'

Blythe is a delicate character who is brimming with reserve and modesty, in contrast to the cooler American characters. His great friend becomes the Scrounger, and together they form a great team, making a valiant bid for freedom late in the film.

The camp commandant is portrayed not as a cartoonish thug but as a human who seems all too aware of the cost of war. It is his response to the events that anchors the film to some degree.

Ives is a man who ultimately cracks under pressure and Danny the tunnel digger experiences similar doubts about himself.

STYLE: *The Great Escape* is a classically styled Hollywood action movie that uses World War Two as the backdrop for a range of macho heroics. Daniel Fapp's cinematography is warm for the most part and there is a prevailing lightness to the film's visual tone that matches the level at which most of its action is pitched.

CRITICAL CROSSFIRE: The film has always been well received as an action movie/war-film classic, with several famous set pieces, none more so perhaps than Hilts's dash for freedom on the motorbike. The *Time Out Film Guide* is less than impressed by the film, describing it as an 'uneven but entertaining World War Two escape drama, which even when it first appeared seemed very old fashioned'. For *Leonard Maltin's Movie and Video Guide* the film is 'beautifully photographed . . . Rip-roaring excitement.'

MEDALS OF HONOUR: The film was nominated for Best Film Editing at the 1964 Oscars and was Golden Globe nominated the same year in the category of Best Motion Picture. The film's screenwriters, James Clavell and WR Burnett, were nominated in 1964 by the Writers Guild of America.

OTHER BATTLEFRONTS: For more prisoner-of-war drama that contrast with the more zestful tone of *The Great Escape*, check out *La Grande Illusion, The Bridge on the River Kwai* and *Empire of the Sun.* For more action adventure in the spirit of *The Great Escape* consider viewing *The Guns of Navarone* and *Where Eagles Dare* (Brian G Hutton, 1974).

THE HOMEFRONT: *The Great Escape* is available as a special edition DVD featuring a number of extra features, including a documentary and a piece about the 'real' Virgil Hilts.

FINAL BRIEFING: *The Great Escape* is a war film that uses war as a playground for boyish invention. It is far more an action film than a comment about war and its effects. Instead it is concerned with how a unit of men function. Only twice is violence portrayed with any chilling effect, once when Ives is shot attempting to climb the wire fence, and late in the film when several of the characters are gunned down.

The film owes more perhaps to the western heroics of Sturges's previous film, *The Magnificent Seven*, than it does to representing an experience of being in a POW camp, though the film does acknowledge that Luftwaffe camps were that bit more civilised than other SS and Gestapo-run sites. *The Great Escape* often comes across as a fairly dull film with occasional moments of humour and energy, notably from McQueen and Pleasence. Why it has gained quite such a following seems a bit of a mysterty though.

FINAL SALUTE: Longtime actor friend of Steve McQueen, Dan Gordon is quoted as saying 'the Steve of *The Great Escape* was . . . cool, together, abstracted from the group, his own guy'.

Das Boot (1981)

Director's Version 200 minutes (original theatrical version
150 minutes; television miniseries version ran to six hours)

Bavaria Atelier
Producer: Gunter Rohrbach, Michael Bittins
Director: Wolfgang Petersen
Co Producer: Michael Bittins
Screenplay: Wolfgang Petersen based on the novel by
Lothar-Guenther Buchheim
Cinematographer: Jost Vacano
Editor: Hannes Nikel

Music: Klaus Doldinger
Production Design: Rolf Zehetbauer
Art Direction: Gotz Weidner
Costume Design: Monika Bauert
Visual Effects: Karl Baumgartner

CAST: Jurgen Prochnow (*Captain*), Herbert Gronemeyer (*Lieutenant Werner/Correspondent*), Klaus Wenneman (*Chief Engineer*), Hubertus Bengsch (*1st Lieutenant/Number One*), Martin Semmelrogge (*2nd Lieutenant*), Bernd Tauber (*Chief Quartermaster*), Erwin Leder (*Johann*), Martin May (*Ullmann*), Heinz Honig (*Hinrich*), UA Ochsen (*Chief Bosun*)

RATING: R/15

TAGLINE: The Other Side of World War Two.

WAR STORY: This outline refers to the Director's Cut of *Das Boot*.

A title card sets the context. By 1941 Hitler was attempting to blockade the United Kingdom, but German efforts in this regard were not successful. Ever more German submarines were launched, crewed by young men. By the autumn of 1941 a battle for control of the Atlantic was in progress.

The story begins with the captain at a German Navy bar popular with the submarine crews; some are just back from combat, others are preparing to head out to sea the next day.

The following morning the captain meets his crew at the shipyard. The submarine crew have a guest in the form of a naval correspondent, who appears out of his depth from the start. The U-boat sets out and the crew settle into their routines. Twenty days go by without the crew being engaged in combat or action of any kind. Frustrations build as the men on the boat wait. Finally the U-boat sees action, but is then found to have gone off course.

One night the U-boat becomes aware of a convoy of British ships, and they successfully torpedo one of the destroyers. The submarine crew then await certain British revenge. Sure enough, the U-boat is hit by British attack and suffers significant damage, so the captain decides they must return to base.

En route the U-boat stops in the ocean to rendezvous with a ship to take on new supplies and to rearm. The submarine command crew are greeted by the clean and tidy crew of the tugboat who are enjoying a lavish, comfortable dinner in stark contrast to the life led on board the submarine. The U-boat returns to action and the captain takes it through the Straits of Gibraltar, a dangerous move because of the shallow waters of the Mediterranean. The submarine is attacked again, with serious repercussions. The submarine drops almost three hundred metres and chaos and terror run rife. The crew struggle to fix the submarine amidst flooding, fire and increasingly mounting pressure, mechanical, physical and emotional. The crew's greatest battle has become one to maintain their sanity. After a great effort the crew just about restore the U-boat and it victoriously resurfaces. The captain sets a course back to the shipyard.

Returning as heroes to the German shipyard, the U-boat and the docks immediately come under fire from British fighter planes. Many of the submarine crew are killed, including the captain who dies having watched his beloved submarine sink.

CONCEPT/THE MISSION: *Das Boot* was screened in Germany as a miniseries in the early 1980s and was an immediate pop culture hit. Overseas, the film was released theatrically.

Initially Bavaria Studios had approached John Sturges, the director of *The Magnificent Seven* and *The Great Escape*, and got as far as pre-production on the project with a set being built in Munich. Robert Redford was due to star as the captain. Don Siegel, who had made *Dirty Harry* and *Escape From Alcatraz*, had then attempted to get the film going after Sturges departed along with Redford. Paul Newman was proposed as the new captain. This attempt, too, failed to materialise. It was only when noted German producer Gunter Rohrbach took the job as head of Bavaria Studios that the project finally moved forwards with an entirely German cast and crew.

CASTING/RECRUITMENT: As the captain, Jurgen Prochnow is the heart and soul of the film. Prochnow went on to appear in *The Keep* (Michael Mann, 1983), *Dune* (David Lynch, 1984), *A Dry White Season* (1989), *Twin Peaks: Fire Walk With Me* (David Lynch, 1992), *In the Mouth of Madness* (John Carpenter, 1994), *The English Patient* (Anthony Minghella, 1996) and *Air Force One* (Wolfgang Petersen, 1997).

BACKUP: Director Wolfgang Petersen went on from *Das Boot* into a feature-film career and swiftly moved to America. Petersen's feature credits to date have been *The Neverending Story* (1984), the science-fiction drama *Enemy Mine* (1985), the action movie *Air Force One* (1997), *The Perfect Storm* (2000) and *Troy* (2004). *Air Force One* and *The Perfect Storm* take Petersen's affinity for trauma in confined spaces to their Hollywood extremes.

The cinematographer for *Das Boot* was Jost Vacano who has gone on to shoot a number of films with Dutch émigré director Paul Verhoeven, namely *RoboCop* (1987), *Total Recall* (1990), *Showgirls* (1995), *Starship Troopers* (1997) and *Hollow Man* (2000).

The film's producer, Gunter Rohrbach, went on to produce *The Neverending Story*. Rolf Zehetbauer, the production designer of *Das Boot*, also returned to collaborate with Petersen on *The Neverending Story* and *Enemy Mine*.

PRODUCTION/IN THE TRENCHES: Filming began in July 1980 at Bavaria Studios in Munich and shooting lasted until July 1981. At the time the film was the most expensive German production ever, costing thirty million Deutschmarks. The film crew consisted of 250 people and more than a million feet of film was shot. Several sets were used for the film including two full-size mock submarine sets of the VIIC-type boat. One was for the above the water section, the other a realistically detailed tube for all of the scenes inside the U-boat. The plans for the basis of the set construction were found in Chicago at the Museum of Science and Industry. This interior set was positioned five metres above the soundstage floor, allowing it to be tilted and rocked. Most of the shooting was done using a hand-held camera and it was modified to capture a steadier image. In order to give the actors that pasty, no-sunlight look, they were not permitted to go out into sunlight. The actors were all trained in submarine drills. The film's production lasted three years and most of the filming took place over one year and filmed in sequence, hence the hair and beard growth is authentic.

At the Bavaria Studios in Munich a conning tower set was built and a third-sized model of the entire submarine was made for underwater shots and when the vessel skims the surface of the sea.

Filming at the submarine pens in La Rochelle (where *Raiders of the Lost Ark* was also shot) meant that all modern vessels had to be moved out of sight. A sixth-scale model of the submarine was used on open water and the camera over-cranked so that when the film was played back the model appeared to have appropriate weight as it pushed through the waves.

The film was re-edited and overhauled in 1997 under the supervision of director Wolfgang Petersen. Previouly unseen sequences were incorporated into the original cut and, making use of improved sound recording and design, the film's soundtrack was reconfigured.

MARTIAL MUSIC: The film is carried by one key theme that is played at either a funereal pace or at a faster, more victorious tempo. Klaus Doldinger's theme music was remixed by a German rave producer, Alex Christensen, in 1991.

REIMAGINING REALITY: *Das Boot* was based on the memoirs of a war correspondent named Lother Gunther Buchheim. The film's captain was inspired by real-life Captain Heinrich Lehmann-Willenbrock. Buchheim had reported from the U-96 submarine that Willenbrock had captained during battle. He had commanded seven missions by late 1941 when Buchheim came aboard to document the submarine's latest voyage. Willenbrock was to take the submarine to Newfoundland Bank in the North Atlantic in order to intercept Allied ships running supplies between Halifax, Nova Scotia and Great Britain. The mission was interrupted by an order from Vice Admiral Karl Dönitz, commander-in-chief of U-boats, for Willenbrock to take his submarine to the Mediterranean. This was a frustrating order, as the Mediterranean was regarded as inappropriate for U-boats – the Straits of Gibraltar were heavily guarded and the Mediterranean Sea is very shallow. Sure enough, U-96 took a hit from 812th Squadron Fleet Air Arm and Willenbrock ordered the submarine drop to 240 feet below the surface for repairs, resurfacing five hours later. The submarine eventually perished in 1946 when an American fighter plane took a shot at it. The vessel's hull was fractured and it sunk. Eventually the U-boat was used for scrap metal.

HEART OF BATTLE: Many war films are marked by a welcome simplicity of plot and *Das Boot* is exceptionally straightforward. As such the plot (or the mission) gives the film the opportunity to cluster a range of characterisations that can express a given theme. *Das Boot* celebrates courage and unity through the prism of tragedy to explore themes of honour, unity, terror under pressure and a sense of national identity under fire. How men cope with pressure during war is key to the film's effectiveness and resonance, and as such there is something universal about the situation the men are in. You don't feel as if you are watching a film about 'the enemy'. The strengthening and moments of fracture within the unit call to mind *Saving Private Ryan*, *Paths of Glory* and *Casualties of War*.

Within the demands of its action-thriller format, *Das Boot* finds chances to dramatise how Germany viewed Britain as a combatant to be truly afraid of. The film also suggests the frustration of the German fighting man at the orders of their High Command. Undeniably the film humanises the German soldier and provides a useful, telling contrast to those British and American films that present the German soldier as an enemy in the most blanket sense of the term. For many audiences, *All Quiet on the Western Front* would be the other film that focuses on German soldiers as heroes. More recent than either of these films is the little-seen *A Midnight Clear* (Keith Gordon, 1991).

CHARACTER: The captain is the focus of the film's drama, which is made so compelling by the physical limitation of the film's setting and subject. He begins the film as a charismatic and contained, clean-shaven, heroic figure. By the close of the adventure he is a broken man, though one who still has huge pride and love for his U-boat and crew. The captain is both steely and compassionate. He is a spiritual man, it emerges, who, in his moment of greatest anxiety, says 'My God, do not turn thy face away from me.' This call to God finds its place in many war films. When the U-boat is fixed and ready to resurface the captain comments, 'All you need is good people.' A very affecting scene occurs late on when the captain and his colleagues board a German tug for provisions. The captain's silence as he looks on at a feast of food says more than any dialogue would. His gaunt face is just a little bit Christlike, and his generally exhausted, dishevelled frame contrasts with the portly and smug tugboat captain.

Throughout the mission he regards himself as a father figure. Early in the film he says, 'I feel ancient around these kids. Like I'm on some Children's Crusade.' The captain's paternal quality brings to mind other father figures. We can look for examples of this in Colonel Dax in *Paths of Glory*, Captain Miller in *Saving Private Ryan*, Elias in *Platoon* and Captain Staros in *The Thin Red Line*, for example.

For the audience, their way into the story is through the 'guest' on the U-boat, Werner the naval correspondent. Werner frets from the moment he boards the U-boat, evidently wishing he were anywhere but in a tin can far beneath the waves.

STYLE: To some degree *Das Boot* amplified the impact of hand-held camera work in communicating the intensity of combat and men under pressure. The film also contrasts its hyper-tense atmosphere with many quiet, reflective moments for the characters, and recognises the power in a simple close-up of a human face. The film excels in communicating anticipation, both of combat and of impending doom and death. Sound rather than image does much to generate this tension and horror. A movingly quiet scene late in the film shows the crew looking through photos of home and family.

The film fuses war movie expectations with a documentary sense of life on board a U-boat and in keeping with this spirit of authenticity the characters speak with a range of specific German dialects.

Much of *Das Boot* is defined by a naturalistic quality, a sense of the real world captured. In its last, action-orientated sequences the visual style becomes more heightened than previously in the film. The film creates a real sense of claustrophobia, and the blue light of torches cutting through darkness anticipates the lighting schemes of James Cameron in his film *Aliens* (1986) and his notable underwater science-fiction drama *The Abyss* (1989), which is something of an anti-war film itself in its complete version.

Das Boot, whilst it does use miniatures to offer some sense of combat, is most effective when it uses sound to express danger. When they strike the British destroyer the sound of the ship going down allied with the close-ups on the German crewmen's faces is truly powerful.

CRITICAL CROSSFIRE: *Das Boot* stands as the most commercially successful foreign-language film to have been released in North America, and its intensity inspired many successive filmmakers in their presentations of wartime terror. When the film was released, however, it was criticised for not admitting enough to fascism so that only one of the men on the ship is overtly fascist.

Roger Ebert wrote of the film when released in its Director's Cut format that: 'The film is like a documentary in its impact.' The *Time Out Film Guide* wrote on the film's release that it 'belongs to that least enticing of genres, the submarine movie . . . Petersen's shooting style displays a breathtaking, if impersonal and faintly academic, virtuosity comparable to that of Lean or Coppola.' *Leonard Maltin's Movie and Video Guide* simply says the film is a 'realistic, meticulously mounted nail biter'.

MEDALS OF HONOUR: *Das Boot* was nominated at the Academy Awards in 1983 for Best Cinematography, Best Director, Best Effects/Sound Effects Editing, Best Film Editing, Best Sound and Best Writing Based on Material from Another Medium. At the BAFTAs in 1983 the film was nominated in the category of Best Foreign Language Film, and the Directors Guild of America nominated the film in the category of Outstanding Directorial Achievement in Motion Pictures. At the Golden Globes it was also nominated for Best Foreign Film and at the German Film Awards the film won Film Award in Silver for Outstanding Feature Film and Film Award in Gold for Outstanding Individual Achievement in Sound/Sound Mixing.

OTHER BATTLEFRONTS: While there have been a number of more recent films with submarine settings, such as *The Hunt for Red October* (John McTiernan, 1990), *Crimson Tide* (Tony Scott, 1995) and *K19: The Widowmaker* (Kathryn Bigelow, 2001), *Das Boot* remains perhaps *the* acknowledged modern classic of the submarine war-film strand.

THE HOMEFRONT: In 1981 *Das Boot* was the most expensive German film that had been produced. The film was made with two specific audiences in mind and as such two different versions of the material were created. For German TV the project was screened as a six-episode miniseries, each episode fifty minutes long. For the overseas market, the material was edited into a motion picture which was subsequently expanded in its Director's Cut format, which this chapter refers to. Both the TV series version and the Director's Cut edition are readily available on DVD.

FINAL BRIEFING: *Das Boot* is astonishing for the way in which it so confidently sustains attention over its long running time. It achieves this not so much through spectacle or sound and fury but through its relentless attention on the captain. His face becomes increasingly bleak as the odyssey develops and our interest is in seeing how he will react as the pressure intensifies.

FINAL SALUTE: Speaking at the time of the re-release of the film, Wolfgang Petersen commented, 'My vision for *Das Boot* was always to show the gritty and terrible reality of war, and to combine it with a highly entertaining story and fast-paced action style that would pull audiences into the experience of these young men out there.'

Saving Private Ryan (1998)

160 minutes

DreamWorks SKG–Paramount Pictures
Producers: Steven Spielberg and Ian Bryce, Mark Gordon
and Gary Levinsohn
Director: Steven Spielberg
Co Producers: Bonnie Curtis and Allison Lyon Segan
Screenplay: Robert Rodat
Cinematographer: Janusz Kaminski
Editor: Michael Kahn
Music: John Williams
Production Design: Thomas Sanders
Art Direction: Ricky Eyres, Tom Brown, Chris Seagers
Costume Design: Joanna Johnston

CAST: Tom Hanks (*Captain Miller*), Matt Damon (*Private James Ryan*), Tom Sizemore (*Sergeant Mike Horvath*), Giovanni Ribisi (*Medic Wade*), Vin Diesel (*Private Caparzo*), Ed Burns (*Private Reiben*), Jeremy Davies (*Corporal Upham*), Harve Presnell (*General Marshall*), Paul Giamatti (*Sergeant Hill*), Ted Danson (*Captain Hamill*), Harrison Young (*Old James Ryan*), Amanda Boxer (*Mrs Ryan*)

RATING: 15

TAGLINE: The mission is a man.

WAR STORY: It is the late-twentieth century. An old man visits the graves of American dead at Normandy and remembers.

Omaha Beach, 6 June 1944 – American soldiers slam across the sea and onto the beach. A furious effort to reach some kind of safety ensues as Captain Miller leads his unit on, and in the carnage of the battle, a soldier named Ryan lies dead on the beach. In Washington it is learned that three of the four Ryan brothers have died in action. Mrs Ryan is informed and a command is issued to rescue the one surviving Ryan brother. Captain Miller and eight men are charged with the mission to locate Ryan.

Miller leads his men on foot across French terrain and they become involved in several skirmishes as they look for Ryan. The unit survives two losses and Miller maintains morale. They find a Private James Ryan, but he is not the one they seek, and the team become ever more unconvinced about the wisdom of their mission. The unit begins to fracture at a critical moment but Miller succeeds in just about holding them together. They then come across a soldier who does know the Private Ryan they are looking for, and gives them some idea of where he might be.

Miller and his unit finally locate Ryan, but he is reluctant to give up his post. They join Ryan in the bombed-out town of Ramelle as they await Rommel's forces, who are looking to use the bridge in Ramelle as a route through. The soldiers put up a last stand in a furious battle amidst the ruins, where Miller is badly wounded, though still managing to destroy an enemy tank. Allied planes swoop in, while Ryan stays with Miller as he dies.

In the final scene, Ryan stands as an old man at Miller's graveside.

CONCEPT/THE MISSION: At the time of the film's release, director Steven Spielberg commented that 'I think people stopped trusting me about ten years ago. I really don't feel people expect from my movies the same kind of Disney enchantment that [was] ascribed to me back in the 70s and first half of the 1980s.' *Saving Private Ryan* represented a shift away from Spielberg's established tone rather in the way that *Schindler's List* (1993) had done. In the fourth decade of his career Spielberg's work has continued to vary from the intense science fiction of *AI: Artificial Intelligence* (2001) to the satisfying comedy of *The Terminal* (2004) to the more recent film *Munich* (2005), which dramatised a recent historical trauma. *Munich* concerned itself with the killing of eleven Israeli athletes at the Munich Olympics in 1972, which then prompted a secret Israeli counter attack on the Palestinians believed to have committed the murders.

In her book *The World War Two Combat Film*, Jeanine Basinger writes that *Saving Private Ryan* 'dared to reactivate World War Two'. The film brought American presentations of the war full circle to the first Hollywood movie about the subject, *Wake Island* (John Farrow, 1942*)*, a successful movie that had been nominated for the Best Picture Oscar. *Wake Island* was the first American film based on an actual World War Two battle and was a major studio production that ignited a period of around thirty years of major studio productions of films about the conflict. Of *Wake Island*, Basinger writes that it 'concerns itself not only with history and battle, but also with the underlying issue of what it means to be an American'. These issues remain a constant in many American war movies, and *Saving Private Ryan* is no exception.

Writer Robert Rodat had been inspired initially to develop the screenplay when he saw an American Civil War monument at Putney Corners, New Hampshire. The monument honoured a family that had lost eight sons in the war (1861–5). In the Second World War a similar incident occurred with the Niland family, where three brothers were lost and the fourth surviving one was tracked down and returned home by an army chaplain.

Screenwriter Frank Darabont, who had written and directed *The Shawshank Redemption* (1994) and went on to write and direct *The Green Mile* (1999) and *The Majestic* (2001), worked on elements of Rodat's script once Spielberg had committed to it. Darabont went on to write a draft of the (long in development) fourth Indiana Jones film.

For one of the few times in Spielberg's career, the screenplay for *Saving Private Ryan* came to him via his agent rather than being developed in-house at Amblin Entertainment/DreamWorks SKG. *Saving Private Ryan* was the second feature Spielberg directed for DreamWorks, the first having been the underrated *Amistad* (1997).

Spielberg worked with screenwriter Robert Rodat, who had written the beautiful *Fly Away Home* (Carroll Ballard, 1995). Of the *Saving Private Ryan* script, Spielberg commented, 'Even though the screenplay wasn't the intense experience that the film became, the screenplay was much more a morality play.'

In part, Spielberg's commitment to directing the film appears to have come out of a desire to honour his father's generation. One of the stories Spielberg often told during discussions about the film was his memory of his dad and fellow soldiers having reunions every few years at Spielberg's home. Spielberg recalled memories of when 'you're a kid and you hear eight or nine guys in a room, adults, your father's age, crying . . .'

In order to enhance the generic aspects of the screenplay (the mission, the unit, the battles) Spielberg spoke to a number of D-Day veterans to gather their personal memories of the event so he could apply these details to the script. Spielberg had previously engaged with World War Two in the knockabout 1979 comedy *1941*, in which the Japanese invade Los Angeles and the common man fights back. He had also directed the elegant and melancholy *Empire of the Sun*, about a British boy surviving in a Japanese prisoner-of-war camp. *Saving Private Ryan*, though, was Spielberg's first combat war movie.

For some the film was not an especially fresh take on the war film beyond its opening sequence. Indeed, the first sequence is so strong that it tends to be this that sticks in the viewer's mind, rather than what follows. For writer Louis Menand, 'There is nothing unconventional about this story. It is possibly the most tried and true dramatic plot known to man: a life is saved . . . It is a plot guaranteed to melt stone.'

CASTING/RECRUITMENT: As an avid collector of *Life* magazine, Spielberg was aware of casting actors whose faces evoked the 1940s, one young man saying he was 'in a face hunt before I was in a talent hunt'.

The only actor Spielberg met prior to filming was Tom Hanks. Spielberg chose the rest based on show-reels and their work in previous films, only meeting them once in Ireland to shoot the Omaha Beach sequence. Part of the preparation for the actors was to attend a week-long boot camp to break them into the idea of the World War Two soldiering experience. The only actor not in attendance was Matt Damon. Clearly the exercise was to encourage the unit of actors to bond, but Tom Hanks found himself having to stave off a mutiny when the actors threatened to quit. Hanks called Spielberg, in America editing *Amistad*, who just told Hanks to keep everyone on board.

Matt Damon, who plays Private James Ryan, had found massive success in 1997 with the film *Good Will Hunting* (Gus Van Sant, 1997), which he had co-written with Ben Affleck and co-starred in alongside Robin Williams. Damon has gone on to star in *The Bourne Identity* (Doug Liman, 2002) and *The Bourne Supremacy* (Paul Greengrass, 2004) as well as *Dogma* (Kevin Smith, 1999) and the underrated *All The Pretty Horses* (Billy Bob Thornton, 2000). More recently, Damon has co-starred in *The Brothers Grimm* (Terry Gilliam, 2005).

When Spielberg came to work with his principal actors on location he found that the boot camp had galvanised them as a team, and it took a little while to prove himself to them.

The squad of soldiers were portrayed by a number of young actors for whom the film served as a showcase for their talents, already established in smaller movies. Vin Diesel has since gone on to star in *xXx* (Rob Cohen, 2002) and voice the Iron Giant in *The Iron Giant* (Brad Bird, 1999). Barry Pepper has appeared in *The Green Mile* and *We Were Soldiers* (Randall Wallace, 2002). Ed Burns had already established himself as a filmmaker with *The Brothers McMullen* (1995) and *She's The One* (1996). Giovanni Ribisi had featured in *Friends* and went on to star in the brilliant Tom Tykwer film *Heaven* (2002) and the zeitgeisty *Lost in Translation* (Sofia Coppola, 2003) and also *Flight of the Phoenix* (John Moore, 2004).

Ted Danson, who appears briefly in the middle of the film, had been a major American TV star with *Cheers* (1982–93). He has also appeared in *Body Heat* (Lawrence Kasdan, 1983), *Three Men and a Baby* (Leonard Nimoy, 1987), *Dad* (Gary David Goldberg, 1989) and *Mumford* (Lawrence Kasdan, 1998). Paul Giamatti, who played the officer at the bombed-out town the unit arrive in during the pouring rain, has gone on to star in *American Splendor* (Shari Springer Burman, 2003) and *Sideways (*Alexander Payne, 2004).

BACKUP: In 1993 Spielberg first worked with cinematographer Janusz Kaminski, who had come to Spielberg's attention with his work on a TV movie for Diane Keaton. Kaminski then lensed the Spielberg TV production *Class of '61* (about Civil War soldiers) before Spielberg brought him on board for *Schindler's List*. Kaminski has since worked on *Jerry Maguire* (Cameron Crowe, 1996), *How to Make an American Quilt* (Jocelyn Moorhouse, 1995), *The Lost World: Jurassic Park*, *Amistad, AI: Artificial Intelligence, Minority Report* (Steven Spielberg, 2002), *Catch Me If You Can* (Steven Spielberg, 2002), *The Terminal* and *War of the Worlds* (Steven Spielberg, 2005).

Editor Michael Kahn, with the exception of *The Sugarland Express*, *Jaws* and *ET: The Extra Terrestrial*, has edited all of Spielberg's films. Kahn's other credits include early career work editing episodes of *Hogan's Heroes* and work on the feature films *A Man Called Horse* (Elliot Silverstein, 1970) . *Table For Five* (Robert Lieberman, 1983), *Alive* (Frank Marshall, 1993), *Casper* (Brad Silberling, 1995) and *Lemony Snicket's A Series of Unfortunate Events* (Brad Silberling, 2004).

Spielberg's other longstanding key collaborator, composer John Williams, scored the film, leaving his musical accompaniment for everything except the battle scenes. As such he had the chance to score music to suit the quieter, introspective sequences. At the scoring session for the film Hanks read out a letter that Abraham Lincoln had written to a grieving mother who had lost children in the Civil War. One imagines this is the same letter that is read out early on in *Saving Private Ryan* by George C Marshall to motivate his staff. Williams's *Hymn to the Fallen* overflows with a sense of tragedy and is suitably Coplandesque, reminding us of Copland's piece *A Lincoln Portrait*, in its support of the sequence when it is realised that the Ryan family has been all but wiped out and that James Ryan must be found.

PRODUCTION/IN THE TRENCHES: Spielberg's films are often associated with a technical, technological gracefulness (those tracking shots, crane shots and beautifully lit close-ups), and *Saving Private Ryan* allowed him to strip down the 'artifice' of the Hollywood production and immerse the audience within the zone of battle, a production approach he had established in *Schindler's List*.

As with *ET: The Extra Terrestrial* (1982) and *Schindler's List*, Spielberg eschewed storyboarding even when it came to filming the Omaha Beach landing, which was shot in sequence.

For the Omaha sequence, the production used up to a thousand Irish soldiers, but when the days of filming proved intense Spielberg was pulled before the Irish colonel and given, in Spielberg's own words, a 'formal dressing down . . . so I just took it. I just sat there and took it.' Spielberg had prepared a statement to praise the Irish soldiers, but it never got an airing.

Whilst running camera tests with Janusz Kaminski, they stripped a Panaflex camera lens of its coating and opened up the shutter to 45 or 90 degrees rather than the usual 180 degrees. This was done to create the clarity and detail of explosions that the film exhibits. The resulting film's nervous energy is in part attributable to an experiment that Spielberg conducted whereby he put a Black and Decker drill, without the bit in place, fixed to the pan handle of a fluid head, and locked an oblong bowl with an eccentric washer in the chuck. The resulting vibration created a nervous energy to the footage captured. For the production a gizmo named a lens shaker was used to create the same effect. Spielberg also often exploded a blood squib directly beneath the camera lens, intending for the lens to be dirtied up even more. Inspired by cinematographer Doug Milsome's work on *Full Metal Jacket*, Kaminski and Spielberg opted to throw the camera's shutter out of sync, thereby creating a streaking effect from top to bottom of the frame.

The film shot for 59 days, of which 24 were given over to the Omaha Beach sequence. The film was shot primarily in England, Ireland and France. Much of the filming in England was based in and around Hertfordshire, where the French village sets were constructed in all their apocalyptic wreckage. In the wake of the success of *Saving Private Ryan*, filming returned to the same locale for the TV series *Band of Brothers* (2001).

MARTIAL MUSIC: Spielberg again collaborated with John Williams. Williams created a score that accentuated the emotion and concern that emerged in the quieter, pastoral phases. The kinetic and traumatic action sequences that start and finish the film are not underscored with any music, in order to keep the sense of realism at full throttle. Williams's highly American score suggests the work of Aaron Copland and also his own earlier scores *The Cowboys* (Mark Rydell, 1972) and *The Reivers*. In an article at the time of the recording of the *Saving Private Ryan* score at Boston Symphony Hall in February 1998, Spielberg said, 'This is a movie about a company of soldiers and it seemed appropriate to use an experienced company of musicians who are all virtuosos.' The Boston Symphony Orchestra had performed the score for *Schindler's List* and also for the special edition sequence of *Close Encounters of the Third Kind*. More recently the orchestra performed the score for *Mystic River* (Clint Eastwood, 2003). Williams's other credits include **Born on the Fourth of July**, *JFK* (Oliver Stone, 1991), *Nixon* (Oliver Stone, 1995) and *Rosewood* (John Singleton, 1997).

REIMAGINING REALITY: Spielberg's film is widely remembered for the intensity of its Omaha Beach sequence which does go some way to indicating the scale of the operation as it had actually occurred. The allied troops that stormed the beaches at Normandy numbered 175,000 and inexperienced though the US Army Infantry were they were very possibly the most educated men to make up an enlisted army in the history of combat. By 30 June 452,000 American soldiers had arrived in France, 11,000 GIs had died in action and 1,000 were missing in action.

To make the staging of Omaha Beach as accurate as possible, the production referred to numerous photos generated by American and British flyovers from the period. The fictional movie towns of Vermeil and of Ramelle, in which the final battle takes place, were based on Carentan and Sainte-Marie Eglise respectively. The other key frame of historical reference was the photographs of Robert Capa, who had been at the Omaha Beach landing. He took around four hundred photos, but the developer was apparently so excited by the images on the rolls of film that he did not pay attention to the process and only eight photos were correctly processed.

Key to Spielberg's sense of how to present the D-Day landing and, indeed, much else in the film was John Huston's film *The Battle of San Pietro* (1945) which documented the mission of American soldiers to secure the Italian village of San Pietro, which was a strategic point in the battle againt the German forces. More than 1,000 American soldiers died in their attempt to secure the village and in some quarters of the American military at the time the film was seen as the work of a pacifist filmmaker who was apparently not only anti-war but anti World War Two also. Lewis Milestone's *All Quiet on the Western Front* is marked by a dirtiness and sense of grime that *Saving Private Ryan* also embeds in its images.

Spielberg's affinity for the paintings of Norman Rockwell, evident in one of the images in *Empire of the Sun* inspired by the painting *Freedom From Fear*, is also apparent in *Saving Private Ryan*, which conjures another particular Rockwell wartime image entitled *Let's Give Him Enough and On Time*. This image depicts an American soldier hunched over his machine gun engulfed by darkness, his face in shadow, his universality assured. Rockwell also created eleven *Saturday Evening Post* covers featuring his own iconic creation Willie Gillis, the all-American GI. In 1945, Rockwell painted a Thanksgiving picture called *Mother and Son Peeling Potatoes* that showed a mother looking lovingly at her uniformed son as he sits on a chair peeling potatoes alongside her. These images inspire much of the feeling towards the American citizen soldier.

HEART OF BATTLE: Like *All Quiet on the Western Front*, *The Deer Hunter*, and *Platoon*, Spielberg's film offers up a story about brotherhood and the community of a unit. In one of the film's quietest and most affecting scenes the unit make camp inside a church. Miller talks with young interpreter Upham, who quotes American philosopher and writer Ralph Waldo Emerson. The reference opens up a field of meaning for the film around transcendental issues, and as such the film makes a connection with *The Thin Red Line*. Where *The Thin Red Line* explored how good and evil exist very explicitly, *Saving Private Ryan* really only alludes to the issue a few times, notably when Caparzo wants to rescue a little girl against the command of Miller. When Caparzo says it's the right thing, Miller angrily retorts, 'We're not here to do the decent thing, we're here to follow fucking orders.'

CHARACTER: For all its dazzling scale and commitment to recreating a sense of the horror of close combat, characterisation is perhaps *Saving Private Ryan*'s strongest element. The plot is simple and functions to contain thematic riffs as expressed by the characters. Many war films allow this valuable opportunity. It's the characters of *The Great Escape* that we most recall, for example. The plot is elemental.

Tom Hanks felt his character of Captain Miller had too much dialogue and so, in consultation with Spielberg, he decided to eliminate three-quarters of it. Hanks's justification was that the character would be too busy just reacting to all that was happening around him. Miller is a decent man, a citizen soldier who becomes like a father to his unit, who spend much of their time trying to work out what Miller's work back home is. At a critical point in the mission Miller tells them what he does for a living – he's a high-school teacher – and it clarifies the way he has behaved with the men under his command and protection.

Caparzo is a tough guy. Mellish is a wisecracking character who is proud of his Jewish heritage. Medic Wade is a considerate and thoughtful soldier who talks movingly about his mother as he sits in the torchlight in the church overnight. Reiben is a hard case from Brooklyn who is most willing to question Miller's authority and Upham is a gentle, non-aggressive soldier who is compelled to change his behaviour at a critical moment in order to survive. The cost of combat on the emotion is the focus of the film rather than any detailed sense of political context. The film is an adventure fused with a morality play. Sergeant Horvath is the tough-talking professional soldier who is shown collecting soil from each of the territories he has fought in. Miller looks to Horvath for backup at critical moments.

Ryan is a stereotypical all-American man who is committed to his brothers in battle. His most affecting comment is when he tells Miller that he cannot remember what his dead brothers' faces look like. The comment recalls Jim's comment to Dr Rawlins in *Empire of the Sun* when he tells him he cannot remember what his parents look like. War distorts everything and Miller testifies to this when he says, 'With every man I kill the farther away from home I feel.' War's ability to distance the soldier from fundamental things that make sense rings loud and clear through so many war films, and again this backs up the notion that many war films are less interested in the specifics of war and historical detail than in the job of showing what conflict does to hearts and minds. This emphasis is what gives the films their endurance.

STYLE: *Saving Private Ryan* appears to have become remembered solely for its opening 25-minute sequence, which some have suggested could be shown as an art installation piece of its own, so cinematic is it in its creation of a moment in time. In *Schindler's List*, Spielberg had advanced his aesthetic of immediacy and 'documentary'. With *Saving Private Ryan* this stylistic approach, this way of representing a moment that occurred, takes on an even more visceral quality. Spielberg said, 'I was concerned about deconstructing this movie, and I was more concerned with putting you through the eyes of someone who couldn't see very well.'

Kaminski rounds out the picture, commenting that 'I deliberately gave some scenes in *Saving Private Ryan* a warm feeling to alleviate the bleakness of the rest of the film.'

For many critics the consensus was that the approach taken in rendering war was informed by footage of the Vietnam War that would have been so familiar to so many of the film's audience. Spielberg's 'favourite' war films had been *Battleground* (William Wellman, 1949), *The Steel Helmet* (Sam Fuller, 1951) and *Hell is for Heroes* (Don Siegel, 1962). For *Saving Private Ryan*, Spielberg looked to *Memphis Belle* (Michael Caton-Jones, 1990), *Why We Fight*, John Ford's *Midway* film and John Huston's wartime documentaries.

For the sequence when the Ryan brother fatalities are realised and Mrs Ryan is informed, Spielberg plays the sequence as something close to a silent film, accompanied by a powerful piece of music. From the elegantly composed shots for this sequence the film then returns to predominantly hand-held images that keep the audience immersed in the trek across country. It is through such an approach that the audience empathises with the soldiers and gets to know them.

The film's action climax allows Spielberg to demonstrate his well-established kinetic sense, and as the P51 fighters fly in to the rescue it recalls the fury of the Mustangs racing by in *Empire of the Sun*.

CRITICAL CROSSFIRE: On several previous occasions, Spielberg's films had been regarded as having tapped into the zeitgeist, and *Saving Private Ryan* seemed to be another such occasion. The cover of *Newsweek* magazine ran the line 'Why a new Spielberg movies draws us back to the horrors of World War Two', whilst *Entertainment Weekly*'s cover raved that the film was 'A masterpiece of terror, chaos, blood and courage.' For *Leonard Maltin's Movie and Video Guide* the film was a 'trenchant World War Two drama . . . Conventional elements in the script are balanced by a genuinely complex examination of heroism in the field . . . the ultimate vision of war as hell on earth.'

MEDALS OF HONOUR: *Saving Private Ryan* had a dazzling degree of success – commercially, critically and through awards. Amongst the awards and recognition it garnered were winning Oscars in 1999 for

Best Director, Best Cinematography, Best Sound Effects, Best Sound and Best Editing. The film was nominated for Oscars in the categories of Best Actor, Best Art Direction, Best Make-up, Best Music, Best Screenplay and Best Picture. At the BAFTAs in 1999, Spielberg was nominated for the David Lean Award for Directing.

OTHER BATTLEFRONTS: Lewis Milestone's *A Walk in the Sun* was especially influential on Spielberg's war odyssey as was his *All Quiet on the Western Front*. *A Walk in the Sun* is one of the most accomplished of war films, made right at the tail end of the Second World War and striving to offer some sense of the emotional toll taken on fighting men. The screenplay had been written by Robert Rossen from the novel by Harry Brown. Early in his career John Ford, whom Spielberg has become something of an echo of since his work on *The Color Purple*, made a film called *Four Sons* (1928), in which a Bavarian mother loses three of her four sons in the First World War.

Notable as one of the few major works about the Second World War made in the late 1970s and early 1980s was the film *The Big Red One* (Samuel Fuller, 1980), the tagline for which was simply, 'The real glory of war is surviving.' The film was originally released with a running time of 113 minutes but in 2004 was reissued at 2 hrs 40 minutes, overseen by film writer and historian Richard Schickel.

In many ways *The Big Red One* came to be regarded as a cult movie and one in need of resuscitation. Richard Schickel led the effort in the years after Fuller's death when the director's kudos was on the up. Twenty rolls of film were found in the vaults but had no accompanying soundtrack. More rolls of film were located and finally the restoration effort had 70,000 feet of negative and 112 reels of location sound to work with. Camera and sound reports were also accessed, as was a copy of Fuller's shooting script. Fifteen new sequences were interpolated and there were insertions of shots and extensions to a further existing 23 sequences. Two new scenes reinstated are a battle between French cavalry and a German tank in a North African amphitheatre and also the inclusion of a German soldier named Schroeder.

Sam Fuller had been a Hollywood film director from the 1950s onwards with films such as *Shock Corridor* (1963) to his name as well *Hell and High Water* (1954) and *Merrill's Marauders* (1961), an action-adventure war movie set in Burma. He began as a journalist and is noted for bringing a journalistic snappiness to his cinema storytelling. Fuller fought in the Second World War, seeing action in North Africa and at Omaha Beach, and was present at the liberation of a Czech death camp. Unlike most film directors of the last thirty years who have made war films, Fuller is unique for having actually been in the war zone. It informs his work on *The Big Red One* with undoubted force and perhaps a sense of first-hand honesty. In his autobiography, Fuller wrote, 'For moviegoers to get the idea of real combat, you'd have to shoot at them every so often from either side of the screen. The casualties in the theatre would be bad for business.' Fuller initially looked to make *The Big Red One* as far back as 1959 with John Wayne in the lead, but his colleagues Richard Brooks and Dalton Trumbo advised against this casting choice. The film finally came together in the late 1970s with Fuller securing backing from Lorimar, who then went out of business just as the film was released.

Kent Jones wrote in *Film Comment* in 2004: 'The spirit of the film seems right, in a way that Malick's and Spielberg's self-important World War Two films don't, their obvious virtues aside.'

The Big Red One opens with a title card that reads, 'This is fictional life, based on factual death.' It's a mantra that stands true for all war films.

In autumn 2001 an American TV series entitled *Band of Brothers* was first broadcast to acclaim and popularity. Building on the success of *Saving Private Ryan*, the series followed American soldiers serving in Europe during World War Two and took the Stephen Ambrose book of the same name as its source. With Steven Spielberg and Tom Hanks serving as executive producers the series was assured massive media interest and the series seemed to connect with viewers young and old, who responded to its realist dynamic.

The early 1990s saw a feature film called *A Midnight Clear* (Keith Gordon, 1991) being released which centred on a US intelligence unit who become very unsettled by a nearby German unit who refuse to fight. The film was notable for its sympathetic view of the German soldiers.

Saving Private Ryan capped a run of films set during World War Two that Spielberg had directed. There was the slapstick comedy of *1941* in which Everyman and Everywoman seek to defend the Californian home front with cartoon-like excess from Japanese invasion. The film is too much of everything, but remains an interesting misfire, a curiosity more interesting than its reputation suggests. Against Spielberg's later, explicit war films it seems amazingly immature. Spielberg's Indiana Jones films *Raiders of the Lost Ark* and *Indiana Jones and the Last Crusade* which both pit their American hero against Nazis in the years prior to World War Two had spiked the action, jeopardy and historical reference points with humour and plenty of inventive sight gags bordering on the balletic. In 1987, Spielberg directed *Empire of the Sun*, the stunning and occasionally eerie adaptation of JG Ballard's autobiographical novel about life for a British boy in a Japanese POW camp. Finally Spielberg directed *Schindler's List* (after offering it to Scorsese and Kubrick in the 1980s) about the efforts of German businessman Oskar Schindler to save the lives of a number of Jewish people in Poland from the Holocaust. At the time of writing, Spielberg is collaborating with Clint Eastwood on the film *Flags of Our Fathers*, based on James Bradley's book about the American soldiers who raised the flag on Iwo Jima during World War Two. That moment is now memorialised in a statue.

THE HOMEFRONT: *Saving Private Ryan* is available on DVD and home video. The DVD features trailers and a documentary about the citizen soldiers.

FINAL BRIEFING: Aware that for some critics the sequences at the graveyard that book-ends the film diminished its impact, Spielberg recognised that for many men of seventy and over those two sequences were the most affecting of all the scenes in the film.

FINAL SALUTE: In an interview with the *Washington Post* at the time of the film's release, Spielberg made an incisive comment: 'When people see World War Two movies, they expect to be entertained. If they see a Vietnam movie they expect to be shocked. But World War Two has become fun: they want a big action adventure. But it wasn't an adventure.'

The Thin Red Line (1998)

170 minutes

Twentieth Century Fox
Producer: John Roberdeau and Grant Hill
Executive Producer: George Stevens Jr, Ross Sheldon and Michael Stevens
Associate Producer: Sheila Davis Lawrence and Michael Stevens
Director: Terrence Malick
Screenplay: Terrence Malick
Cinematographer: John Toll

Editor: Billy Weber
Music: Hans Zimmer
Production Design: Jack Fisk
Art Direction: Ian Gracie
Costume Design: Margot Wilson

CAST: Sean Penn (*Sergeant Edward Welsh*), Adrien Brody (*Corporal Fife*), Jim Caviezel (*Private Witt*), Ben Chaplin (*Private Jack Bell*), George Clooney (*Captain Charles Borsche*), John Cusack (*Captain John Gaff*), Woody Harrelson (*Sergeant Keck*), Elias Koteas (*Captain James Staros*), Jared Leto (*2nd Lieutenant Whyte*), Dash Mihok (*Private Doll*), Tim Blake Nelson (*Private Tills*), Nick Nolte (*Lieutenant Colonel Gordon Tall*), John C Reilly (*Sergeant Storm*), Larry Romano (*Private Mazzi*), John Savage (*Sergeant McCrow*), John Travolta (*Brigadier General Quintard*)

RATING: 15

TAGLINE: Every man fights his own war.

WAR STORY: The Pacific, 1942. On one of the Solomon Islands a young American solider, Witt, revels in the freedom of not being a soldier. He has gone AWOL. He enjoys his time spent with the Melanesian villagers and contemplates his place in the world, but his idyllic life is interrupted by the arrival of an American ship. Witt is brought on board, where Welsh questions him about going AWOL for the third time. The ship is bound for the island of Guadalcanal, where the American soldiers are to take the island from the Japanese, who are using it as an airbase by which they hope to open up a route to Australia and thus control the seas to the United States. Lt Col Tall talks with the Brigadier about the mission – evidently Tall is a captain frustrated by his military experience.

The soldiers ride out to the island and nervously anticipate whatever awaits them. Arriving on the island they find themselves overwhelmed by its beauty and danger as they make their advance on their target, and tension develops between Captain Staros and Lt Col Tall. One of the soldiers, Private Bell, thinks endlessly about his wife back home, while Witt focuses on his pacifist view of the world. As they advance they are attacked in a ground battle with the unseen Japanese troops. Staros's unit are beleaguered and Tall angrily berates Staros for not taking his men directly into the firing line. Eventually the ridge is taken, and Tall relieves Staros of his post out of frustration.

Having secured the ridge, the soldiers move on and confront Japanese troops in a village, where a brutal face-to-face skirmish ensues. After this the American troops are granted a week's respite at the American base. Bell receives a letter from his wife announcing she wants to divorce him.

The troops then go back into action and find themselves in danger of being surrounded by Japanese soldiers. Witt and two younger soldiers make the journey back to base to inform the unit, but Witt is caught by the Japanese and shot dead. Welsh oversees Witt's burial before the soldiers leave the island and return to their command vessel.

CONCEPT/THE MISSION: Throughout 1997 and 1998, when it became evident that writer–director Terrence Malick was in the process of making a new film, there was a sense of great anticipation amongst film fans. Malick had not made a feature film since 1978 when his beautiful second film *Days of Heaven* was released. His first film had been the lovers-on-the-run film *Badlands* in 1974. Like *The Thin Red Line*, *Badlands* pitched its young protagonists into the wilderness.

The title of James Jones's novel is derived from an American Midwestern saying that goes, 'There's only a thin red line between the sane and the mad.'

Malick had become a moviemaker of mystery, totally disconnected from the promotional buzz so central to the popular American film form. Let the work speak for itself is the implication. Hype passed Malick by and yet ultimately, a little like Stanley Kubrick, his absence made him all the more present. According to cinematographer John Toll, Malick, who himself does not give interviews, 'loves to speak in metaphors, and he kept saying "It's like moving down a river, and the picture should have that same kind of flow".'

Over the 1980s and 1990s apocryphal stories of Malick's whereabouts and return to cinema were heard, but nothing concrete emerged until 1997 when *The Thin Red Line* was announced with Malick as screenwriter adapting the James Jones novel. Jones's novel had previously been adapted by Hollywood in 1964. With this iteration, Malick substantially adapts the plot and elected to not include any of the novel's concerns with racism and homophobia. Malick's film also elects to make Witt, a supporting character in the novel, into the major voice of the film.

His previous two features had been marked by their poetic, lyrical approach, infusing mainstream storytelling with an unexpected reluctance to haste and explication. Malick was regarded as a personal filmmaker, apparently unswayed by the commercial imperative. *The Thin Red Line* was filled with movie stars, all eager to work with the director (who knew when he might make another feature?). During production on *Apocalypse Now* Malick had been approached to shoot some second-unit footage, but it never happened.

Malick's first two features had displayed an affinity with and rapture in images of nature and *The Thin Red Line* supersedes both previous efforts in its pantheistic approach. For Malick the context of war allowed for the drama of his script to explore issues of evil and goodness and whether these forces exist within or without an individual, with the machinery of war invading the Edenic island where the film is set. Intriguingly, Malick's most recent film *The New World* (2005) dramatises the arrival of white Europeans to the North American continent and their conflict with the native people.

CASTING/RECRUITMENT: *The Thin Red Line* is packed out with new and established film actors, some of whom put in the briefest and most understated of cameos. Sean Penn had starred in *Taps* (Harold Becker, 1981), *Fast Times At Ridgemont High* (Amy Heckerling, 1982), *Racing With The Moon* (Richard Benjamin, 1984), *The Falcon and the Snowman* (John Schlesinger, 1985), *Colors* (Dennis Hopper, 1988), *Casualties of War*, *We're No Angels* (Neil Jordan, 1989), *State of Grace* (Phil Jounao, 1990), *Carlito's Way* (Brian De Palma, 1993) and *Dead Man Walking* (Tim Robbins, 1995). Penn has also directed three very fine films: *The Indian Runner* (1991), *The Crossing Guard* (1995) and *The Pledge* (2000). Ben Chaplin can also be seen in *The Truth About Cats and Dogs* (Michael Lehmann, 1996). Nick Nolte had starred in *48 Hours* (Walter Hill, 1982), *Cannery Row* (David S Ward, 1982), *Under Fire* (Roger Spotiswoode, 1983), *Down and Out in Beverly Hills* (Paul Mazurksy, 1985), *Farewell to the King* (John Milius, 1988), *Life Lessons* (Martin Scorsese, 1989), *The Prince of Tides* (Barbra Streisand, 1991), *Cape Fear* (Martin Scorsese, 1991) and more recently *The Hulk* (Ang Lee, 2003) and *The Good Thief* (Neil Jordan, 2002).

John Travolta made *The Thin Red Line* during that initial burst of post *Pulp Fiction* revival. Travolta's other films include *Saturday Night Fever* (John Badham, 1977), *Grease* (Randall Kleiser, 1978), *Urban Cowboy* (James Bridges, 1980), *Blow Out* (Brian De Palma, 1981), *Pulp Fiction* (Quentin Tarantino, 1994), *Michael* (Nora Ephron, 1996), *Get Shorty* (Barry Sonnenfeld, 1995) and *A Civil Action* (Stephen Zaillian, 1998).

Bell's wife back home in America was portrayed by Miranda Otto, who plays Ray Ferrier's ex-wife in *War of the Worlds* (Steven Spielberg, 2005). Otto has also appeared in *What Lies Beneath* (Robert Zemeckis, 2000), *Lord of the Rings: The Two Towers* (Peter Jackson, 2002) and *Lord of the Rings: The Return of the King* (Peter Jackson, 2003).

Jim Caviezel appears briefly as Wyatt Earp's younger brother in *Wyatt Earp* (Lawrence Kasdan, 1994) and most famously went on to portray Jesus Christ in *The Passion* (Mel Gibson, 2004).

John Cusack has starred in *Sixteen Candles* (John Hughes, 1984), *The Journey of Natty Gann* (Jeremy Kagan, 1985), *Stand By Me* (Rob Reiner, 1985), *Eight Men Out* (John Sayles, 1988), *Say Anything* (Cameron Crowe, 1988), *The Player* (Robert Altman, 1992), *Map of the Human Heart* (Vincent Ward, 1992), *Shadows and Fog* (Woody Allen, 1992), *Bullets Over Broadway* (Woody Allen, 1994), *Grosse Pointe Blank* (George Armitage, 1996) and *Serendipity* (Peter Chesholm, 2002).

Elias Koteas has also appeared in *Gardens of Stone* (Francis Ford Coppola, 1987), *Some Kind of Wonderful* (Howard Deutch, 1987), *Tucker: The Man And His Dream* (Francis Ford Coppola, 1988), *Crash* (David Cronenberg, 1996), *Gattaca* (Andrew Nichol, 1997) and *Simone* (Andrew Nichol, 2002).

John Savage has also appeared in *Bad Company* (Robert Benton, 1976), **The Deer Hunter**, *Salvador* (Oliver Stone, 1986) and *Do The Right Thing* (Spike Lee, 1989).

BACKUP: Malick's key collaborator on the film was cinematographer John Toll and production designer Jack Fisk. Malick and Fisk had worked together on Malick's previous two features, *Badlands* and *Days of Heaven*, and Fisk also provided production design for the brilliant and warm *The Straight Story* (David Lynch, 1999) and the intense, astonishing and corkscrew-plotted *Mulholland Drive* (David Lynch, 2001). Most recently Fisk has collaborated with Malick on *The New World* (2005).

John Toll had not worked with Malick before but is notable for having lensed *Legends of the Fall* (Ed Zwick, 1994) and *Braveheart* (Mel Gibson, 1995), winning back-to-back Oscars for these films. Toll's other credits include *Wind* (Carroll Ballard, 1992), *Jack* (Francis Ford Coppola, 1996), *The Rainmaker* (Francis Ford Coppola, 1997), *Almost Famous* (Cameron Crowe, 2000), *Captain Corelli's Mandolin* (John Madden, 2001) *Vanilla Sky* (Cameron Crowe, 2001), *The Last Samurai* (Ed Zwick, 2003) and *Elizabethtown* (Cameron Crowe, 2005).

PRODUCTION/IN THE TRENCHES: The film was shot largely in Port Douglas, Australia with other footage shot at San Pedro in California. Filming took place primarily in Australia for eighty days. A remaining twenty days were given over to 'improved' filming on Guadalcanal itself, where Malick and his crew captured the images of Witt musing and meditating and footage of the Melanesian life. As such this segment of filming was a little closer to gathering documentary footage, much of which comprises the first thirty minutes of the film.

MARTIAL MUSIC: Hans Zimmer was brought on board to compose the dreamlike score. He had established himself with a vast number of scores from the late 1980s onwards for films such as *Rain Man* (Barry Levinson, 1988), *Driving Miss Daisy* (Bruce Beresford, 1989) and *Backdraft* (Ron Howard, 1991) and more recently *The Lion King* (Roger Allers and Rob Minkoff, 1994), *The Peacemaker* (Mimi Leder, 1997), *The Prince of Egypt* (Brenda Chapman, Steve Hickner and Simon Wells, 1998), *Gladiator* (Ridley Scott, 2000) and *Black Hawk Down* (Ridley Scott, 2002).

The music for *The Thin Red Line* is marked by its hypnotic, mournful quality. Rather than provide a kinetic, highly charged accompaniment to battle it is instead slow and funereal. During one of the film's critical dialogue scenes – Witt and Smart sit out in the moonlight in a passage that may be the core of the story – we hear a statement of the film's main theme.

In his book on *The Thin Red Line*, author Michel Chion notes that at one moment in the film Malick interpolates into the original score a segment of classical music, an extract from American composer Charles Ives's *The Unanswered Question*, a piece that was intentionally composed to give musical voice to metaphysical issues. Ives's composition is one of the most popular pieces of American 'classical' music. Two previous titles considered by Ives for the piece were *A Contemplation of Serious Matter* and *The Unanswered Perennial Question*. The piece was composed in 1906 and the 'question' of the title is 'What is the meaning of existence?' Sure enough, the same big idea obsesses Witt in the film.

REIMAGINING REALITY: The film shows the rifle unit of the US Army's 25th Division making their assault on Japanese defences to secure the island of Guadalcanal. True to the historical truth, the Japanese soldiers on the island were malnourished and badly hit by malaria. During the sequence where the American troops fight the Japanese in the village in the latter part of the film, the Japanese are presented as frail, though the film does not explain this context. The American troops were repeatedly victorious over Japanese forces and eventually they overwhelmed the lightly defended Japanese airstrip at Lunga Point.

For Malick the specifics of the Guadalcanal campaign are incidental to his use of the situation to offer up a sense of how battle can alter one's sense of self. In this respect the film shares a commonality with *The Deer Hunter*. Rather like *A Matter of Life and Death*, *The Thin Red Line* is a metaphysical war movie.

HEART OF BATTLE: *The Thin Red Line* is notable, and admirable, for being a war film that, though set against a specific historical combat, is only marginally concerned with fighting. For this film the heart and soul of the story is to offer a meditation on good and evil. The idea of compassion in the most abrasive of situations is key to the film. Military manoeuvres are really incidental. Tall notes that 'nature's cruel' in his description of the jungle, and the film dramatises how that cruelty can be countered by gentleness.

The film suggests that one person can make a positive difference to the life of another, even though Smart evidently does not believe this. Witt's job throughout the mission seems to be to provide some calm and protection for others. He never really seems to engage in combat as he drifts spirit-like in and out of the story.

CHARACTER: The prism through which the concepts and emotions of *The Thin Red Line* are most clearly expressed is the pacifist soldier Witt. It is his voice we first hear when he says, 'What's this war in the heart of nature? Why does nature vie with itself?' Throughout the film, Witt offers up these philosophical, questioning statements, to the frustration of his commanding officer, Smart. Where Witt is an idealist, Smart is a realist, a man who has no faith in something more transcendent.

Witt belongs to the American transcendental tradition that began with writers such as Ralph Waldo Emerson and, perhaps most strikingly, Henry David Thoreau, whose book *Walden* we can imagine Witt would enjoy reading. Smart does not even see the war as a moral battle but instead, in the heat of battle, makes the bold statement, 'Property. Whole fucking thing's about property.' By the film's end, Welsh's view of life as being only in the here and now ('There's not some other world out there where everything's gonna be OK') is unchanged. As he stands over Witt's grave he asks 'Where's your spark now?' Smart is gruff on the surface but throughout the film displays some compassion.

By contrast Lt Col Tall is a career soldier who is frustrated at never having had a career, boldly exclaiming, 'This is my first war!' He is hellbent on achieving military glory, and in pursuit of his goal to take the ridge never even considers that his men have not enough water to sustain them. Tall cracks and crumbles as the mission proceeds, distorting the rules and the integrity of his position. Captain Staros, by contrast, is a compassionate soldier who Tall regards as being 'too soft'. Staros is portrtayed as a spiritual man in a brief but affecting scene, where he prays to God by candlelight. He is in a way very much an older version of Witt. Staros's refusal to go with the questionable command of his superior recalls the dramatic conflict that runs through **Paths of Glory**.

When Staros packs up to leave he talks with the young men he has led and his sense of fatherly responsibility shines through when he says, 'You are my sons, my dear sons. You live inside me now. I'll carry you wherever I go.'

All of the men in *The Thin Red Line* are ultimately battling loneliness. When Witt asks Smart, 'You ever get lonely?' Smart replies, 'Only around people.'

STYLE: Malick's approach to the war film with *The Thin Red Line* eschews to some degree those elements we would expect to see in a combat film set during World War Two. In doing so, his stylistic choices morph the movie into something other than only a film about fighting. Certainly when combat is shown it carries a kinetic energy, but for the most part the film is far more concerned with placing men in the wilderness and offering images that portray their emotional and spiritual breakdowns in this otherworldly environment. To some degree the film has a point of similarity with Kevin Costner's era-defining movie *Dances with Wolves* (1990) in which paradise is invaded by white men and violence.

The film is relatively quiet and meditative for a combat movie, the gentleness of certain key characters pervading this approach. The film, like Witt and Smart, meditates on the world. During the heat of battle Malick's camera cuts away to an image of a newborn bird struggling to stand as on the soundtrack we hear the noise of warfare. What chance does new life have in such a world? The first image of the film is also of nature as a crocodile submerges itself in the water. The jungle is presented as blissful, with man and the machinery of warfare invading it.

In Malick's previous films, *Badlands* and *Days of Heaven*, he similarly explored natural landscapes onto which human endeavour intrudes. Malick's most recent feature, *The New World*, also considers the culture clash between nature and human intrusion. Like those films, too, *The Thin Red Line* is characterised by visual pauses in the action where the film diverts our attention from the human story to images of wildlife and nature, suggesting a whole other world that is observing the human folly. With *The Thin Red Line* it is rather like there are two films being made: one a war film in the traditional sense, the other a series of contemplative sequences about how the individual makes sense of the world or crumbles before it. At one point in the film, one of the soldiers appears to break down in the pouring rain, whilst earlier another suddenly snaps during battle and never really recovers.

Perhaps the most striking image to suggest the contrast between fragile men and the war zone is a shot of a man playing a violin in the time spent anticipating the launching onto the beaches.

The film also emphasises how many soldiers were merely teenagers, barely more than boys.

For Bell, the key to his narrative, his memory of his wife, allows the film to intercut the savage war and wilderness with the comfort of a sunlit afternoon at home making love to his wife.

For cinematographer John Toll, his initial concept was to be considerably graphic in depicting the horror of armed combat, but Malick chose not to take that approach. Toll, Malick and Fisk were influenced in their image-making by a book of paintings by artists on front lines in the Second World War called *Images of War: The Artist's Vision of World War Two*. Toll commented that 'the graphic and visceral aspects . . . weren't nearly as important to Terry as the individual soldier's reaction to the situation. Therefore, our presentation of that type of action isn't hyper-real as it is in *Private Ryan*.'

CRITICAL CROSSFIRE: Released just six months after Steven Spielberg's immensely popular and more traditionally designed war movie **Saving Private Ryan**, *The Thin Red Line* was subject to critical confusion, writers unable to gauge whether they had just watched a war film or something other than that, something more openly philosophical.

Leonard Maltin's Movie and Video Guide wrote that the film was an 'ethereal, moodily philosophical interpretation of James Jones's novel . . . Those wanderings turned many viewers off.' For *Time Out* magazine the film seemed very welcome as 'a genuinely epic cine poem that essentially sidesteps history, politics and conventional ethics'.

MEDALS OF HONOUR: The film was nominated at the 1999 Oscars for Best Cinematography, Best Director, Best Music, Best Picture, Best Sound, Best Editing and Best Adapted Screenplay. At the 1999 American Society of Cinematographer awards the film won for its cinematography.

OTHER BATTLEFRONTS: *The Thin Red Line* is perhaps the most lyrical war film yet made, at least within the American popular cinema format. It is a very different version of the James Jones novel than the more literal adaptation of the 1960s. Other films that share *The Thin Red Line*'s sense of a mysterious landscape which possesses a mystic and metaphorical value are *Apocalypse Now* and *Ran*.

The Guadalcanal conflict and the Pacific theatre of war are also featured in *From Here To Eternity* (Fred Zinneman, 1953) and *Pearl Harbor* (Michael Bay, 2001).

THE HOMEFRONT: *The Thin Red Line* is available on DVD and VHS.

FINAL BRIEFING: *The Thin Red Line* is an astonishing war film for its conscious decision to minimise battle and combat talk in favour of examining essential human concerns around love, community and faith in the unseen and maybe the unknowable. The battle sequences, when they arrive, are arresting. The film's emphasis on the 'philosophical' is very much in contrast with the other war film released in 1998, *Saving Private Ryan*, which offers a more genre-based story.

FINAL SALUTE: In a retrospective essay on *The Thin Red Line*'s reception, Martin Flanagan wrote 'Where [*Saving Private Ryan*] had been opportunistically promoted as an event of huge public significance, a chance to remember and pay tribute, *The Thin Red Line* was marketed as a cineaste's dream, an aesthetic event.'

Vietnam

The American combat in Vietnam is perhaps the most vividly remembered war of the post-WW2 world, because it was covered so thoroughly in the media.

During the 1950s and early 1960s America understood that dealing with Indo-China would be central to security in Southeast Asia.

The American government went on to back the conservative South Vietnam administration against their communist North Vietnamese neighbours. America was committed to keeping South Vietnam as an 'ally' of the West in order to ensure that India and Australia were not to be subverted. However the South Vietnamese government was a fragile one and President Johnson was advised that more American support was needed. Soon after, American air attacks on North Vietnam occurred and American troops began arriving.

The Vietcong were the communist underground movement in South Vietnam. In 1962 President Kennedy sent 4,000 'advisers' to South Vietnam to support the government. American involvement in Vietnam had swiftly assumed a massive status that became ever more difficult to extricate itself from. By the end of 1968 some 500,000 American troops were in South Vietnam and a heavier tonnage of bombs had fallen on North Vietnam than fell on Germany and Japan together throughout World War Two. By 1970 Nixon began withdrawing troops, and the final bombing campaigns took place at the end of 1972. The war in Vietnam seriously damaged America's diplomatic prestige.

The Deer Hunter (1978)

183 minutes

EMI/Universal
Producer: Michael Deeley, Barry Spikings, Michael Cimino and John Peverall
Director: Michael Cimino
Screenplay: Deric Washburn (based on a story by Michael Cimino, Deric Washburn, Louis Garfinkle and Quinn K Redeker)
Cinematographer: Vilmos Zsigmond

Editor: Peter Zinner
Music: Stanley Myers
Art Direction: Ron Hobbs and Kim Swados
Costume Design: Eric Seelig
Visual Effects: Fred Cramer

CAST: Robert De Niro (*Michael*), John Cazale (*Stan*), John Savage (*Steven*), Christopher Walken (*Nick*), Meryl Streep (*Linda*), George Dzunda (*John*), Chuck Aspergen (*Axel*), Shirley Stoler (*Steven's Mother*), Rutanya Alda (*Angela*), Pierre Segui (*Julien*)

RATING: R/18

WAR STORY: The late 1960s/early 1970s. In the steel-mill town of Clairton, Pennsylvania, a group of friends – Michael, Axel, Nick, Stan and John – prepare for the wedding of their friend, Steven. They are mainly single, blue-collar guys, with the exception of Nick, who has a girlfriend, Linda.

The friends all work at the steel mill and hang out in the local bar, and Michael has arranged for them all to go hunting after Steven's wedding.

The wedding is a communal celebration and also something of a sendoff for several of the men, as Michael, Nick and newly married Steven are soon heading for Vietnam. The deer-hunting trip takes place and is by turns raucous and solitary. Michael is in his element in the mountains.

The film then cuts to Vietnam and the thick of battle. Michael lies dazed in the overgrowth, but moments later he is fighting again, raising a flame-thrower to immolate a village. Michael, Steven and Nick are captured by the Vietnamese and held in cages submerged in a river. Steven breaks down, and Nick and Michael are forced by their captors to play one another at Russian roulette. The three men eventually break free and escape the prison. They are picked up downriver by an American helicopter but Steven falls from the chopper and Michael goes after him, getting Steven to safety and a hospital. Nick is also in hospital and is finding it very hard to cope with the toll of combat. It has been life-changing for him and he remains in Saigon.

Michael returns to Clairton and is greeted as the returning hero. He develops a relationship with Linda, Nick's former girlfriend, and they fall in love. Michael finds it very difficult to adjust to all aspects of life back at home. Michael goes deer hunting with Stan, John and Axel.

Returning from the hunt Michael learns that Steven has returned home and is in a veterans' hospital. When Michael visits Steven he finds that his legs have been amputated. Steven is reluctant to leave the hospital but Michael convinces him and takes him back to Clairton.

In an effort to track down Nick and bring him home, Michael returns to Saigon. Michael eventually finds him earning money by gambling as a Russian roulette player. He tries to persuade Nick to return home, but it is no use. Nick kills himself and dies in his friend's arms. Nick is buried in Clairton, and after the funeral the friends gather for breakfast. Steven sits with his wife and this 'extended family' sing 'God Bless America' and drink to Nick.

CONCEPT/THE MISSION: *The Deer Hunter* is a major work of the Vietnam War film canon. Michael Cimino had studied art at Yale University and had begun his career as a successful director of commercials. Cimino made his break into feature films as a writer on *Silent Running* (Douglas Trumbull, 1971), working with Deric Washburn.

As an emerging screenwriter Cimino had also written *Magnum Force* (Ted Post, 1973) for Clint Eastwood to star in, and then *Thunderbolt and Lightfoot* (1974), which Cimino also directed, with Eastwood and Jeff Bridges co-starring. Cimino was not really a part of the 'Movie Brat' scene so defined by Scorsese, Spielberg, De Palma, Lucas and Coppola, and yet he made two films that bridged the late 1970s and early 1980s that are absolutely as vital and important to that era as the work of the other named filmmakers.

A key element in the development of the screenplay for *The Deer Hunter* was an original script by two unknowns named Louis Garfinkle and Quinn Redeker, who had written *The Man Who Came To Play*, a script that focused on the game of Russian roulette. Cimino was intrigued by this concept and encouraged Washburn to work it into *The Deer Hunter* screenplay. Sure enough, the Russian roulette scene became one of the definitive moments of the film, even forming the basis for one of the images used to advertise the movie. The contribution to Cimino and Washburn's screenplay resulted in arbitration by the Writers' Guild of America, and the story credit for the film was shared by all four writers.

The story was concerned more with the physical and emotional scars that war creates, rather than being too concerned with the Vietnam War specifically. For Cimino, 'The film is really about the nature of courage and friendship. Even the landscape is surreal.' Indeed, *The Deer Hunter* shares more in common with a film such as *The Best Years of Our Lives* (William Wyler, 1946), about American World War Two veterans returned home, than it does with **Apocalypse Now** or **Platoon**.

CASTING/RECRUITMENT: At the time that Cimino was developing *The Deer Hunter* one of American cinema's notable emerging actors was Roy Scheider. He had co-starred alongside the great Gene Hackman in *The French Connection* (William Friedkin, 1972) and then alongside Robert Shaw and Richard Dreyfuss in *Jaws* (Steven Spielberg, 1975). Cimino was keen for Scheider to portray Michael. However, when Universal Studios would not release Scheider from his *Jaws 2* contract, Cimino had to look elsewhere for a lead actor. Scheider was rightly frustrated by this turn of events, given the richness of the story that Cimino wanted to tell. On producer Michael Deeley's advice, Cimino then turned to Robert De Niro, who had been discovered by Brian De Palma in the late 1960s and then become a movie star and icon through his collaboration with Martin Scorsese on films such as *Mean Streets* (1973) and *Taxi Driver* (1976).

At the time of development on *The Deer Hunter*, De Niro was especially keen to star in a film called *Prizefighter*, later retitled *Raging Bull* and released in 1980 with Martin Scorsese directing. Ultimately, *The Deer Hunter* would be as important a part of De Niro's notable work of the 1970s, playing not only to his affinity for moments of anger and aggression, but more significantly to his evident skill in expressing moments of quiet and uncertainty. De Niro is a softer actor than many people think.

For Michael's close friends, Cimino cast the emerging Christopher Walken and the frail and mesmerising John Cazale. By the late 1970s Cazale had starred with Al Pacino in *Dog Day Afternoon* (Sidney Lumet, 1975) and also alongside Marlon Brando, James Caan, Robert Duvall and Al Pacino (again) in *The Godfather* (Francis Ford Coppola, 1972) and *The Godfather Part Two* (Francis Coppola, 1974). Cazale had also played the jittery sound-surveillance accomplice to Harry Caul (Gene Hackman) in *The Conversation* (Francis Coppola, 1974). Cazale was always a reluctant film actor, enjoying the theatre more. Tragically Cazale had been diagnosed with terminal bone cancer before filming on *The Deer Hunter* began, and he died soon after the film was made.

Christopher Walken has had an incredible career in films such as *Annie Hall* (Woody Allen, 1977), *The Dogs of War* (John Irvin, 1981),

Brainstorm (Douglas Trumbull, 1983), *The Dead Zone* (David Cronenberg, 1983), *King of New York* (Abel Ferrara, 1990), *Pulp Fiction*, *Sleepy Hollow* (Tim Burton, 1999) and *Catch Me If You Can* (Steven Spielberg, 2002).

At the time of production on *The Deer Hunter* John Cazale's girlfriend was a young actress named Meryl Streep, and Cazale suggested her to Cimino. Sure enough, Streep was cast in the role of Linda and went on to be the most highly regarded film actress of the late 1970s and throughout the 1980s, starring in *Sophie's Choice* (Alan J Pakula, 1982), *The French Lieutenant's Woman* (Karel Reisz, 1982) and *Out of Africa* (Sydney Pollack, 1985).

Portraying Steve was John Savage, who also appeared in *Do The Right Thing* (Spike Lee, 1989) and was in **The Thin Red Line** as the soldier who loses his composure totally on the battlefield.

George Dzunda has appeared in many films including *Streamers* (Robert Altman, 1983), *No Way Out* (Roger Donaldson, 1987), *White Hunter Black Heart* (Clint Eastwood, 1990), *Basic Instinct* (Paul Verhoeven, 1992) and *Crimson Tide* (Tony Scott, 1995). Chuck Aspergen only ever appeared in *The Deer Hunter*.

BACKUP: The cinematographer for *The Deer Hunter* was Vilmos Zsigmond, whose credits include *Close Encounters of the Third Kind*, *Heaven's Gate* (Michael Cimino, 1980), *The River* (Mark Rydell, 1984), *The Crossing Guard* (Sean Penn, 1995) and more recently *The Black Dahlia* (Brian De Palma, 2006).

Deric Washburn has also written *Extreme Prejudice* (Walter Hill, 1987).

The producer Michael Deeley has also produced *The Italian Job* (Peter Collinson, 1969) and *The Man who Fell to Earth* (Nicolas Roeg, 1976).

PRODUCTION/IN THE TRENCHES: *The Deer Hunter* was an expansive production, being filmed whilst Francis Coppola was still busy putting a shape to his sprawling Vietnam adventure epic **Apocalypse Now**.

Production on *The Deer Hunter* was immediately affected by the revelation of John Cazale's terminal illness. Inevitably, EMI considered shutting down the film if Cimino did not write the Cazale character out. Admirably, Cimino would not revise his screenplay in this way and instead the filming schedule was rearranged, with all the material involving Cazale being shot first.

EMI in England invested $7.5m into the film with Michael Deeley (who went on to produce Ridley Scott's 1982 movie *Blade Runner*) and Barry Spikings. The Appalachians were chosen as the location for the deer-hunting segments of the story, with extra filming taking place in the Cascade Mountains to expand the view. The production also moved to Thailand for the Vietnam sequences, even filming on the River Kwai, something David Lean had failed to do for **The Bridge on the River Kwai.**

For the scene where the three soldiers escape the Vietnamese and are rescued by helicopter, tragedy almost ensued when the helicopter seemed on the verge of crashing, leading DeNiro and the other actors to drop into the river.

For the tiger-cage sequence where the friends are imprisoned in the river in bamboo cages, real rats and insects proliferated.

During the now famous, if culturally inaccurate, roulette sequence, Cimino told Walken to spit at De Niro, but didn't tell De Niro this is what would happen. De Niro, in turn, was directed to slap Walken and Savage as hard as possible.

When the film came to be edited Cimino insisted on it being a three-hour film, and the publicity agent Alan Carr set up screenings in December 1978 so the film could qualify for Oscar nomination the following winter. Carr had not been especially keen on the subject matter and yet recognised the power of the film, famously saying that it was a masterpiece at three hours and a flop at two hours.

MARTIAL MUSIC: The music most associated with the film is the piece that Stanley Myers composed, entitled *Cavatina for Guitar and Orchestra*; a wistful and melancholy piece that swiftly became part of the popular cultural landscape. The music has nothing to do with combat and everything to do with a sense of grief and loss. The film begins with its title cards being accompanied by the Myers theme. Only occasionally does music feature in the film and it is never used to underscore battle or time spent in the combat zone. Rather, it is used sparingly and affectingly for moments of loss and contemplation, such as when Michael, having returned home, stays in a motel rather than attend his welcome-home party. Michael sits alone in the motel room painfully adjusting to being home. It is a sad moment and the music speaks on Michael's behalf.

REIMAGINING REALITY: *The Deer Hunter* has been widely criticised for presenting the Vietcong as sadists. There was no evidence to suggest

Russian roulette was played in Vietnam and the film was regarded as right-wing and attacked for playing fast and loose with historical accuracy. Protesters picketed the film on Oscar night. The film does not really engage with the pro- and anti-war stances, but instead uses the war as the context for a morality play and reflection on aspects of America in the 1970s. For its first hour *The Deer Hunter* charts a very naturalist line as it documents the details of everyday working-class American life in a Russian Orthodox community. In many ways the film is most affecting in this opening hour, offering a welcome contrast to the more comfortable middle-class lives that American cinema typically presents to the world.

HEART OF BATTLE: *The Deer Hunter* is ultimately interested in dramatising the cost of war on emotional lives. It is less interested in the political and far more invested in the strains that veterans face when they return home and find they have changed when life at home has not. The film also implicitly expresses the inherent violence and aggression in men. Even the good-natured bonhomie of the friends is underscored by aggression. Late in the film Michael compellingly and tensely illustrates to pistol-toting Stan that guns are not toys, and the film could be said to express a pacifist message. Whereas initially Michael is committed to killing the deer in the mountains, after experiencing warfare he cannot bring himself to kill again and lets the deer run free. These quiet moments are where the film excels.

CHARACTER: De Niro has commented, 'I liked the characters. I liked that they didn't say much.' De Niro, so noted for his immersion in characters and committed research, spent time at Mingo Junction and Steubenville in Ohio to familiarise himself with the blue-collar world in which the character of Michael lives.

Several critics have observed that Michael's character owes a huge debt (either intended or otherwise) to the eighteenth-century American novelist James Fenimore Cooper's character 'The Deerslayer', an American frontier character who features in several of Cooper's novels, stories that played their part in defining the American man in relation to native Americans, the wilderness and violence.

Through Michael the film is able to more vaguely address the concept of war because he becomes so symbolic. In an essay about *The Deer Hunter*, Leonard Quart observes that Michael echoes '. . . Hemingway's notion of grace under pressure'. Michael is a contained and thoughtful character even amidst the raucous, male bonding that dominates the first third of the film. In war Michael's contained, controlled emotion becomes his greatest ally. As Steven loses his composure in the prison compound, Michael quietly tries to maintain Steven's rapidly breaking sanity. In the larger picture Michael attempts to redeem Nick from the life he has chosen to lead in Saigon. For Michael the core issue upon his return home is of feeling disconnected from everything. He tells Linda, 'I feel far away.'

Ultimately, Michael is different from the other men throughout the film. It is indicated that Michael is more cosmically inclined. Early in the film, as they leave work and head for the bar, Mike notes the sundogs (a solar phenomenon) that can be seen and how this is a good omen for the hunt. Michael's journey is a spiritual one.

Whilst Michael is contained, with an undercurrent of suppressed aggression (at least prior to going to war), Nick is the most gentle and playful of the characters at the beginning of the film. By its close he has become its most brutal and has lost all sense of value.

Steven is an anxious man whose frail emotion cannot sustain itself in war. As a veteran he wants to remain institutionalised at the hospital but by the end, as the closing scene indicates, he has begun to renew his relationship with his wife and find new strength.

Prior to going to fight, Michael, Nick and Steven are easygoing, naïve men, whose immaturity and forgivable ignorance about the war is clarified when they meet a Green Beret at Steven's wedding reception. They ask him what the war is like and imagine it to be the chance for glory. The Green Beret says barely anything other than 'Fuck it.' This foreshadows Mike's own muted stance when he returns.

Of the friends who do not go to fight the most vividly drawn is Stan, a mouthy man who thinks that toting a gun is fun.

Linda and Angela are the two women in the film. Angela is shown having had a breakdown in the aftermath of Steven's return. Linda has longed for Nick to return but finds herself falling in love with Michael, though by the film's end their future together has not been defined.

STYLE: Cimino adopts a very unfussy and naturalistic style for this film. There is the sense that the film is keen to somehow document working-class life as a context and certainly the Clairton-based sequences are the most quietly affecting. Cimino revels in close-ups to communicate intensity during the first Russian roulette sequence. By contrast the deer-hunting scenes are marked by an airy, big-sky quality that immediately communicates the sense of freedom and cleansing that the hunt means, for Michael especially. The images of the American wilderness recall the paintings of Albert Bierstadt, and contrasts so clearly with the grime and close quarters of life in Clairton. For the sequences in Saigon in the last part of the film there is the sense of it being a living hell – cars stand aflame on roadsides and a red hue dominates several of the night-time scenes as Mike goes to find and hopefully rescue Nick.

The domestic scenes in Clairton – on streets, at bars, in homes – have a naturalistic, unobtrusive quality. A wintry feel hangs over all the home-town sequences, lending them yet more sadness and quiet despair.

Cimino favours wide shots that contain groups of people, communities. He applies the same approach in sequences from his next film, *Heaven's Gate*, an undervalued film if ever there was one.

CRITICAL CROSSFIRE: The *Time Out Film Guide* records the film's reception in Britain in 1978 as very strong, saying, 'This is probably one of the few great films of the decade ... Moral imperatives replace historical analysis ...' For *Leonard Maltin's Movie and Video Guide*, 'this sensitive, painful, evocative work packs an emotional wallop'.

MEDALS OF HONOUR: *The Deer Hunter* enjoyed serious commercial and critical response through late 1978 and into spring 1979. At the 1979 Oscars the film won Best Director, Best Film Editing, Best Sound, Best Director and Best Picture. There were Oscar nominations too for Best Actor, Best Supporting Actress and Best Cinematography. At the BAFTAs the film won Best Cinematography and Best Editing and was nominated for Best Actor, Best Director, Best Actress, Best Film and Best Screenplay. In 1996 the film was included on the National Film Registry (USA) of the National Film Preservation Board.

OTHER BATTLEFRONTS: *The Deer Hunter* had a contemporary rival with a similar story to tell of returning Vietnam veterans, *Coming Home* (Hal Ashby, 1978), which starred Jon Voight. In the same year two other films about the experience in Vietnam were released: *The Boys in Company C* (Sidney J Furie) and *Go Tell The Spartans* (Ted Post). Oliver Stone's **Born on the Fourth of July** also expressed the plight of the Vietnam veteran through its dramatisation of the life of veteran and campaigner Ron Kovic.

Michael's character gets a more immediate update in *First Blood* (Ted Kotcheff, 1982) in which a Vietnam veteran, named John Rambo, runs into trouble with the local sheriff. The vet goes on the run and takes to the wilderness, where he is more at home than in the town. Rambo's emotional lifeline is his connection to his former commander, who is drafted in to help bring John in. When Rambo returns to town he vents his anger and resentment at the plight of the veteran back home. It is a point of view more thoroughly expressed in **Born on the Fourth of July**, though *First Blood* has a legitimate and valuable place in the chronology of Vietnam war films. *First Blood* was conceived as an action thriller that plays the war-zone concept out in the American Northwest.

Francis Coppola, who had directed **Apocalypse Now** (and even attended a publicity screening of *The Deer Hunter* by invitation whilst completing his own Vietnam film) made a quietly powerful, small-scale drama called *Gardens of Stone* (1987) about the military unit that supervises the National Military Cemetery at Arlington. The film charts the emotional toll of the Vietnam war on the families at home with real force and in many ways is, one feels, a more telling indictment of war than the surreal, super-symbolism of *Apocalypse Now* and, indeed, *The Deer Hunter*.

THE HOMEFRONT: *The Deer Hunter* is available on VHS and a two-disc DVD edition.

FINAL BRIEFING: *The Deer Hunter* is a bleak film. Even though the Russian roulette scenes have become the film's most celebrated sequences, especially the first of them, the segment directly about combat occupies the smallest part of the film. The remaining two thirds are all about life at home, before and after war. Some found the film cruel in itself rather than being a critique of cruelty, and there is a sense that the film rubs the audience's face in the horror of war in a most desperate way. Ultimately, the hysteria of the Vietnam scenes in the film are less telling about the cost of war than Steven's reaction to Michael arriving at the veteran hospital.

The film's final moment, as the friends sing 'God Bless America', does not suggest that a definitive happiness will return to their lives. Instead the film acknowledges the need for community and belonging in order to cope with the suffering of war and the battle of living.

FINAL SALUTE: For Cimino *The Deer Hunter* was never intended as a factual piece, and to those who opposed the film aesthetically and politically he replied by saying, 'You're fighting a phantom, because literal accuracy was never intended.'

Apocalypse Now Redux (1979/2001)

195 minutes

Omni Zoetrope
Producer: Francis Coppola
Co-Producers: Gray Frederickson and Fred Roos
Associate Producer: Mona Skager
Screenplay: John Milius and Francis Coppola
Cinematographer: Vittorio Storaro
Editor: Walter Murch, Gerald B Greenberg, Lisa Fruchtman
Music: Carmine Coppola
Sound Montage/Design: Walter Murch
Supervisory Sound Editing: Richard Cirincione
Production Design: Dean Tavoularis
Art Direction: Angelo Graham
Second Unit Photography: Stephen H Burum
Costume Design: Charles E James
Visual Effects: Joe Lombardi, AD Flowers

CAST: Marlon Brando (*Colonel Walter E Kurtz*), Robert Duvall (*Lieutenant Colonel Bill Kilgore*), Martin Sheen (*Captain Benjamin L Willard*), Frederic Forrest ('*Chef*' *Hicks*), Albert Hall (*Chief Phillips*), Sam Bottoms (*Lance B Johnson*), Larry Fishburne ('*Clean*'), Dennis Hopper (*Photo Journalist*), GD Spradlin (*General Corman*), Harrison Ford (*Colonel Lucas*), Jerry Ziesmer (*Civilian*), Scott Glenn (*Captain Richard Colby*)

RATING: R

TAGLINE: Francis Ford Coppola presents *Apocalypse Now*.

WAR STORY: Captain Benjamin Willard is in Saigon, his tour of Vietnam duty over. Willard is divorced and has been waiting a week for details of his next mission. He is called in by Intelligence to be told that his task is to go upriver into the deep jungle of Cambodia (where America has no reason to be). Once there he must terminate a renegade American colonel named Kurtz. Willard is handed a dossier on Kurtz, which includes correspondence and images, and is played a tape of what is believed to be Kurtz's voice. Willard accepts the mission and boards a PBR (a river patrol boat) crewed by four men: Chief, Clean, Chef and Johnson.

For the early part of the journey the Air Cavalry are to escort Willard upriver. AirCav is commanded by Captain Kilgore, soldier and surfer. Kilgore calls up an air attack on a village and Willard and his men take a ride in one of the choppers to see the village destroyed.

They now continue their long journey without military support. Willard keeps his mission a secret to the PBR crew, but the men bond as the river trip goes on. Willard spends a lot of time trying to understand what kind of character Kurtz is by reading through the dossier. One night the PBR comes across a US supply station where a United Services Organisation (USO) entertainment is being prepared, so Willard and his men stay overnight and attend a Playboy-bunny show.

The next day they continue upriver and arrive at the deserted and dishevelled MedEvac station where a couple of the Playboy bunny girls are. The river narrows and the PBR arrives at the last American line, the Do Long bridge, where a chaotic battle scene is taking place, and Willard speaks to some of the dazed and confused troops in an effort to get some idea about what is going on. The journey continues and Willard learns that several months previously another soldier had been sent on the same mission as Willard and had not returned, apparently choosing to stay at Kurtz's camp. The PBR comes under fire and Clean is killed. They halt and bury him. The next day, Willard, Chief, Johnson and Chef carry on with their journey. Willard finally confides to Chief the specifics of the mission. Johnson, meanwhile, is becoming increasingly primal and whacked out, whilst Chef becomes increasingly worried and uneasy. Chief is then killed when the boat again comes under fire, and his dead body is taken by the river.

With just Johnson and Chef remaining, Willard continues his mission and finally reaches the riverbank where Kurtz's compound is located amidst an ancient temple. Hundreds of Ifuago indigenous people are there and Montagnard soldiers line the riverbank. Willard is met by a talkative photographer and then taken to Kurtz, who imprisons Willard in a bamboo cage and then in a container. Chef is killed by Kurtz.

Finally, Willard is taken into Kurtz's inner sanctum and is confronted by the colonel, who talks about his disillusionment with the world and the military. Willard listens patiently and finally prepares to kill Kurtz, which he does brutally with a machete. He emerges into the night where he is greeted by the soldiers as their new leader. Willard returns to the boat with Johnson, the boat pulls away from the temple and Kurtz's face is shown for the last time. Willard starts the journey back to the known world and the film fades to black.

In the *Apocalypse Now Redux* version (2001) Willard and his crew arrive at a French plantation house in an extensive sequence and dine there overnight, while the French explain their resolve to stay there. This sequence is the most significant restored material to the edit and occurs in the film after the death of Clean.

CONCEPT/THE MISSION: Coppola's energy and imagination are not to be disputed and *Apocalypse Now* is one of the boldest films of the 1970s, reminding audiences again of just how powerfully quest narratives and adventures speak to us. There is something of the *Boys' Own* adventure about the film, but Coppola and his creative team ally this with a genuine desire to invest the adventure genre with a philosophical soul.

Apocalypse Now is one of the few films – and Coppola has directed a couple of the others – whose title and concept has transcended the immediate realm of film and become a major part of contemporary pop culture.

The film presents a torrent of images of man and the nature of light and darkness. The all-consuming character of the film's creation and the obsessional nature of the quest undertaken in the film eerily, powerfully and excitingly mirror one another, and have plugged into our pop-culture psyche. With the world still confronting a regular display of First World military might the film continues to carry a strain of social significance and protest.

Vital to the eventual conception of *Apocalypse Now* was the fact that America had only very recently ended their intervention in Vietnam. During the conflict John Wayne had directed the tub-thumping, pro-American movie *The Green Berets* (1968), designed to explain to movie audiences why American troops had to be in Vietnam. Wayne even wrote a letter to President Lyndon B Johnson in December 1965 expressing his intention with the film.

When Coppola took on the challenge of making *Apocalypse Now* he was well aware of the problems and tensions inherent in the task. Coppola commented that 'I'll be venturing into an area that is laden with so many implications that if I select some aspects and ignore others, I may be doing something irresponsible.'

With some irony, it was *The Deer Hunter* (Michael Cimino, 1978) that made the biggest impact on audiences in the late 1970s and which predated *Apocalypse Now* by one year. When Coppola's film was released there was the sense that it might play its cultural part in purging recent history. Maybe even more importantly was the recognition that a Vietnam movie could not claim to be some version of the truth if it portrayed the American experience there as victorious.

Famously, the origins of *Apocalypse Now* lay in the late 1960s, when George Lucas concocted the idea of a Vietnam movie shot on 16mm in the rice fields of northern California. Speaking about the project with his friend and fellow film student John Milius ignited the project further, and Milius began work on a screenplay, which at one point had been called *Psychedelic Soldier*, and the resulting film adheres to this sense of reality being out of kilter. Coppola's old colleague Carrol Ballard had also wanted to make a movie based on Joseph Conrad's 1902 novel *Heart of Darkness*, set in the African jungle. Screenwriter and Zoetrope founder member John Milius had a keen interest in the military and was an aspiring screenwriter. It was he who responded to a badge popular at the time, emblazoned with the legend 'Nirvana Now'. Milius dipped into the Bible and recalled the phrase 'Apocalypse now'.

For Milius, *Heart of Darkness* suggested itself as a powerful framework and metaphor with which to enhance the basic concept. The involvement of George Lucas in the project eventually lessened and he became busy with *American Graffiti* (1973). By this time, Lucas had also begun developing what would become *Star Wars*, which to editor and sound man Walter Murch's eyes and mind is a transposition of the essence of *Apocalypse Now* at that point, namely that a primitive race, working with invention and great courage, could overcome the challenge of a mighty empire of machines. It remains a central motif in Lucas's prequel trilogy nearly thirty years later.

In due course, the narrative of the film's developing screenplay would be clarified by journalist Michael Herr's war reports in *Esquire* magazine. These pieces went on to form the basis of Herr's celebrated book *Despatches*. Herr's most notable *Esquire* piece was an article entitled 'The Battle for Khe Sanh', which certainly inspired the Do Long bridge sequence in the eventual film.

Milius's first draft of the script was dated 15 December 1969. One of the major questions has always been his identification with the maverick,

Above *All Quiet on the Western Front:* Paul Baumer (Lew Ayres) lies on the First World War battlefield, a place that expresses all of man's potential for cruelty, despair and violence.

Below *La Grande Illusion:* Maréchal (Jean Gabin) and de Boeildieu (Pierre Fresnay) enter into the world of the prisoner of war.

Left *Gallipoli:* Archie (Mark Lee) and Frank (Mel Gibson) race one another through the streets of Cairo during their preparations to fight at Gallipoli.

Below *The Dambusters:* Guy Gibson (Richard Todd) readies himself to ride out on the mission of a lifetime.

Right *The Bridge on the River Kwai:* Defiant, proud and hell bent on military honour, Nicholson (Alec Guinness) stands firm with his men in the face of prison camp life.

Below *Kanal:* Strong and determined Daisy (Teresa Izewska) endures the trauma and tragedy of the desperate race to hoped-for freedom through the sewers of Warsaw.

Left *The Great Escape:* Virgil Hilts (Steve McQueen) prepares for one last ride to glory.

Below *Saving Private Ryan:* Captain Miller (Tom Hanks) takes a quiet and pensive moment to reflect on the mission that lies ahead.

Right *The Thin Red Line:* Pacifist soldier Witt (Jim Caviezel) tends to the injured, his far off gaze seeking to understand the reasons why war exists and what battles are fought in the heart and mind.

Below *The Deer Hunter:* Mike (Robert De Niro) finds solace, security and understanding in his retreats to the mountains.

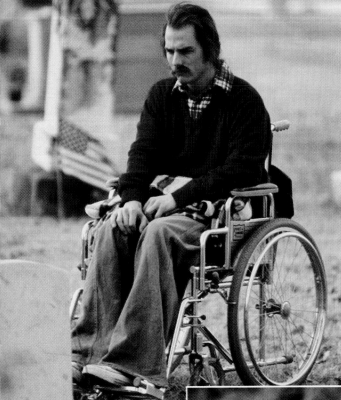

Left *Born on the Fourth of July:* Exhausted and alone, Ron Kovic (Tom Cruise) confronts the tragedy of war. In this moment of home-front despair and regret, Ron will begin to revive and restore his life.

Right *Casualties of War:* Fear and anger become all consuming in the wilderness of Vietnam as Eriksson (Michael J. Fox) desperately tries to stop Meserve (Sean Penn) causing further atrocities.

Above *Ran:* The resplendent samurai embellishes death on the battlefields of *Ran*.

Below *Aliens:* Ripley (Sigourney Weaver) goes the industrial gladiator route in order to wage war, one on one, with her alien enemy.

Above *Welcome to Sarajevo:* Taking cover, news reporter Michael (Stephen Dillane) confronts the trauma and tragedy of Sarajevo and his life will change forever.

Below *Glory:* The members of the 54th Massachusetts regiment confront their destiny in a blaze of courage and brotherhood.

martial, primordial Kurtz character. In an interview with *Film Comment* in 1976, John Milius tells interviewer Richard Thompson that he regards Willard's trip upriver as akin to Homer's *Odyssey* narrative, with the character of Kilgore representing nothing less than the Cyclops. For Milius, had he been director, the film's inspiration would have been *The Bridge on the River Kwai*, suggesting the more explicitly adventure-based narrative the screenplay originally took; unsurprising perhaps, given George Lucas's initial involvement in the concept. It has been reported that when Lucas and Milius saw the eventual film many years later in 1979 they were uneasy with the way in which Coppola had transformed the material. It seems as though Coppola transcended the concept and took it away from a pulpy sense of adventure to something more rooted in mythology and symbolism.

So, having taken on the job of developing *Apocalypse Now* in the early 1970s, Coppola finished a rewrite of Milius's script in late 1975. Famously, Coppola would rewrite the screenplay endlessly through the seemingly interminable filming period of 1976–7.

One early draft of the screenplay began with Willard back in America, working as a bodyguard to a businessman on a boat. Willard begins to tell a woman on board about the trials of being in Vietnam. The film was originally to have concluded with Kurtz and Willard fighting alongside one another against the Vietcong and succeeding. When a helicopter comes in to fly them out, Kurtz guns the chopper down. Coppola discarded this conclusion in favour of the material in Kurtz's compound.

As with any movie adaptation of a source text, there is fun to be had in noting what has been transformed or eliminated in the process. In the movie, the shower of arrows that strikes the PBR just before it arrives at Kurtz's compound recalls a particular instance in *Heart of Darkness*. 'Exterminate all the brutes' is a line in Conrad's novel which has an echo in the movie line 'Drop the bombs, exterminate them all.' In the film, Willard calls himself 'caretaker of Kurtz's memory'. In Conrad's text, the narrator Marlowe says, 'I was to have the care of his memory.' In both the film and the book, Kurtz's last words are the same, 'The horror, the horror' – a line that inspired TS Eliot's poem *The Waste Land* which is suggested as being part of Kurtz's reading in the film.

Ernest Hemingway once noted that all of American literature flows from Mark Twain's landmark novel *Huckleberry Finn*. In turn, a number of films have been buoyed along by that great book, and *Apocalypse Now* is one of them.

Orson Welles, Coppola's 1940s equivalent, had attempted his own version of *Heart of Darkness*. Like Coppola, Welles's Hollywood star burned very bright very early and much of his career thereafter was one of battles. Welles had attempted *Heart of Darkness* as early as 1939 at RKO Pictures, but he would not comply with budgetary cuts that the studio wanted to make.

When Coppola was at UCLA film school, a classmate named Jack Hill (who went on to be a low-budget movie producer) made a short called *The Host*, which was inspired by the book *The Golden Bough*. It told of a young man taking refuge in an Aztec temple. Coppola has joked since that *Apocalypse Now* was just a splashy remake of the same concept.

Heart of Darkness was the film's most prominent influence, and as Coppola ventured towards shaping the conclusion of the film he paid more attention to Conrad's text than to the screenplay, drawing from the prose a sense about the primitive and the savage. The film makes a quantum leap from notionally being a war movie to being an exploration of the wildness in man.

For the end of the film, Coppola sought much inspiration in TS Eliot's *The Waste Land*. Eliot's landmark poem explores the post-World War One world and alludes to a range of tensions and associations between the modern and the ancient, just as *Apocalypse Now* does.

As mentioned above, the other key influence on the film (and it earns a visual reference towards the end of the picture) is James Frazer's book *The Golden Bough* (1887). This was the first in a series of volumes (the final one published in 1915) detailing and comparing world rituals and mythic narratives. In keeping with the apocalyptic nature of the film, Frazer published a supplement to *The Golden Bough* in 1936 called *Aftermath*. The inspiration for the title *The Golden Bough* was Virgil's poem *Aeneid*, which in turn influenced elements of the *Apocalypse Now* narrative. As is certainly clear, Willard's journey takes him into a kind of Underworld where he experiences a death and resurrection.

There is an appeal in knowing that the journey Willard takes into a mythic zone was matched by Coppola's own legendary creative entanglements. The mythological associations and influences on the film manifest themselves further in shots of Kurtz's library that show Jessie L Weston's *From Ritual to Romance*, a study that is concerned with Grail mythology, one of whose most prominent narratives is the myth of the Fisher King.

Coppola and John Milius dominate the conceptual proceedings in most accounts of the creation of *Apocalypse Now*. There is, apparently, an unsung hero of sorts in Dennis Jakob, a film editor and long-time associate of Coppola's. He was on the *Apocalypse Now* set much of the time, particularly during the filming of Kurtz's scenes, and with his interest in mythology Jakob was able to advise Coppola on how the film could best incorporate and allude to ancient narratives and motifs. Indeed, it was Jakob who suggested the Fisher King narrative reference to Coppola in his refinement of the screenplay.

There were three military advisers on the project: Pete Kama, Paul Hender and Doug Ryan.

As a result of creating the *Apocalypse Now Redux* edit from the original negative, this negative of the film in its original form now no longer exists.

The film once clocked in at around seven and a half hours. Three and a half of these hours covered the journey upriver and the remaining four were at Kurtz's compound.

CASTING/RECRUITMENT: Most famously, Coppola reteamed with Marlon Brando, whose role is essentially an extended cameo during the end sequence of the film. Brando had been contracted for fifteen days work over a three-week period.

However, when Brando arrived on set the first three days were spent huddled with Coppola going through the script. Brando had not realised that the screenplay was not a direct adaptation of *Heart of Darkness*. When he read the book once arriving on set, everything Coppola and Milius's script laid out was clarified for him and allowed him to move ahead with his performance.

As with so many Coppola films, familiar faces reappear in *Apocalypse Now*, notably Robert Duvall in a very showy and loud role as Kilgore, quite in variance to the thoughtful quietness of his Tom Hagen character in *The Godfather*.

Laurence Fishburne, back then Larry Fishburne, appears as the young soldier Clean, the youngest soldier on the boat that Willard takes upriver.

Frederic Forrest also reprised his relationship with Coppola after the success of *The Conversation*.

Amazingly, Steve McQueen had been first choice for the role of Willard but he declined. His take on the character was that he should essentially be cool, but this did not sit well with Coppola. Furthermore, McQueen did not want to be away from his family for an extended period of time. Coppola, in his keenness to work with McQueen, said that the production would let McQueen bring his family to location, but to no avail. McQueen was then offered the role of Kurtz and he declined that too. Keith Carradine, Tommy Lee Jones, Nick Nolte and Frederic Forrest were all candidates for Willard. Even more amazing, perhaps, was that Clint Eastwood had been considered for the role of Willard, as had Yves Montand.

After McQueen pulled out of the project, Coppola went to Al Pacino, Jack Nicholson, Robert Redford and James Caan before finally casting Harvey Keitel. This decision proved to be something of a misjudgement. After a few weeks' filming Keitel's style of performance (for which he is recognised as one of the modern greats), as the astonishing *Ulysses Gaze* (Theo Angelopoulos, 1995) demonstrates, was considered not quite what the film needed. Coppola felt that Willard needed to be a more passive entity than Keitel was portraying, and so Martin Sheen was cast, and was working on the movie by 26 April 1976.

Sheen had auditioned for the role of Michael Corleone in *The Godfather*. Harrison Ford, on the cusp of breaking through as a leading man, was cast in the small role of Colonel G Lucas, an affectionate homage to George Lucas, with whom Ford had recently finished working on *Star Wars: A New Hope*. Ford looks very young and bookish in the film's briefing scene with his thickset glasses and clean-cut haircut.

Dennis Hopper was cast during Coppola's summer 1976 return to America and for Hopper the role was something of a career revival, no less, restoring his profile with both the industry and audiences. On location, Hopper was taken to heart by the Ifuago tribe, who made him a badge of honour from pine needles.

Martin Sheen was a star with a strong run in television shows. His credits have included: *Badlands*, *Gandhi*, the TV miniseries *Kennedy*, *The Dead Zone*, *Wall Street* (Oliver Stone, 1987), *Da* (Matt Clark, 1988), *JFK* (narrator only) and *Catch Me If You Can*. Frederic Forrest appeared in Coppola's *The Conversation*, *The Missouri Breaks* (Arthur Penn, 1976), *The Rose* (Mark Rydell, 1979), *Hammett* (Wim Wenders, 1982), *Music Box* (Costa Gavras, 1989) and *Falling Down* (Joel Schumacher, 1993).

Larry Fishburne changed his name to Laurence Fishburne and has lit up the screen in *Death Wish 2* (Michael Winner, 1982), *The Color Purple* (Steven Spielberg, 1985), *A Nightmare On Elm Street 3: Dream Warrior* (Chuck Russell, 1986), *Gardens of Stone* (1987), *Boyz n the Hood* (John Singleton, 1991), *Higher Learning* (John Singleton, 1993), *What's Love Got to Do with It?* (Brian Gibson, 1993) and *The Matrix* (The Warshowski Brothers, 1999).

Robert Duvall is one of the finest American actors of the modern era and has appeared in *To Kill A Mockingbird, Countdown* (Robert Altman, 1968), *Bullitt, True Grit* (Henry Hathaway, 1969), *The Great Northfield Minnesota Raid* (Philip Kaufman, 1972), *Network* (Sidney Lumet, 1976), *Tender Mercies* (Bruce Beresford, 1982), *Colors, Falling Down* and the great, recent western *Open Range* (Kevin Costner, 2003). Duvall also directed *The Apostle* (1999) and *Assassination Tango* (2003). Marlon Brando starred in *A Streetcar Named Desire* (Elia Kazan, 1951), *Viva, Zapata!* (Elia Kazan, 1952), *Julius Caesar* (Joseph L Mankiewicz,1953) and *On the Waterfront* (Elia Kazan, 1954).

Dennis Hopper has had an immensely long career that has included *Johnny Guitar* (Nicholas Ray, 1954), *Rebel Without a Cause* (Nicholas Ray, 1956), *Hang 'Em High* (Ted Post, 1967), *Easy Rider* (Peter Fonda, 1969), *The Last Movie* (also directed, 1971), *River's Edge* (Tim Hunter, 1986) and *Hoosiers* (David Anspaugh, 1986), *The Indian Runner* (Sean Penn, 1991), *True Romance* (Tony Scott, 1993), *Speed* (Jan DeBont, 1994).

BACKUP: *Apocalypse Now* consolidated the team that Coppola had built, starting with *The Rain People*, through *The Godfather, The Conversation* and *The Godfather Part II*. Many of the *Apocalypse Now* creative and managerial crew would continue to work with Coppola for the next twenty years. Returning to Coppola's moviemaking fold were Gray Frederickson and Fred Roos, fresh from the success of *The Godfather Part II*. Frederickson was responsible for the locations of *Apocalypse Now* and Roos for the logistical issues that were massive and many.

Once again, Dean Tavoularis reprised his duties as production designer, a monumental task in this instance. Walter Murch headed up the post-production effort.

Screenwriter John Milius, one of the Movie Brat gang, has also written *Dirty Harry, Jeremiah Johnson* (Sydney Pollack, 1973), *The Life and Times of Judge Roy Bean* (John Huston, 1972) and *The Wind and the Lion*. He had also written and directed *Dillinger* (1973) for Roger Corman and went on to direct intermittently through the 1980s and 1990s including the adventure *Conan The Barbarian* (1982), *Red Dawn, Farewell to the King* and two TV movies, *Motorcycle Gang* (1994) and *Rough Riders* (1997). Milius may yet team up with the Warshowski Brothers (*Bound, The Matrix* Trilogy) to make another *Conan* movie. Milius has also written the screenplay for *Geronimo: An American Legend* (Walter Hill, 1993).

Apocalypse Now marked Coppola's first collaboration with Vittorio Storaro, whose work Coppola had been impressed by on *The Conformist* (Bernardo Bertolucci, 1970). Storaro had originally been unsure about committing to an American film where he had no obvious personal connection or 'interest' in the subject, but his mind was changed when he read the *Apocalypse Now* screenplay on a flight to Australia to recce locations for the film before the Philippines was finally decided on. Storaro's other credits include *The Spider's Stratagem* (Bernardo Bertolucci, 1969), *Last Tango in Paris* (Bernardo Bertolucci, 1972), *1900* (Bernardo Bertolucci, 1976), *Agatha* (Michael Apted, 1979), *Reds* (Warren Beatty, 1981), *Ladyhawke* (Richard Donner, 1985), *The Last Emperor* (Bernardo Bertolucci, 1987), *The Sheltering Sky* (Bernardo Bertolucci, 1990), *Little Buddha* (Bernardo Bertolucci, 1993) and *Bulworth* (Warren Beatty, 1998).

Storaro was the youngest fully ranked cinematographer in Italian film history, achieving this position by the age of 26. His intensity and intellectual integrity enriches his work. As happened on *The Conversation* and *The Godfather Part II*, Coppola committed to a concentrated period of research, which was undertaken and led by Deborah Fine, research which ran from spring 1975 until summer 1977. Information about the North Vietnamese army, Cambodian ruins, China Beach, PBRs and USO shows amongst many other minutiae was part of Fine's fact-finding mission.

PRODUCTION/IN THE TRENCHES: The making of the film, fraught with struggle, has assumed a mythical status and in the process Coppola became real moviemaking legend, his name (even today) immediately conjuring images of the brave and grandiose. For many observers, the film marked a cruel watershed in Coppola's creative output and industry standing. It was as if he had gone upriver himself and in a sense never returned with the same vigour.

It was initially thought that the shoot would last around four months, but *Apocalypse Now* went thirty-seven weeks over schedule, filmed over a fifteen-month period. At a certain point, Coppola referred to the film as the 'idiodyssey'.

To say that Coppola faced challenges and setbacks with the production of *Apocalypse Now* is one of the great understatements. The shoot fused financial, personal and even spiritual concerns as Coppola struggled to make a movie that would make sense to him and the world.

Unsurprisingly, one of the first hurdles was the attempt to secure the support of the American military. This was not forthcoming, as the screenplay was regarded as ultimately unpatriotic, and may have been why the Australian military was not keen to support the movie either. Coppola had considered basing the movie in Cairns on the northeast coast of Australia, but with the objection of the military another location would have to be found, and so the Philippines became the production's base.

For the film's finance, the Bank of America lent seven million dollars to Coppola Cinema Seven, the company Coppola had formed after the initial 'failure' of the first iteration of American Zoetrope. This money was forthcoming because United Artists had agreed to distribute the film. At this point in his career, Coppola was the Spielberg of the era.

In a neat parallel, Coppola began shooting *Apocalypse Now* on the same day that George Lucas began filming in the Tunisian desert on *Star Wars: A New Hope*. Throughout its production, the *Apocalypse Now* crew were challenged by the problems of shooting in such a remote location with little infrastructure. The project was affected especially badly when Typhoon Ruby demolished a set on the South China Sea coast. Two PBRs were utterly demolished by the weather. The typhoon cost the production over a million dollars and the film shut down in early July to recover from the impact of the storm. Coppola returned to his California base to think through the film and was back on location on 25 July. In August the Saigon hotel scenes were shot.

Famously, Coppola convinced President Marcos of the Philippines to loan the shoot a number of the country's helicopters. US insignia would be painted on them and if necessary the Philippine Air Force logos would be repainted at the end of the shooting day.

As with the *Godfather* films, Coppola pushed production designer Dean Tavoularis's creativity and pragmatism. His challenges included overseeing the construction of an immense Cambodian temple complex at the Pagsanjan riverbank location. In all Tavoularis had the task of creating the sets for 292 scenes.

For the Saigon Hotel scene that intensely opens the film, Coppola encouraged Sheen to improvise. According to Jerry Ziesmer, who was also an assistant director on the film, Sheen smashed the mirror when he miscounted his steps and so was nearer the mirror than he thought when he lashed out and connected with it. Coppola encouraged Sheen to continue when he registered no dismay at cutting his hand. 'I felt as if

Francis was pulling Marty inside out,' Ziesmer comments in his book *Ready When You Are, Mr Coppola, Mr Spielberg, Mr Crowe*.

When Ziesmer arrived on set the first conversation he had with Coppola was about the number of helicopters available, as Coppola had not been told how many he would have. For the Kurtz compound scenes two hundred extras were required on set every day, and on one occasion there were nine hundred.

The Ifuago natives would work as crew on the production, carving props and totems and building the cages that Willard and his crew were imprisoned in.

It was a happy accident that Eleanor Coppola (shooting 16mm footage of the production, that became the foundation footage for *Hearts of Darkness*, the 1991 documentary about the filming of *Apocalypse Now*) saw the Ifuago slaughtering a water buffalo, an action that sparked concepts in Coppola's mind for the primal finale.

One of the biggest logistical problems in staging the battle scenes was that some of the American soldier extras were indeed Vietnam veterans. When the helicopters flew in for the shot the vets would become very intense and almost manic, and then when the brief moment of filming was over a sort of depression would kick in.

It may well have been post-typhoon, during the summer of 1976, that the shoot became more chaotic than anybody could have predicted. Sometimes, though, it is the films made under great duress and tension that seem to yield astonishing results.

Coppola began doubting his ability to deal with the material adequately and felt that he was cheapening the subject. Symptomatic of this were Coppola's constant rewrites as he wrestled with how best to suggest that Willard's trek upriver takes him and the crew effectively into the past and something primal and disturbing, something that civilisation had covered over.

Coppola found the French Plantation sequence especially vexing and the production spent two weeks shooting it, as the sequence became weighed down by an obsession with detail, right down to the inclusion of a 1954 bottle of Latour wine that was shipped in from Coppola's own home in California.

On the 15 September 1976, Coppola considered calling everything to an end and returning to California. Storaro encouraged him to continue and to keep pushing the symbolism of Kurtz's character and situation.

As December 1976 approached and filming continued, Coppola came under studio pressure to complete the shooting. He had just shot the

USO concert sequence, which included 1,500 extras. In dealing with United Artists at this time, Coppola insisted they drop his middle name Ford from any of their advertising on the movie. Over Christmas 1976, Coppola returned to northern California and viewed five hours of footage. The film was now way over budget but Coppola still needed to shoot images of the boat going upriver and the destruction of Kurtz's compound, and the movie was evidently going to finish up costing about $25m. It was with filming going into 1977 that Coppola's experience of the directing of the film became especially intense. On 5 March 1977, Martin Sheen suffered a heart attack, which was initially denied by the film's publicity so as not to cause investors any alarm, instead being described as heat exhaustion.

Filming continued and the sequence of the destruction of Kurtz's compound was shot over nine nights using ten cameras, some of which used infrared film to lend the images a surreal quality. The location shoot finished on 21 May 1977, just four days before *Star Wars* was released.

In spring and early summer of 1978, pickup filming was done in northern California around Sacramento along the Napa River, including a scene of Chef and one of the Bunny girls (Colleen Camp) inside a helicopter. Insert shots of Willard were also shot at this time.

MARTIAL MUSIC: Carmine Coppola's score is a synthesizer piece that emphasises the dissonant, ambient, hallucinatory and eerie, suggesting the nightmare that Willard is caught in. At no point is the music triumphalist or sentimental. Most famously, the film features Wagner's *Ride of the Valkyries*, the inclusion of which was suggested by screenwriter John Milius, in his enthusiasm for all things grandly martial. The music had been played live on set for the scene and was taken from a Georg Solti-conducted version. Securing the rights to this piece of music had been difficult and resulted in Walter Murch buying up eighteen other versions in an effort to tie the image and sound together perfectly. However, Murch found that no recording was as appropriate as Solti's. Murch even noticed how in one shot of the ocean the blue of the water, in his mind, somehow rhymed with the sound of the brass being played. Eventually, the Solti version was acquired. When the music hits a certain crescendo this is matched by a cut to a wide shot of the helicopters swooping in.

Music helps establish the time period, so that the soundtrack includes the Rolling Stones' classic 'Satisfaction' playing on the PBR radio. Most famously, the Doors' song 'The End' opens and closes the film.

The film's drumming music was provided by Mickey Hart, a percussionist for the Grateful Dead, and he put together a group called the Rhythm Devils. Coppola got them to provide percussion for the entire film, which they improvised as the film was screened for them.

REIMAGINING REALITY: An extremely heightened sense of reality is evident from the start of the film. The Vietnam War has often been invoked as one underscored by drugs and music, a rock 'n' roll war, and that is the reality that the film goes for. Yes, the jungle is shown, the scale of the military operation is made evident, but in turn is presented in such a way as to heighten a sense of absurdity. What counts most in the film is its emotional truth rather than its presentation of the Vietnam War as a specific historical moment, and indeed as the film progresses it detaches itself evermore from anything identifiably 'Vietnam' in its images and interests.

HEART OF BATTLE: One of the key themes of *Apocalypse Now* is the conflict between civilisation and the primitive, and in terms of the wider American narrative culture *Apocalypse Now* feeds into the stream of native consciousness, of the frontier and wilderness mythology (this cultural progression is stunningly mapped out in Richard Slotkin's book *Regeneration Through Violence*). The beginning of *Apocalypse Now* functions somewhat like a musical overture, introducing and associating a range of diverse themes and settings. All the core concepts of the film fuse in this dreamy and nightmarish opening sequence, which functions as a miniature of the entire film, a symbolic device.

There are sounds before there is an image. The sound of helicopters begins the film and the first image is a long lens, locked off shot of a portion of the Vietnamese jungle. The choppers swoop across frame, initially out of focus. The helicopters move closer to the jungle and are seen in full. The forest erupts in a fireball, establishing clearly the sense of apocalypse. This is followed by a dissolve to a close-up on the face of Willard. This inverted image then dissolves to show a ceiling fan, whose movement and sound rhymes with that of the chopper blades. There is a dissolve to a blood-red sky behind a silhouette of trees, and another dissolve brings in the element of an ancient jungle statue.

The camera revolves as we watch Willard on a bed with letters at his bedside and a picture of his ex-wife. Willard sleeps and the camera reveals a glass of whisky. Another dissolve shows a gun lying next to Willard and we see his face in near darkness. He goes to the window and a point-of-view shot through the blind shows a street as we hear Willard's weary voice: 'Saigon. Shit. I'm still only in Saigon. Every time I think I'm going to wake up back in the jungle.' The scene continues, plunging the action further into the angst of Willard. There is a dissolve to Willard on the floor and he looks at the camera directly. A dissolve to flames is then followed by an image of Willard executing several drunken karate moves, and he smashes his hand in the mirror. He smears his face with the blood and a jump cut shows him naked on the floor, crying. He has been reduced to an animal state – by the end of the film he will have come full circle.

CHARACTER: The heroes of *Apocalypse Now* are the young men on the PBR escorting Willard upriver. They do their job without questioning its integrity or worth. As one character says in Coppola's later film *Gardens of Stone*, the army is not the place for an opinion. In the same breath, though, this sense of duty is presented as honourable and responsible. Willard, of course, is the film's protagonist, the one who endures the adventure and emerges from its crucible of trial and terror. Willard spends much of the time observing the craziness around him, only coming into his own in the last phase of the film, when we are asked to consider who the villain is. It is an indefinite, ever-shifting line as uncertain as the many faces in the shadows. Willard is an emotionally contained young man focused on his goal (rather like Michael in *The Deer Hunter*), not given to wild displays of emotion, unlike the other men on the boat. By the end of the film Willard has divested himself of the trappings of his civilisation and become utterly primal – he becomes what had scared him, he has become wild Willard. He enters a corrupt world and becomes corrupted by it.

Having seen Willard in broad daylight for most of the film, with Kurtz dead he stands in half-light, half-shadow. Finally he walks with Johnson towards a literal and symbolic light on the riverbank, returning to the world after his adventure and test.

The characters of the men on the PBR are economically sketched out in simple shots showing them doing things, not saying things. Verbal characterisation comes a little later. Chef reads, Johnson suns himself, Clean brushes his teeth and Chief is at the helm. Clean and Johnson represent the unquestioning, uninformed young soldiers drafted for the war as cannon fodder.

Johnson is the surfer-dude kid whose ignorance is maybe what keeps him sane, a point made especially clearly when he stands on the PBR deck with a purple flare blazing and says, 'This is better than Disneyland.'

Chef is the older, more cynical and realistic of the group, and the soldier who seems to least want to be in the jungle.

Inevitably, the spectre of Colonel Kurtz hangs over the action and the journey of the heroes, although he is not revealed until the final part of the film, true to the way in which Kurtz is revealed in Conrad's novel. Once Willard arrives Kurtz is able to define his motives, actions and outlook. He is somebody for whom power has become all-consuming, but he does believe he is acting out of genuine disillusionment with the American military. Kurtz may be brilliant, but brilliance is only valuable when used compassionately. In *Apocalypse Now* the duality of dark and light is explicitly expressed by the French woman when, talking to Willard, she says, 'There are two of you, one that kills, one that loves.' In some sense, Kurtz is less a character and more a vessel to contain a wealth of ideas, and he may even be the film's moral compass, offering up two lines that would not be out of place coming from Vito Corleone in *The Godfather*: 'You have to have men who are moral,' and 'It's judgement that defeats us.'

The other force that engulfs the film is that of Imperialism and in the French plantation sequence it is the basis of a major dinner discussion. The Frenchman talks about property: 'This piece of earth, we keep it!' He then goes on to say they want to stay in Vietnam because being there 'keeps our family together'. At other points in the film, Imperialism and American intervention is alluded to. The political and social dynamic of Imperialist activity is made somewhat understandable by having it personalised. In *The Thin Red Line* this relationship between war and property is commented on by one of the soldiers early in the film.

Kilgore is based on real-life military man, Colonel John B Stockton. Kilgore serves as a key guide in the adventure of Willard. To some degree he is a whacked-out wisdom giver who begins the process of illuminating Willard about the journey ahead.

Finally, the jungle itself is a character in the story. The wilderness is both a threatening and beautiful place, and for all the pain it contains it is the means of salvation for the hero of the film.

STYLE: Vittorio Storaro, the cinematographer on the film, invested it with a visual plan very different from what would usually be seen in a war film. The psychedelic emphasis on surreal pictures and juxtapositions of unexpected images runs through *Apocalypse Now*.

Storaro has spoken of three phases to his career: the first investigated the properties of light, the second the properties of colour and the third the properties of earth, water, air and fire. *Apocalypse Now* places itself neatly in this final phase of his work. For Storaro, *Apocalypse Now* represented the culmination of his moviemaking experience to that point, and he regards darkness not as an absence of light but the antithesis of light. The film's final sequence is an investigation of this theory.

Storaro said, 'The original idea was to depict the impact of one culture which had been superimposed over another culture.' The film disturbs our perception and juxtaposes contradictory elements, such as surfing in the jungle waters. Countless images suggest a world gone utterly mad, tipping frequently towards the surreal. Late in the film the image of the tail of an American plane jutting out of the river suggests a high-tech ruin.

In the scene where Willard and Chef go mango-hunting, Storaro constructs a majestic and terrifying shot of the two men, tiny against the immense, primordial roots of a tree. It is evident that the men, and the military generally, are strangers in a land that is gradually consuming them.

Contrasting with the expansive and chaotic vistas of the riverboat journey that comprises most of the film, there are scenes near the beginning that exist on a much smaller scale, though no less quirky. For the briefing scene Coppola instructed his camera operator to pan whenever he felt bored in order to give some sense of Willard's disorientation at being badly hung over.

Key to the interest of the *Apocalypse Now Redux* edit is the inclusion of the long-discussed French plantation sequence. The sequence begins with the PBR arriving at the site on the riverbank, engulfed in deathly smoke. Once inside the property it is a very different and far more opulent world than Willard might have imagined. The dinner scene is lit with a gold light, partly to suggest the setting sun (symbolic of the sun setting on the French Empire) and also to bathe the meal (decorous and delicate) in a sense of old-world glory.

The duality of the jungle's beauty and danger runs right through the visuals. Indeed, this aesthetic, which partly recalls some of the paintings of Henri Rousseau, can also be seen in **The Thin Red Line.** The PBR is often shown cutting through the golden, sunlit water. Contrasting with the stillness and calm of the river (a far safer place than the jungle around it) are the immense battle scenes, which are at their most intense when the camera tracks at speed through the carnage and confusion, dragging the audience right into the chaos.

As a film with a distinctly episodic structure, born of the adventure format, the film's culmination point in Kurtz's temple becomes virtually a film of its own. The sequence emphasises the central conflict between, and closeness of, dark and light. Kurtz ducks in and out of the shadow like the Minotaur in the labyrinth. Coppola's penchant for tableaux shows Kurtz in silhouette in the doorway to his inner sanctum, which is a portal to another world.

For the sequence that brings the film to its climax, Coppola reprises his intercutting crescendo technique (famously wrapping each episode of *The Godfather* trilogy) so that as Willard hacks into Kurtz we see the Indians hacking into a water buffalo. The build-up to Kurtz's death employs the same narrative tricks that Coppola uses for the killing of gangsters in *The Godfather* and music is central to this design. As Willard moves in for the kill, cast in silhouette, divested of anything recognisably human, the song 'The End' by the Doors plays on the soundtrack. Kurtz is then seen in silhouette and the mute intercutting lends the scene a nightmarish, almost unreal quality.

When *Apocalypse Now* comes to its exhausted close it repeats the dissolves that began the film, associating apparently disparate elements, the meaning of which is now more vivid. The fade-out ends the film with a sense of uncertainty and ambiguity about the fate of Willard.

The film is a strong example of an effort to elevate the role and density of sound, combining the demands of realism with the allure of more symbolic uses of sound. Coppola's brief to Walter Murch for the sound was to make it quintaphonic, authentic and psychedelic. The sound is working to express the theme that the civilised world of presumed human achievement is gradually being consumed by the natural order and chaos.

The film has enormous rigour and vitality in its sound recording and sound design. *Apocalypse Now* was one of the first films with split stereo sound. For the *Redux* release, several of the actors were called back into the studio to re-record certain lines of dialogue being included in the film for the first time. The narration that accompanies the onscreen action is one of the highlights of the film, material that was authored by Michael Herr. The film is very much like a silent film and it is the voice-over that contributes much of the film's metaphorical weight and investigation. To get the narration just perfect, between 35 and 40 voice-over sessions were conducted.

Great pains were taken over the intensity of its frequently naturalistic sound effects. For the sound of a helicopter crew in transit, four veteran pilots were brought into a studio where a mute image of the scene played. The vets were asked to improvise their wild chatter in flight, whilst at the same time on speakers the loud sound effect of chopper wings in motion added to the ambience.

For Storaro one of the principal influences was Paul Gaugin's work, particularly his painting *Where Do We Come From? What Are We? Where Are We Going?* Gauguin also influenced Coppola in describing Kurtz to Brando as a man who had gone native.

Apocalypse Now adheres to Hollywood's long-standing commitment to descriptive realism in terms of military clothing. For the final phase of the film, the material becomes more symbolic and abstract. Willard dresses very conventionally, befitting his straight-arrow status within the film. For the confrontation with Kurtz, Willard's emotional transformation is mirrored by his mud-caked, shirtless body. He has divested himself of civilisation completely. As the film progresses, Coppola's symbolic ambitions and metaphor overwhelm all. Johnson liberates himself from his army outfit and paints his face, and even Chef gets into the spirit of things, wearing a hat made of immense leaves.

CRITICAL CROSSFIRE: For *Empire* magazine the film pitches 'Vietnam as an epic, psychotic nightmare . . . with almost every line in the script sounding like a classic quote.' And for the *Time Out Film Guide* the film is 'brilliant as moviemaking, but it turns Vietnam into a vast trip, into a War of the Imagination'.

MEDALS OF HONOUR: At the 1980 Academy Awards the film won for Best Cinematography and Best Sound. It was nominated for Best Actor in a Supporting Role (Robert Duvall), Best Art Direction and Set Decoration, Best Director, Best Film Editor, Best Picture and Best Written Screenplay. The film won the 1980 Golden Screen award in Germany and in 1981 took home the London Critics' Circle Film Awards Film of the Year award. In the 1980 National Society of Film Critics Award, it won Best Supporting Actor (Frederic Forrest) and in 1980 the Writers Guild of America nominated it for Best Drama Written directly for the Screen. The American Cinema Editors, USA 1980, nominated it for Best Edited Feature, and at the 1980 American Movie Awards it won Marquee for Best Supporting Actor (Robert Duvall) and was nominated for Best Actor (Martin Sheen) and Best Film.

At the 1980 BAFTAs the film won for Best Director and Best Supporting Actor (Robert Duvall) and was nominated for the Anthony Asquith Award for Film Music, Best Actor (Martin Sheen), Best Cinematography, Best Editing, Best Film, Best Production Design and Best Soundtrack. At the 1979 British Society of Cinematographers awards the film was nominated but did not win and at the 1979 Cannes Film Festival the film was submitted as a work in progress and went on to win the Palme D'Or. The film was nominated for Best Foreign Film at the 1980 Cesar awards and won the 1980 David di Donatello Award for Best Director (Foreign Film). At the 1980 Golden Globes awards the film won for Best Director, Best Motion Picture Actor in a Supporting Role (Robert Duvall) and Best Original Score. It was nominated for a Golden Globe in the category of Best Motion Picture. In 2000 the National Film Preservation Board (USA) placed the film on the National Film Registry and in 2001 the Boston Society of Film Critics Awards acknowledged the *Redux* version.

OTHER BATTLEFRONTS: In 1977 a TV movie had been aired in America. Called *Limbo* it focused on the wives of American POWs and how their husbands' fates impacted on life at home. Coppola's later film *Gardens of Stone* would deal with this very subject. *Heroes* (Jeremy Paul Kagan, 1977) starring Henry Winkler, Sally Field and Harrison Ford had failed to make much impact and *Coming Home* dramatised the experience of the Vietnam veteran back home with far more success. Another film that centred on the soldiers in the battlefield of Vietnam was *The Boys from Company C*. By 1986 director and screenwriter Oliver Stone began work on an informal trilogy of Vietnam movies, starting with **Platoon,** detailing life in Vietnam for a young American civilian soldier. In **Born on the Fourth of July** Stone dramatised the experience of Vietnam vet Ron Kovic and finally with *Heaven and Earth* (1993) explored the relationship between a Vietnamese woman and an American soldier. In 1987, Stanley Kubrick released *Full Metal Jacket*. Over all of these films, and indeed any movie set during the Vietnam War, the grandiose *Apocalypse Now* continues to throw its shadow.

THE HOMEFRONT: Both the region 1 and region 2 DVDs of *Apocalypse Now Redux* are the same. There are no featurettes, though the disc includes a booklet that outlines Coppola's decision in creating the *Redux* edition and also lists all the scenes reinstated. The disc has an interactive menu, scene access and has been formatted in widescreen 2.10:1

The VHS of *Apocalypse Now Redux* is also available.

Key to the longstanding cult following of *Apocalypse Now*, and possibly accountable for renewed interest in the film in the early 1990s, is the stunning documentary *Hearts of Darkness: A Filmmaker's Apocalypse*. This is a documentary by Fax Bahr and George Hickenlooper, which was released in 1991. It combines the wealth of footage shot by Eleanor Coppola on location with clips from the film and more recent, retrospective interviews with many of the film's principal players.

FINAL BRIEFING: Both the original *Apocalypse Now* and *Apocalypse Now Redux* remain an intense and arresting experience. For some the film is no more than a trashy adventure set against war. For others it hints at the miasma of madness that the American intervention in Vietnam became. In an age where the cinema of spectacle dominates the mainstream movie world, *Apocalypse Now* stands tall, allying its big pictures and adventure engine with the fuel of powerful ideas and associations. Coppola goes for philosophical and metaphorical integrity in *Apocalypse Now*, as the story charts the fall of two men, one from a position of grace, the other from a position of humility, as the primal instinct overwhelms both of them, their spirits consumed by the unconscious forces of the jungle. Hearts of darkness is absolutely the concern. The war element and critique seems secondary, regardless of intent – it is present, but it is overwhelmed by the personal drama. This is very much a hero's journey film, taking its protagonist through the highs and lows of self-discovery, so that he returns to the world bruised, broken, illuminated and somehow stronger. It is a spiritual film with a social inflection.

FINAL SALUTE: 'This new, complete and definitive version extends this idea (of the lie) to all young people, boys and girls, who are sent out to function in an established immoral world expected to function in a moral way.' – Francis Ford Coppola

Platoon (1986)

111 minutes

Hemdale (US)
Producer: Arnold Kopelson
Director: Oliver Stone
Screenplay: Oliver Stone
Cinematographer: Robert Richardson
Editor: Claire Simpson
Music: Original music by George Delerue. Source music:
Samuel Barber's *Adagio for Strings*
Production Design: Bruno Rubeo
Art Direction: Rodel Cruz, Doris Sherman Williams
Costume Design: Kathryn Morrison
Visual Effects: Yves De Bono

CAST: Tom Berenger (*Sergeant Barnes*), Willem Defoe (*Sergeant Elias*), Charlie Sheen (*Chris*), Forest Whitaker (*Big Harold*), Francesco Quinn (*Rhah*), John C McGinley (*Sergeant O'Neill*), Richard Edson (*Sal*), Kevin Dillon (*Bunny*), Reggie Johnson (*Junior*), Keith David (*King*)

RATING: R/15

TAGLINE: The first casualty of war is innocence.

WAR STORY: It is September 1967: the scene is a US army base in Vietnam, near the Cambodian border. Yet another planeload of young recruits is flown in. One of these men is Chris Taylor.

Chris is with his platoon trekking through the jungle, rapidly acquainting himself with the horrors of war. The platoon make camp and Chris is on watch, but falls asleep and awakes just in time to sight the silhouettes of approaching Vietnamese soldiers. There is a skirmish, and, as Chris is held responsible for the unit being taken by surprise, he is put on light duty at base camp, cleaning out the latrines. Chris is then invited into the barrack of Sergeant Elias, a place that is markedly different to that of Sergeant Barnes. In his barrack, Barnes and his men sit and play cards, but in Elias's barrack the emphasis is on smoking pot and listening to good music.

On manoeuvres the unit comes across an enemy camp and there is a battle. The soldiers then arrive at a village and chaos ensues as the pressure mounts and the unit's composure self-destructs. Chris shoots at the feet of a Vietnamese man but one of the other soldiers then comes in and kills the man, who was defenceless. Outside, Barnes puts a gun to a Vietnamese child's head until Elias breaks up the craziness, intensifying the tension between Elias and Barnes. At night Chris and Elias talk about the war.

The platoon's mission continues and as the enemy close in Elias heads off alone to engage the enemy. Barnes and Elias come face to face in the jungle and Barnes shoots at Elias, then returns and tells Chris that Elias is dead.

As the unit lift off from the battle zone Chris sees that Elias is still alive and outnumbered by Vietnamese soldiers. He sees Elias being gunned down by the enemy.

Back at camp, Chris says to the others in the unit that they should do something about Barnes. Barnes overhears and comes in to confront Chris, leading to a fight where the sergeant slashes his blade across Chris's face. One more battle remains and it is fought in the jungle. Many of the American soldiers are killed and injured, but Chris survives. He sees that Barnes has been badly wounded.

At the end of the film Chris is finally flown out of Vietnam.

CONCEPT/THE MISSION: Oliver Stone's compelling characteristics as a film director and writer include his energy and commitment to storytelling, and his desire to engage the audience in some awareness of what could be considered 'the bigger picture'. In his film *JFK*, Jim Garrison (portrayed by Kevin Costner) talks about not wanting to sleepwalk through life. This is the guiding Oliver Stone principle, it would seem. Sure enough, and with appealing consistency, as a young man Stone had converted his Vietnam experiences into an unpublished novel entitled *A Child's Night Dream*.

In 1986 Oliver Stone's latest directorial effort *Platoon* was released by Orion Pictures (who now no longer operate). The film proved a watershed in American depictions of the Vietnam War and was hugely controversial at the time. The film placed Stone at the forefront of popular American filmmakers. Stone wrote the screenplay, basing it on his own experiences of soldiering in the Vietnam War, where he was twice awarded the Purple Heart with Oak Leaf cluster and also the Bronze Star for valour. Returning from Vietnam, after time spent teaching and in the Merchant Navy in Southeast Asia in 1965–6, Stone attended film school at New York University. A very early script that

Stone wrote was entitled 'Break' and can be considered the seed idea for what became *Platoon*.

One of Stone's student films was entitled *The Last Year in Vietnam*. Martin Scorsese was one of Stone's tutors for a period of time. Soon after completing film school, Stone's first directorial effort was a low-budget feature in Canada entitled *Seizure (Queen of Evil)* (1974) and then *The Hand* (1981). He finally broke into the film industry as a screenwriter of *Midnight Express* (Alan Parker, 1978), *Conan the Barbarian*, *Scarface* (Brian De Palma, 1983), *Year of the Dragon* (Michael Cimino, 1985) and *Eight Million Ways to Die* (Hal Needham, 1985).

As a writer–director Stone's breakthrough came in 1986 with *Salvador*, which was shot in Mexico and proved Stone's commitment to making the political personal and accessible. *Salvador* tells of a photojournalist (portrayed by James Woods) exploiting El Salvador's internal conflict for his photographs.

Across his body of work one of Stone's recurrent interests has been, in significant part, to consider the role of masculinity in the America that has developed since the 1960s. Whilst some may find Stone's cinematic language lacking subtlety, it does not lack in sincerity.

Platoon was a watershed film. The first half of the 1980s had been bereft of any Vietnam-themed films. The 1970s had accumulated a number of significant films on the subject, most famously *Coming Home*, **The Deer Hunter** and **Apocalypse Now**. There had also been *Heroes* (starring Harrison Ford in his second Vietnam movie appearance) and *Who'll Stop the Rain?* (Karel Reisz, 1978). By this time American television had even tried to mount a number of Vietnam-set sitcoms, notably *The Bureau* (CBS), *The 6:00 Follies* (NBC) about the Armed Forces TV network in Saigon, and finally *Bringing It Home* (ABC).

Platoon's success heralded a new phase of Vietnam War films, including *Full Metal Jacket*, which had been in production at the same time as *Platoon*. Then too there was *Hamburger Hill* (John Irvin, 1987), the comedy *Good Morning, Vietnam* (Barry Levinson, 1987) and Stone's **Born on the Fourth of July** and *Heaven and Earth*. More recently there has been *Tigerland* (Joel Schumacher, 2001).

Interestingly, *Good Morning, Vietnam*, starring Robin Williams, did as much as *Platoon's* combat-set film to hard-wire Vietnam hard and fast into the popular imagination and cinematic terrain of teenagers in the middle and late 1980s.

It is hard to doubt Stone's sincerity when he says that his trilogy of Vietnam films have only 'deepened my interest [in the war]. There was no plan for a trilogy. But they complement each other.' Rather like Elia Kazan and William Wyler, and other Hollywood directors of old, Stone has shown a longtime commitment to making socially engaged films.

Stone had written the first draft of *Platoon* in the summer of 1976 during the bicentennial American celebrations. He found that after the release of *The Deer Hunter* and *Apocalypse Now*, even though they had been commercial and critical hits, Hollywood was not especially interested in further films about the Vietnam War, so he had not taken the project any further. Intriguingly, Stone had been inspired to reactivate his interest in *Platoon* in the early 1980s after watching the epic *Reds* (Warren Beatty, 1981). *Reds* had been very popular and well received, a film with a David Lean kind of scale to it as it combined an expansive historical situation with personal stories. It had been based on the book *Ten Days in May* by American journalist John Reed.

In the wake of *Platoon*'s eventual success, Stone looked back at his struggle to get the film financed and made: 'I got the message. America didn't really care about the truth of the war. It was going to be buried.' At one point Michael Cimino, who had collaborated with Stone on the thriller *The Year of the Dragon*, said that he would produce *Platoon* for Stone. It was not to be. Eventually, a producer named Arnold Kopelson would help Stone to realise his cinematic dream. Dino De Laurentis had expressed interest early in *Platoon*'s development but ultimately backed out. Of the screenplay, Stone commented that the story was very simple and 'probably the least writing I've ever done, more like a newspaper report'.

In creating *Platoon*, Stone's modus operandi was to counter the more mythical scale and tone of *The Deer Hunter* and *Apocalypse Now*. *The Deer Hunter* had stark and stunning allusions to American literature and the concept of the wilderness and the frontier as embodied in the novels of James Fenimore Cooper and brilliantly dissected in Richard Slotkin's expansive study *Regeneration Through Violence*. *Apocalypse Now* became a Fisher King myth set within the context of a jungle adventure. All three films, different though they are in tone and scale, share an intention to chart the American male's shift from innocence to experience. Whether Chris, Michael or Willard would ever get on together over a beer is another matter, and a movie scenario to imagine in itself.

In *The Thin Red Line* the character of Lt Col Tall explicitly references Homer's description of the rosy-fingered dawn. For Oliver Stone, *Platoon* also had its Homeric reference point when he said at the time of the film's release, 'I was thrown into a war, just a kid from New York, and suddenly everything I had read in Homer was coming true.'

The symbolic value of the developing *Platoon* screenplay was built up over the drafting process, and it was only in 1984 that Stone wrote in the moment when Chris confronts Barnes at the end of the story.

CASTING/RECRUITMENT: *Platoon* was a film that defined the careers of several actors, showcasing them and introducing them as a new generation of performers. Charlie Sheen (as Chris Taylor) was the son of Martin Sheen, who had portrayed Willard in **Apocalypse Now**. When Stone recollected the casting of Sheen in the role he spoke of it as being a fateful moment, acknowledging the closeness in Sheen's appearance and his own saying, 'He looks like me when I was that age: a dark, dreamy air, as if he wasn't really there.' Sheen went on to star in Stone's *Wall Street*. Tom Berenger had co-starred in *The Big Chill* (Lawrence Kasdan, 1983) but *Platoon* showed a performer capable of nastier characterisation. Berenger went on to star in *Deadly Pursuit* (Roger Spottiswoode, 1987), *Someone To Watch Over Me* (Ridley Scott, 1987) and the recent western miniseries *Into The West* (2005).

It was Willem Defoe, though, who was most powerfully presented in the film. Like Christopher Walken in **The Deer Hunter** and subsequent films, Defoe possesses a compelling, otherworldly quality. He went on to star in the astonishing and beautiful *The Last Temptation of Christ* (Martin Scorsese, 1988), *Wild At Heart* (David Lynch, 1990) and in *Finding Nemo* (Andrew Stanton, 2003). Defoe also played the Green Goblin in *SpiderMan* (Sam Raimi, 2002). Forest Whitaker went on to star as Charlie Parker in *Bird* (Clint Eastwood, 1988) and *Ghost Dog* (Jim Jarmusch, 2000) and has moved into his own career as a director.

Kevin Dillon has also featured in *The Doors* (Oliver Stone, 1990) and the World War Two film *A Midnight Clear* (Keith Gordon, 1992).

If you look quickly you'll sight Johnny Depp as one of the soldiers. From his sideline appearance in this film Depp has gone on to star in a successful TV series, *Twenty One Jump Street*, and is an actor totally in sync with the spirit of the new millennium's film fans. He has appeared in *Edward Scisssorhands* (Tim Burton, 1990), *What's Eating Gilbert Grape* (Lasse Hallstrom, 1993), *Donnie Brasco* (Mike Newell, 1997), *Fear And Loathing in Las Vegas* (Terry Gilliam, 1998), *Pirates Of The Caribbean* (Gore Verbinski, 2003), *Finding Neverland* (Marc Forster, 2004) and *Charlie and the Chocolate Factory* (Tim Burton, 2005).

The film's military adviser Dale Dye appears as a commander. Dye is also in *Casualties of War* and *Saving Private Ryan*.

BACKUP: Cinematographer Robert Richardson, who has gone on to collaborate with Stone on several other features, had a background in documentary filmmaking. Richardson's work as a cinematographer has defined a number of key American films of the last twenty years. His credits include *Salvador*, *Eight Men Out*, *Casino* (Martin Scorsese, 1995), *Bringing Out The Dead* (Martin Scorsese, 1999), *Kill Bill Vol1 and Vol2* (2003/04) and *The Aviator* (Martin Scorsese, 2004).

PRODUCTION/IN THE TRENCHES: Rather like *Apocalypse Now*, *Platoon* was denied the support of the Pentagon on the grounds of it being an inaccurate presentation of war. By contrast, the US Navy had readily supported *Top Gun* (Tony Scott, 1986), which had been released in the same year as *Platoon* but which glorified the naval experience and functioned as something of a recruitment video. *Platoon* was the first feature film to be directed by a Vietnam veteran.

The film cost $8m, with $6m coming from Hemdale and $2m from Orion.

Prior to filming the key actors were put through a boot camp run by Dale Dye. They had to contend with explosions being set off at night, all as part of an effort to instil in them the feeling of being 'irritated, worried, frightened . . .'

Like *Apocalypse Now*, *Platoon* filmed in the Philippines with the support of their army – Stone's only problem was that it was a time of unrest there, so the army could have pulled out of the film at any time had civil war broken out.

MARTIAL MUSIC: Famously, *Platoon* showcased Samuel Barber's melancholy and expansive *Adagio for Strings*, which runs under the opening sequence of the film and then refrains in part throughout the film, most powerfully during the death of Elias. Supplementing the classical, source music is film composer Georges Delerue's contribution. Delerue was a major composing figure in the business, having worked on projects since the 1950s in France and then in America. His credits include *Hiroshima Mon Amour* (Alan Resnais, 1959), *Jules et Jim* (Francois Truffaut, 1962), *A Man For All Seasons* (Fred Zinneman, 1966), *The Day Of The Jackal* (Fred Zinneman, 1973), *Salvador*, *Joe Versus The Volcano* (John Patrick Shanley, 1990) and *Amelie* (Jean Pierre Jeunet, 2001).

REIMAGINING REALITY: *Platoon* was marketed and promoted as being authentic in a way that previous Vietnam-set films had not been. Oliver Stone had served a fifteen-month tour of duty in Vietnam. The film was also recognised for casting actors much closer to the age of soldiers: teenage men, the least-liked strata of mainstream society. In his essay *Hollywood and Historical Memory: the Road to Platoon*, Michael Klein writes that 'At a deeper level . . . the film substitutes a psychological and metaphysical interpretation for a historical understanding of the genocidal aspects of war.'

Platoon received criticism from both the left and right for its apparently apolitical stance on the one hand, and on the other its valorisation of the troops. For left-wing critics the film glorified American military involvement and offered no real assessment of the reasons for the American intervention in Indochina. For Stone, the overriding concept was to counter the image of war as adventure that had permeated so many films, and which was certainly true of contemporary films such as *Top Gun* and *Rambo: First Blood Part II* (George Pan Cosmatos, 1985).

In his book *The Penguin History of the World*, JM Roberts writes, 'It was in Southeast Asia that the powerlessness of the United States to obtain any results she wanted at any reasonable cost was at last borne in on many of her citizens.' This historical point is certainly expressed in Stone's film.

In developing the film, Stone did not seek to make a war film but instead document a moment from a life that had been lived. As such, Stone adopted far more the role of reporter rather than dramatist, even though the narrative that unfolds against the context of the war and jungle combat is archly mythic and spiritually dramatic, befitting the term used to describe the jungle by the Vietnamese, namely 'Beyond'. In the film, Elias is wounded by Barnes when they come across one another during a combat; the bullet weakens Elias, who is then finished off by Vietnamese soldiers. Elias was based on a real sergeant who Stone served with whose name was Elias, though it is unknown whether this was the real soldier's first or last name, and in reality Elias had died under slightly uncertain circumstances, to the effect that he may have been killed by one of his own grenades (Elias and Barnes were not in the same platoon). Stone has described the real-life Elias in very romantic terms as a kind of Jim Morrison figure whom Stone idolised.

For Stone, the *Platoon* screenplay was fifty per cent a version of his own direct experience and fifty per cent based on stories and incidents he heard and read about.

HEART OF BATTLE: *Platoon's* opening title card (redolent of the spirit of Scorsese in his *Raging Bull* era), quotes the book of Ecclesiastes: 'Rejoice, O young man in thy youth . . .' Stone's film is what could be called a *Bildungsroman*; it is a story about the onset of maturity in a young man. The Vietnam War is the backdrop for the protagonist's emotional development and recognition that good and evil reside in us all.

Platoon does not extensively explore the political and social aspects of that particular war but instead posits the battlefield as the zone for a young man's emotional and spiritual development. To some degree, Stone saves those debates for his follow-up Vietnam films, and he also interpolates such matters into his films *JFK* and *Nixon*.

Platoon celebrates the sense of brotherhood that combat engenders and, given that Stone saw combat, we take it on good faith that the film's depiction of those bonds and tensions are accurate.

Perhaps the most arresting image in the film comes at the very end with the shot of the crater filled with dead bodies. It's a shot that expresses the mass carnage of war more clearly than any dialogue could.

Platoon captures much of the spirit of an equivalently important Vietnam document, the book *Dispatches* by Michael Herr. Herr, as a young journalist at *Esquire* magazine, had asked to be posted to the war in order to report on it and in the late 1970s, seven years after his return from the battle zone, the book was published.

Herr's text conjures the chaos and camaraderie that *Platoon* visualises, and perhaps more than anything it is that celebration of unity that fuels the success of all war films that endure. Herr's book includes this passage: 'Men on the crews would say that once you'd carried a dead person he would always be there, riding with you. Like all combat people (they were) incredibly superstitious and invariably self-dramatic . . . even bone-dumb grunts seemed to feel that something weird – extra – was happening to them.'

CHARACTER: Chris Taylor is the character through whose eyes the audience sees combat, as he arrives in Vietnam for his tour of duty. Chris is very much Oliver Stone's alter ego. Taylor's middle-class background is similar to that of Stone's and this prompts him to be ridiculed by many of the other soldiers in his platoon who have been conscripted. Taylor is a democratic man who strives to understand the situation and who sees the tragic circumstance of the young American men who comprise the foot soldiers, describing them as being from 'the end of the line. They're the poor, the unwanted . . .' They are the 'social undesirables' that Ferol talks about in *Paths of Glory*. As Chris's experience of combat deepens, it takes its toll on him, as evidenced when they reach a village and Taylor unleashes a barrage of bullets at the feet of a Vietnamese man. Taylor is the moral focus of the film and his voice-over material focuses on the spiritual aspect of the combat. As such it ties him back into the film's excerpt from Ecclesiastes in the Bible.

When Chris arrives at the base he is momentarily transfixed by the gaunt, skeletal face of a soldier passing by. Combat has stripped that nameless man of youth and hope. The initial struggle that Chris confronts in trying to understand what is happening is akin to the moral turmoil that Baumer experiences in *All Quiet on the Western Front* and that Upham deals with in *Saving Private Ryan*. As Chris exits combat his voice-over states, 'We did not fight the enemy. We fought ourselves.' For Stone, Chris belonged not immediately to a cinema tradition but to a literary one, seeing a relationship between his protagonist and the young man at the centre of Stephen Crane's landmark American Civil War novella *The Red Badge of Courage*. Crane's book had been adapted into a feature film by John Huston, who had notably made three stunning and arresting documentaries about the American involvement in World War Two combat zones.

In contrast to the fresh-faced Taylor is the monstrous, vicious-looking Barnes, his face heavily scarred like some Frankenstein's monster. Barnes is a creation of war and is committed to the combat. He appears to be without weakness, though Chris wanders in upon Barnes at one point and sees him momentarily contemplative and maybe even worried. When Barnes and Chris are face to face at the end of the film Barnes is like a wounded animal. He is truly a soldier who treats it as a vocation, as seen when one of the unit lies injured and he shouts at him, 'Take the pain!' In his most egotistical moment Barnes announces, 'I am reality. There's the way it ought to be. There's the way it is.'

Where Barnes is a 'raging bull', Sergeant Elias is a benevolent character who serves as a peacemaker and something of a protector figure to Chris. Chris and Elias make a connection as they talk one night under the stars, as Elias says, '. . . the stars. There's no right or wrong in 'em. They're just there.' Elias then goes on to offer the film's one 'critique' of the war, saying, 'We've been kicking other people's asses for so long, I figure it's time we got ours kicked.' When Elias is killed, his arms reach out and he resembles Christ crucified for an instant. This image formed the basis for the poster advertising the film. In *Born on the*

Fourth of July, Ron prays to Jesus via a crucifix icon on his bedroom wall. In *Platoon*, O'Neill says of Elias 'Guy's in three years and thinks he's Jesus – fucking – Christ.'

Forest Whitaker's soft-speaking soldier and the soldier named King both offer Chris the brotherhood and solace he needs at critical moments.

Of the character configurations in the film, Stone once said, 'It's a *Moby Dick* type thing, with the kid as Ishmael, one of the captains as Ahab, and one of the sergeants a bit like Billy Budd. It's about this platoon at sea, and the white whale is a gook.'

Stone's literary inspirations also extended to Joseph Conrad and perhaps even Jack London, with their stories of men and their identity.

STYLE: Stone and his cinematographer Robert Richardson invest the jungle with beauty and menace. The first sequence to take place in the jungle at the start of the film renders it in a blue-green hue that turns it into an 'alien' place, both mesmerising and terrifying. It recalls the Storaro approach to lighting the forest in *Apocalypse Now* when the soldiers come across the tiger. Ironically, though, Stone and Richardson did not have the resources to spend so much time lighting a scene. The film shot for just 54 days and Stone wanted to avoid it looking too beautiful. The aestheticisation of war can be hard to avoid, however, and it is the bind that filmmakers and audiences will always find themselves in with war films.

For those sequences set at the military base, *Platoon* adopts a more vérité approach that lends a useful throwaway quality to the action (just another body bag) and contrasts the red earth of the hillsides and high ground with the rich colour of the jungle.

In his later films Stone would go on to play with a range of visual textures and devices. *Platoon* is marked by a fundamentally plain quality, though there are moments where Stone's visual flair shines through. For the death of Elias, the film makes emotional use of slow motion to accentuate the moment. For the final battle at night, instead of using spotlights to illuminate the action, bright explosives were employed, again lending the staging of action more immediacy and, we assume, realism.

When Barnes and Elias confront one another in the jungle they exchange stares in extreme close-up and it brings to mind the moment in *The Deer Hunter* when Michael confronts the deer late in the film. Stone's film has an atavistic quality to it whereby the characters occupy an archetypal zone with Chris as the initiate. When the film begins the plane that brings in new American troops is imaged so as to evoke a sense of an animal opening its jaws and releasing the men from it. When Chris awakes in the jungle with his unit he sees approaching enemy soldiers; a heartbeat pounds quietly on the soundtrack and an extreme close-up on his eyes emphasises the terror. At the end, when Chris lifts off in the helicopter, one of the platoon beats on his chest with primal rage.

Platoon is a small film, punctuated by larger-scale moments of combat. In *Film Comment* an interview with Stone included a general assessment of the film's effect, commenting that '*Platoon* is very assured, lyrical at moments, even in its grotesque images of battle and death.'

CRITICAL CROSSFIRE: The *Time Out Film Guide* revelled in the film's vivid images: '. . . a savage yet moving account of a 19-year-old under fire . . . eye-blistering images possess an awesome power, which sets the senses reeling and leaves the mind disturbed'. For Vincent Canby at the *New York Times* the film was 'the best work of any kind about Vietnam since Michael Herr's book *Dispatches*'. *Leonard Maltin's Movie and Video Guide* summed it all up by saying the film is 'harrowingly realistic and completely convincing'.

MEDALS OF HONOUR: The film won the 1990 Oscar for Best Director and Best Film Editing. It was also Oscar nominated for Best Actor, Cinematography, Music, Sound, Screenplay and Picture. At the BAFTA awards the film was nominated for Best Actor and Best Screenplay.

OTHER BATTLEFRONTS: *Platoon* was followed by Stone's **Born on the Fourth of July**, which was adapted from a memoir by Vietnam veteran Ron Kovic, who went from being an all-American idealistic soldier to a war-torn, politically aware activist in the years following his recuperation. Stone's final Vietnam trilogy film was *Heaven and Earth*. This film was based on the memoirs of a Vietnamese woman Phuang Thi Le Ly Haylsip and the film explores the Vietnam War from the perspective of a Southeast Asian; a fairly remarkable aspect of this American film.

Stone was also influenced in creating *Platoon* by two films by director Pierre Schoendroffer, namely *The Anderson Platoon* and *The 317th Platoon*.

Anticipating the great success that *Platoon* would find with its story of the Vietnam War, in 1984 a film was released dealing with another intense and violent aspect of the Indochina region, namely Cambodia. The film was *The Killing Fields* (Roland Joffé, 1984). It was produced by David Puttnam, who had also produced *Chariots of Fire* (Hugh Hudson, 1982) and prior to that *Midnight Express*, with its script by Oliver Stone. *The Killing Fields* was based on a piece of journalistic writing by Sydney Schamberg for *Time* magazine. The article, published in 1980, was entitled, 'The Death and Life of Dith Pran'. The rights to the article were soon bought up and British producer David Puttnam commissioned Bruce Robinson to write the screenplay. The story charts the life of one man against the backdrop of the Khmer Rouge's effort to turn Cambodia into what effectively resembled a Gulag.

THE HOMEFRONT: *Platoon* is available on DVD with a commentary track.

FINAL BRIEFING: Twenty years after its release, *Platoon* can clearly be seen as having initiated a particular way of visualising combat and stripping away at artifice so that there is some sense of honesty and accuracy in the portrayal of death. Evidently it made a huge aesthetic mark on virtually all combat films that followed and indicated that integrity and entertainment value could combine with great effect.

FINAL SALUTE: For Stone, 'In *Platoon* I was as authentic to my own feelings as much as I could be within the dramatic form I was creating.'

Born on the Fourth of July (1989)

140 minutes

Universal
Producer: A Kitman Ho and Oliver Stone
Director: Oliver Stone
Screenplay: Oliver Stone and Ron Kovic (Based on *Born on the Fourth of July* by Ron Kovic)
Cinematographer: Robert Richardson
Editor: David Brenner
Music: John Williams
Production Design: Bruno Rubeo

Art Direction: Victor Kempster and Richard L Johnston
Costume Design: Judy Ruskin
Visual Effects: William Purcell

CAST: Tom Cruise (*Ron Kovic*), Bryan Larkin (*Young Ron*), Raymond J Barry (*Mr Kovic*), Caroline Kava (*Mrs Kovic*), Josh Evans (*Tommy Kovic*), Seth Allen (*Young Tommy*), Jamie Talisman (*Jimmy Kovic*), Sean Stone (*Young Jimmy*), Anne Bobby (*Susanne Kovic*), Jenna von Oy (*Young Susanne*), Kyra Sedgwick (Donna), Frank Whaley (*Tommy*)

RATING: R/18

TAGLINE: A story of innocence lost and courage found.

WAR STORY: 1961, Massapequa, New York State. Ron Kovic is a ten-year-old all-American boy. He rushes through the woods playing 'army' with his friends. It is Ron's birthday on the fourth of July and he, his family and friends go into town and watch the parade pass by. The parade includes war veterans and Ron is transfixed. At home the family watch President Kennedy delivering a stirring speech in which he commits the nation to a renewed sense of pride. As they watch the broadcast Ron's mum says that she dreamed she saw Ron speaking to a large number of people.

As an intense and competitive teenager Ron is heavily into wrestling and other sports.

Ron's high school is visited by a recruitment officer from the marines called Sergeant Hayes. Ron is totally absorbed, and ultimately transformed, by what he hears. Afterwards his friends wonder whether enlisting is the right thing to do. Ron and his friend Timmy decide to go to Vietnam, believing they need to fight Communism, but their friend Stevie is going to stay at home.

Ron asks his 'girlfriend' Donna if she is going to the prom, but she has already planned to go with some other guy. Ron looks miserable. As the prom arrives, Ron is at home preparing to leave. He prays to God, asking for guidance as he looks to the future in the military, and then runs to the prom to see Donna, with whom he has one dance.

The scene cuts to Vietnam, the Cua Viet River, October 1967. Ron, now a seasoned recruit, is on a mission. The unit Ron is in attack an unarmed village and chaos ensues. The unit is ordered out when Vietcong advance on them and Ron then kills one of his own men,

Wilson, in the chaos. He goes to report the act but his superior blanks Ron – he does not want to know.

It's now January 1968, and Ron is on patrol again. His unit are attacked by Vietnamese troops and Ron takes cover, but as he reloads his gun he is shot in the chest. He is Medevacced out and, as he lies in a field hospital, a priest reads him the last rites, presuming that he will die.

Ron wakes in a run-down, decrepit veteran hospital. He is in a wheelchair, paralysed from the chest down, but determined to walk again. As he does all he can to regain his motion he falls and injures himself, and any dream of walking is severed. Ron becomes increasingly dishevelled.

He finally returns home to Massapequa and is greeted by friends, neighbours and, of course, his family. Ron's brother Tommy looks uneasy and his mother touchingly has to go indoors to gather herself after first seeing her son in his wheelchair. Going into town Ron reunites with his old friend Stevie, who runs a chain of burger stores. At the dinner table Tommy voices his anti-war stance and Ron is perturbed and angered.

A parade is held in town in honour of Ron, the returning hero. Ron goes to make a speech but falters and is unable to complete it. He sees his friend Timmy, also back in Massapequa from combat in Vietnam. They sit out in the garden at Ron's family home and talk about how they cope and how perceptions of the war have changed. Ron recalls how he had always thought of it being like playing John Wayne, even on the day he was shot. He talks about wanting to be whole again, both physically and emotionally. He seems to have become the silhouette that war showed him as.

Ron goes to Syracuse University to see his childhood friend (Kyra) for the first time since he left for the war. She is heavily involved with student anti-war demonstrations, and Ron witnesses one such demonstration with concern and quiet anxiety.

Ron returns to Massapequa. At a club back home Ron, drunk and angry, voices his first dissenting opinion about the war in a drunken state. He returns home, cursing and self-pitying and argues with his parents, especially his mother. His father, ever gentle, suggests Ron take a break from Massapequa.

Ron decides to go to Mexico, and there he meets a bunch of ragged, drunk, gambling veterans, the most charismatic of whom is Charlie. Having been worried about how he would ever enjoy sex as a paralysed man, Ron visits a prostitute, but the experience is saddening. Ron unravels further. He argues with Charlie about their war experiences and Ron suddenly realises that there is more to life than indulging his insecurities. He leaves Mexico and travels to the home town of the soldier he killed, Wilson.

Ron visits Wilson's grave and then goes on to see Wilson's parents, where he also meets Wilson's widow and son. Painfully, Ron explains it was he who killed their son.

The scene moves to 1972. Ron is part of an anti-war protest of many wheelchair-bound veterans and supporters. They crowd into the Republican convention in Miami where Richard Nixon accepts the candidacy to run for the Presidency. Ron leads the protest inside the hall, garnering some live news coverage. Eventually, the protesters are evicted from the hall and a riot ensues outside, during which Ron is dragged across the ground by the authorities. He is then 'rescued' by supporters as though being rescued from a war zone, before leading the protesters back into the centre.

Four years later and Ron is at the Democrat National Convention. He is readying himself to address the convention about the experience of the Vietnam War and the reality that veterans face when they return home from combat. Ron has fulfilled his mother's dream.

CONCEPT/THE MISSION: *Born on the Fourth of July* was Stone's self-claimed second film in a Vietnam trilogy (unplanned though it was) that began with *Platoon* and would conclude with *Heaven and Earth*.

Born on the Fourth of July was based on the book of the same name by Vietnam veteran Ron Kovic. Since his return from the Vietnam War, Ron Kovic has remained politically and socially engaged as a peace activist. Kovic had been arrested twelve times during his anti-Vietnam War protests. His book *Born on the Fourth of July* was recently reprinted and in his updated introduction to the book Ron Kovic writes: 'To kill another human being, to take another life out of this world with one pull of a trigger, is something that never leaves you.'

Where *Platoon* took a young man and plunged him into conflict, *Born on the Fourth of July* makes an attempt to measure the cost of that conflict when the veteran returns home and attempts to rebuild his life. Perhaps this is the more effective and affecting of the two films, a bold claim given the emotional impact of *Platoon* as it pummels our heart and mind.

Stone had attempted to make *Born on the Fourth of July* in the 1970s. He got as far as working with Al Pacino on the project with William Friedkin, director of *The Exorcist* (1973) and *The French Connection*

(1971), though he ultimately dropped out to be replaced at that time by Daniel Petrie. Painfully, and in keeping with many films that experience that extra difficult journey to the screen, *Born on the Fourth of July* was cancelled just four days before it was due to begin filming on account of the proposed German investors not coming up with the money.

Where **Platoon** was designed far more as a singularly spiritual journey for Stone, *Born on the Fourth of July* was the opportunity to couch the drama in some wider sense of the political and social context of the Vietnam War. The film is interested in showing how far and fast Ron's youthful certainties fall away when he is forced to reconsider the bigger picture. Of Kovic's involvement with the project, acting as the genesis for it, Stone commented with a familiar sense of grandiosity and the mythic, 'It was as if we had been linked by destiny. Chosen as God's instrument to get a message, a memory out about the war.'

CASTING/RECRUITMENT: By the late 1980s, Tom Cruise had established his clean-cut credentials. In the best way, *Born on the Fourth of July* was a chance to rip that image to shreds. Tom Cruise essayed the Kovic role and offered one of his most affecting and nuanced performances. By this time in his career he had shown his facility at portraying confident, cocky young men who always win out in the films *Risky Business* (Paul Brickman, 1983), *Top Gun*, *The Color of Money* (Martin Scorsese, 1986), *Cocktail* (Roger Donaldson, 1988) and *Rain Man*. Cruise is often best when cast against type in some way and we can see how his established, most popular image is muddied up, physically, emotionally or both as in *Born on the Fourth of July*. Who can forget the moment when Kovic returns home from war in a wheelchair and embraces his mum on the autumnal lawn? Cruise really communicates the sense of a man physically and emotionally paralysed. His performance goes from wide-eyed, naïve young man to bitter war veteran and then motivated anti-war campaigner for whom so many losses of so many kinds have resulted in a far clearer insight and sense of self-understanding.

Kovic is an updated version of Paul Baumer in **All Quiet on the Western Front**. Kovic runs the gauntlet of growing up and, like all of us, recognises his limitations and his capacities. After *Born on the Fourth of July* Cruise went on to star in *Days of Thunder* (Tony Scott, 1990), *Far and Away* (Ron Howard, 1992), *A Few Good Men* (Rob Reiner, 1992), *The Firm* (Sydney Pollack, 1993), *Interview with the Vampire* (Neil Jordan, 1994), *Mission: Impossible* (Brian De Palma, 1996), *Jerry*

Maguire, Eyes Wide Shut (Stanley Kubrick, 1999), *Magnolia* (Paul Thomas Anderson, 1999), *Mission: Impossible 2* (John Woo, 2000), *Vanilla Sky, Minority Report, The Last Samurai* and **War of the Worlds**.

Frank Whaley has also featured in *Field of Dreams* (Phil Adlen Robinson, 1989) and also *JFK* and *Pulp Fiction*. Caroline Kava has appeared in *Heaven's Gate* and *Year of the Dragon*. Raymond J Barry has appeared in *Falling Down* and *Dead Man Walking*.

Tom Berenger, cameoing as the recruitment officer, has starred in *The Big Chill* (Laurence Kasdan, 1983), **Platoon**, *Someone To Watch Over Me* (Ridley Scott, 1987), *Gettysburg* (Ronald Maxwell, 1993) and the TV movie *Rough Riders* (John Milius,1998).

BACKUP: Stone's key collaborator was Robert Richardson, who had also been cinematographer on **Platoon**. Richardson's impressive list of credits includes *Salvador* (Oliver Stone), *Eight Men Out* (John Sayles, 1988), *Casino, Bringing Out the Dead* (Martin Scorsese, 1999), *Kill Bill Vol 1 and Vol 2* (Quentin Tarantino, 2003/04) and *The Aviator* (Martin Scorsese, 2004).

PRODUCTION/IN THE TRENCHES: Somewhat unusually for Hollywood, Ron Kovic, whose book had been the basis for the film, was on set much of the time to advise and guide the accuracy of the movie and Tom Cruise's portrayal of him. Stone urged Cruise to investigate and research his subject and character, and from all accounts Cruise seems to have been exhausted by the role but only in a way that was to the great benefit of his characterisation of Kovic. The film clearly aims to document a time, a place and a range of emotions from hope to despair and back to hope again.

The film reconstructed Kovic's home on location at a Dallas warehouse and the Vietnam and Mexico scenes were both shot in the Philippines. At the end of production Kovic gave Cruise his Bronze Star combat medal in recognition of his commitment to the role.

MARTIAL MUSIC: As with many films, contemporary music tracks provide a sense of a specific time and also comment on the larger action. 'A Hard Rain's Gonna Fall', 'Brown Eyed Girl', 'Born on the Bayou' and 'Moon River' all chart the transition of a life from naïvety to understanding of self and the wider world.

The film also utilises an original orchestral score. John Williams provided his first of three orchestral scores for Oliver Stone films, the other two being for *JFK* and *Nixon*. With *Born on the Fourth of July*,

Williams's rich and melancholy score surges with energy and optimism early in the film, before soaring with lament for lost innocence and finally a celebration of courage. It is a pastorally influenced score that recalls the music of Samuel Barber (whose *Adagio for Strings* had featured as a signature piece in **Platoon**) and Ralph Vaughan Williams, who himself composed music for a number of films during the Second World War.

Contrasting with Stone's **Platoon**, John Williams's music underscores battle as well as the domestic scenes. The music creates a link between Ron as boy, soldier and war veteran. Typically the rich score amplifies the American sense of home, such as in the moment when Ron returns home and sees his mother for the first time as she rushes out to greet him. The theme for Ron's character is used for both moments of trauma and of glory. The music lends a grandiose quality to the battle scenes and it is as though Stone is experimenting with form in his presentation of combat. The music works to add tragedy combined with valour when a helicopter erupts in flames as it falls out of view and at times the music shifts into very discordant strains to express the chaos and lack of harmony in the battlefield.

REIMAGINING REALITY: Stone observed of his films that 'I never put out a history, I put out a dramatic history.' *Born on the Fourth of July* seeks to recreate not only the battlefield but also give some sense of the 'war zone' that was surviving a veteran hospital and finally, the most trying conflict of all, the effort to reintegrate amidst political and social unrest.

Kovic continues to be an active anti-war demonstrator. He was a speaker in Washington in January 2003 at a mass demonstration to protest at the possible invasion of Iraq by American forces.

HEART OF BATTLE: Stone had been described as 'the aloof kid with the preppie perks, driven to seek the heat and corruption underlying the ordered world'.

At the centre of *Born on the Fourth of July* is the concept of how an idealistic and naïve young man comes to understand that events around him are more complex than he first imagined. It is a film about change – how war changes the individual. Specific to the American experience it gives some expression to the sense of loss and being in limbo that veterans found when they returned home from Vietnam. 'I don't think we've got a fucking friend left,' Timmy observes. For Stone, 'Ron's story is a coherent vision of the whole Vietnam experience . . . the concept being there was a second war when we came back.'

Where *Platoon* clearly focused on a spiritual story in charting the combat experience of a new recruit, *Born on the Fourth of July* looks to offer some sense of political context for the Vietnam War. Characters such as Ron's anti-war brother Tommy and Ron's girlfriend confront him with the possibility that the war is neither justified nor useful. Ron moves from being the most all-American patriot imaginable to someone who questions everything. The hospital sequence provides a sense of how the American people began to lose interest and conviction in the Vietnam War to the point that they did not care about it.

As In *Casualties of War*, the superior officers are shown as blanking any chance of a problem. When Ron reports that he believes he killed one of his own platoon he is ignored.

CHARACTER: Ron Kovic is portrayed as a typical American teenager with a buoyant social life and so much to offer. His experience in the battlefield strips away this essential niceness. Initially this lost innocence is replaced with raging self-pity, which then transforms into something nobler and more thoughtful as Kovic fights a new cause. Ron is defined as a fighter throughout the film. When told he is paralysed he challenges the doctor and says he will walk again. Of Ron Kovic as a 'character' in the film, Stone says, 'I just think I like the way he re-integrates himself at the end of the movie. He finds his path, which is not that far from where he started actually, because he was very zealous as a boy but he was very zealous at the end . . . too.'

When Kovic returns home from battle and reunites with his old home-town friends there is the clear and unsettling sense of a disparity and gulf between their take on America's foreign policy and Ron's stance. It takes time for Ron to realign his view.

Perhaps the most powerful tension and struggle is within Ron's family home as the Kovics try to renew their sense of family and as his parents try to understand their changed son. Ron tearfully asks who will love him in his broken state, and this is so affecting because everyone can relate to his wish to just belong and be cared about. He shouts and screams at his family in his emotional meltdown, but from this point on he will gradually rebuild himself, becoming conscious of the value of the anti-war movement. Ron's physical, facial appearance alters radically and is made acute during his dream in the hospital when he sees his teenage self rising up from a wheelchair and running. Ron's Catholic upbringing fuses with and intensifies his guilt around his actions in the war zone. We see him praying and asking God for guidance at the beginning of the film, and an image of the crucifix fills the screen. Symbolically, Ron endures his own death and rebirth and as such assumes some of the quiet sagacity of Elias in *Platoon*. Ron is defined as a winner from the start, his anguish at losing the wrestling match evident as he lies on the mat crying. This moment of failure and sadness seen from above will be repeated later as he lies distressed in his hospital bed, his scream at one point an echo of Paul Baumer's trauma in the field hospital in *All Quiet on the Western Front*. Just as everything spiralled out of sense for Baumer and for Michael in *The Deer Hunter*, so it does for Ron Kovic, who says to his fellow veteran Charlie, 'Do you remember things that made sense?' The question is a wake-up call for Kovic.

Ron's father is a very ordinary man who is established as having fought in World War Two. He seems uneasy about Ron's desire to enlist, concerned about how far his son will be going. One of the strongest scenes in the film encapsulates the warmth of the relationship between Ron and his quiet, reserved dad. Back home, Ron goes to his childhood bedroom. His dad talks to him, close to tears, and then leans over and embraces his son. The camera holds the tableau that says so much about the difficulty of fathers and sons have in verbally expressing their love. Ron's father is quiet and tolerant of his son in his most difficult time. By contrast, Ron's mother believes it is God's will that Ron goes to war. The fact she idolises her son makes it all the more difficult for her to accept Ron's change.

The character of Charlie (portrayed by Willem Defoe) could perhaps be summed up as Elias from *Platoon* had he survived. Charlie is lost in a haze and his self-pity is his undoing. Ron's home-town buddy Timmy is a veteran who is trying to confront the reality of life back in America. He and Ron share their difficulty in understanding why they went to war and how they can restart their lives.

STYLE: Throughout his career Oliver Stone has often been discussed and debated in terms of his deployment of a political point of view. Equally compelling, if not more so, is his deployment of filmmaking technique. *Born on the Fourth of July* takes the aesthetic of *Platoon* and elaborates and enriches it.

The film emphasises the emotional dislocation of war through its stylistic devices. The emotional whiplash of Ron's experience is expressed through abrupt transitions, such as from the prom to the eerie, orange skies of the combat zone. Silhouettes of soldiers give them a universal quality and also indicate a darkness and absence. These men are ghosts of their former selves. The silhouettes also contrast with the bright, clear images of Ron as a boy and a teenager back home. In battle Ron is presented in silhouette at a critical moment as he kneels, the camera zooming in slowly on his profiled face. He has become a shadow and a void.

The film is textured, and Stone's films from *Born on the Fourth of July* onwards are replete with these visually charged and inventive displays to express character and perception. For just an instant Stone uses an accelerated frame rate as Ron lies in bed during his nightmare in Mexico. The image is jittery and unsettling. Sound is as powerful as image in the film. The memory of the attack on the unarmed villagers and the crying baby haunt Ron when he returns home and, when giving a speech, Ron falters when he hears a baby crying in the crowd.

The re-creation of demonstrations and riots is rendered like another combat zone and there is a moment where Ron, motionless and 'helpless' in his wheelchair, watches it unfold.

There are moments of humour in the film too, such as when Ron intentionally angers his mum by blaspheming and swearing, and there is a Beckett-like comic desperation to the scene of Ron and Charlie arguing and then falling from their wheelchairs to fight in the Mexican desert.

The part of the film's prologue showing Ron as a boy playing 'army' with his friends applies the devices with which Stone re-creates the battlefield – edgy camera moves, quick cuts, kids pursuing one another as shadows and glimpses against the sunlight. The image of Ron's idyllic youth and home life contrasts with the harshness and brutality and decay of the world he moves into as a soldier. For the rest of the prologue sequence the film bathes the action in gently gliding camera work, slow motion (as when the young Ron sits on his dad's shoulders and watches a veteran parade pass by, spellbound by the armless soldier, just as Chris is transfixed by the man in the first moments of *Platoon*) and a golden patina.

The combat scenes take *Platoon*'s hand-held approach and amplify it. Enhancing the visual chaos is the collision of radio chatter with gunfire and indistinct shouts and orders. We are given the chance to understand how easily mistakes of judgement and perception are made.

The scenes in the veteran hospital have a pallid, dead quality to them, whereas the sequence in Mexico is marked by a fuller, more saturated palate.

Contrasting with the leafy sun-bathed neighbourhood Ron grows up in are the scenes late in the film where we see the home of the soldier

Ron killed in battle. The scene has a wintry, dead feel to it (recalling scenes in *The Deer Hunter*) and the use of a split-screen composition, with Ron's face in profile as he 'confesses' to Wilson's family, has a simply rendered psychological intensity. The image of Ron by himself hunched in his wheelchair at Wilson's grave encapsulates the loneliness of Ron's situation.

Throughout the film the American flag functions as a motif. The image of the sunlit flag erases its colour and makes it lifeless, as in the opening image of *Saving Private Ryan*. These visual echoes and variations play across the film in various other ways. In the prologue the camera drops down on little Ron in the woods during combat play. When he is in Vietnam and his gun jams and he is in a fix, we see Ron from overhead, recalling his childhood. Small moments echo: in the film's opening parade one veteran (a cameo by Ron Kovic) flinches as blanks are fired. Later in the film, when Ron returns home and is paraded as the town's hero, blanks are fired and Ron flinches.

When Ron rolls out to speak to the Democratic Convention the image fades to white, a sense of absolution, of a fresh start, the end and beginning of Ron's spiritual journey from anguish to harmony and peace.

History repeats itself.

CRITICAL CROSSFIRE: *Leonard Maltin's Movie and Video Guide* describes the film as 'relentlessly realistic and powerful . . . Stone's finest film to date.' For the *Time Out Film Guide*, the film is an 'intense depiction of a man stripped of dignity and sexuality . . . vigorous . . . elegiac'.

MEDALS OF HONOUR: At the Oscars in 1990 Stone won Best Director.

OTHER BATTLEFRONTS: Perhaps the two most significant 'veteran' films are *Coming Home* and *The Deer Hunter*, or rather its last third. Consider too *The Best Years of Our Lives* (1946), which William Wyler made as his first film upon returning to Hollywood after documenting World War Two combat. That film is distinctive for the detail and thoroughness and emotional honesty of its performances, and is carried by a score by Hugo Friedhofer as affecting as John Williams's music for *Born on the Fourth of July*. Wyler's effort charts the pain and frustration in veterans attempting to reintegrate into mainstream life. Stone went on to chart other elements and aspects of American culture and modern mythology with *The Doors*, *JFK*, *Nixon* and far more recently the documentary *El Commandante* (2004). As of this writing, Stone is due to direct a feature film about a moment of heroism during the 9/11 terrorist attacks. It is not hard to imagine the vibrant and vivid cinematic treatment this subject will receive, and one imagines he will bring to it that sense of memorial that pervades *Born on the Fourth of July*.

A very different Vietnam veteran film that does not receive much widespread notice any more is *Birdy* (Alan Parker, 1984) in which the friendship of two young soldiers back at home is charted. The title character is obsessed with birds and the war has compelled him to believe he really is a bird. Because of this mindset he is confined to a mental hospital. The film won the 1985 Special Grand Jury Prize at Cannes.

In 1994 a very small-scale film was released by Universal Pictures entitled *The War*, directed by Jon Avnet. Whilst ostensibly a film about rival gangs of rural American children in the early 1970s, the film explores the life of one father returned home from Vietnam and struggling to find work. The film features one of Kevin Costner's finest performances, and one that seems barely known.

THE HOMEFRONT: *Born on the Fourth of July* is available on VHS and a special edition DVD that includes a commentary and a short featurette.

FINAL BRIEFING: *Born on the Fourth of July* is arguably the greatest film Oliver Stone ever made. It has a complete quality, immersing us in both the trauma and confusion of war and also the story of a young man's battle to resurrect himself and cure himself of his loneliness. It manages to shift from the alien territory of combat to the familiarity of home that in turn distorts and becomes unknown as Ron 'dies' and then revives and resurrects himself. What comes through most powerfully is the loneliness of Ron Kovic.

FINAL SALUTE: In the summer of 2005 Jane Fonda, who had been a vocal anti-war protester, recalled standing with Ron Kovic at a demonstration once, and that he said to those present, 'I may have lost my body but I have gained my mind.'

Casualties of War (1989)

120 minutes

Columbia
Producer: Art Linson and Fred Caruso
Director: Brian De Palma
Screenplay: David Rabe (based on the article by Daniel Lang)
Cinematographer: Stephen H Burum
Editor: Bill Pankow
Music: Ennio Morricone
Production Design: Wolf Kroeger
Art Direction: Bernard Hayes
Costume Design: Richard Bruno

CAST: Michael J Fox *(Eriksson)*, Sean Penn *(Sergeant Meserve)*, Don Harvey *(Clark)*, John C Reilly *(Hatcher)*, John Leguizamo *(Diaz)*, Thuy Thu Le *(Oahn)*, Erik King *(Brown, Radio Man)*, Jack Gwaltney *(Rowan)*, Ving Rhames *(Lieutenant Reilly)*, Dan Martin *(Hawthorne)*

RATING: R/18

TAGLINE: Even in war ... murder is murder.

WAR STORY: A title card announces that the film is based on an event that actually happened.

It is the early 70s and Nixon has resigned from the office of American President. A young man named Eriksson is asleep on a subway train; he awakes and sees a young Vietnamese woman sitting a little way down the carriage. Eriksson is beguiled by the young woman.

The scene goes back to Vietnam, 1966. In the jungle, Eriksson and his unit are under enemy fire at night. They are led by Sergeant Meserve, a bullish, tough young soldier. Eriksson falls through the ground and hangs suspended over a tunnel filled with Vietcong, but at the last minute, Meserve rescues Eriksson from being captured and killed.

The unit move on by day to a village. They pause for a while there, Eriksson even helping the farmer with his work. The soldiers come under fire again and one of their team, Brownie, is shot dead. Back at Basecamp Wolf the unit take time out while Meserve gives the men details of their next mission, scheduled to begin the following morning.

Meserve explains that they will leave an hour earlier than necessary and, when asked why, he explains that it will give them the chance to detour and kidnap a young Vietnamese woman so they can use her for sex during their mission. Eriksson is unnerved and in disbelief about Meserve's plan and goes to his superior, Rowan, to tell him.

The long-range reconnaissance begins the next morning as planned. Sure enough, in the darkness before dawn a village is found and Meserve sets about kidnapping a teenage girl. The soldiers march on with the young girl and make a camp in the jungle. With the exception of Eriksson, each young soldier takes turns at raping the girl, and Eriksson finally challenges Meserve's actions.

The next day Meserve and his men go to survey a river village, while Eriksson remains with the girl to watch over her. Eriksson tends to the girl's wounds and then tries to set her free, but he is unable to. Eriksson and the girl are taken to join the unit at the railway line. A number of American helicopters swoop in and Meserve orders one of his men to kill the girl. Panic fills the unit and Meserve bullies Diaz into the murder, but Diaz is unable to, and so one of the other soldiers, Clark, makes an attempt on the girl's life. Eriksson distracts the unit by firing his gun and then a battle ensues. Clark assumes he has killed the girl, but she stands and walks along the track to the horror of the men. Eriksson runs to save her but the other soldiers shoot her dead, and Eriksson is struck down by Meserve.

Eriksson wakes at a camp hospital. He finds Rowan and tells him that Meserve followed through with his brutal plan. Clark then interrupts the conversation between Rowan and Eriksson and attempts to cover up the story. Frustrated, Eriksson goes to see his superiors, neither of whom are willing to listen or support his accusations.

In retribution for upsetting the status quo, Clark then attempts to murder Eriksson.

Sitting at a bar Eriksson tells an army chaplain what happened and finally an investigation proceeds. There is a court martial and the guilty men are all sentenced to prison. Meserve whispers something as he passes Eriksson on his way out of the court martial.

The scene changes back to the train in 1973. People disembark and the Vietnamese girl gets off the train but leaves behind her scarf, so Eriksson runs after her and returns it. The woman is grateful and seems to connect with Eriksson, if only for that brief moment. Eriksson has awoken from his nightmare.

CONCEPT/THE MISSION: *Casualties of War*, like many films, found its wellspring in a piece of journalism. This article by a writer named Daniel Lang was based on an extensive conversation with the real-life Eriksson and was published in the *New Yorker* on 18 October 1969. This led to a small book of just 123 pages being published about the incident. The events that Lang narrated occurred in October 1966, when a five-man squad of the army's First Air Cavalry Division were sent to survey an area that was heavy with Vietcong activity. As they left the area the sergeant of the squad decided to kidnap a teenage girl from a 'friendly' village. She was subsequently raped and then killed when the troops realised she might report them. One of the squad, Eriksson, did not partake in the rape and then informed his superiors about what had occurred. The film clearly remains close to the essentials of the event.

Director Brian De Palma, had been intent on developing the project since the 1970s. Given the difficult and repellent nature of the subject matter, the proposed film never found a home with any of the studios, its incendiary material proving too intense. In a sense the intense, concentrated focus of the narrative makes it a more disturbing portrayal of war than any of the situations drawn from real life that are shown in a film as expansive, surreal and mythic as *Apocalypse Now*.

A contemporary of film directors such as Martin Scorsese, George Lucas and Steven Spielberg, Brian De Palma's directorial career had not enjoyed the commercial popularity and outright acclaim of the other young directors. De Palma had more of an evident cult following from the start and his precise style often achieved chilling effects. His intense and visceral thrillers and horror movies such as *Carrie* (1976), *The Fury*, *Obsession* (1980) and *Dressed to Kill* (1982) had an adult sensibility to them at odds with the more youth-orientated charms of the Lucas and Spielberg movies of the 1970s and 1980s. De Palma had also often been accused of misogyny and unnecessarily graphic material in his work. Perhaps it is no surprise that given his uncertain commercial appeal other directors were considered for *Casualties of War*, notably British director John Schlesinger, who had directed *Midnight Cowboy* (1969). There has also been speculation that the great Elia Kazan, director of *Wild River* (1960), *East of Eden* (1955) and *On the Waterfront* most famously, might have been inspired by Daniel Lang's article in the creation of his film *The Visitors* (1972).

Throughout the 1980s, De Palma's moviemaking fortunes continued to fluctuate. In 1987, though, he released his feature-film version of the TV series *The Untouchables* for Paramount Pictures and it was a smash success with both critics and the public, combining characterisation with mood, tension and action. Suddenly De Palma was a more commercially viable director than ever before, and he seized on the chance to finally make *Casualties of War*. Paramount Pictures had turned the film down, so De Palma took it to Columbia, where the late Dawn Steel, a De Palma supporter, was now studio head, and the film was given the green light.

De Palma developed the screenplay with David Rabe. De Palma commented, 'It expresses the Vietnam dilemma in a particularly dramatic and terse form. The whole experience of our involvement there is in this kind of mini tragedy.' Rabe remained committed to Lang's book, though inevitably created a number of scenes and incidents to further round out a sense of motivation.

CASTING/RECRUITMENT: *Casualties of War* starred Michael J Fox and Sean Penn, both perfectly cast. By the time of the late 1980s Fox had established himself as a major TV and movie star through his work as the clean-cut Alex Keaton on the sitcom *Family Ties* and then his role as Marty McFly in the *Back to the Future* series (1985, 89, 90). He had also appeared in *The Secret of My Success* (Harold Becker, 1986) and *Light of Day (Paul Schrader, 1988)*. Fox's image was one of an upbeat, positive, good-natured, young man, so his role as the morally correct Eriksson suited him perfectly. In a sense Fox had done a brave thing by challenging his typical image by starring in a film that was far, far removed from the comedy format.

Sean Penn, by contrast, had established a career for himself as an edgy performer not interested in 'cute' characters. As Sergeant Meserve his tough demeanour was absolutely perfectly pitched. Penn had starred in *Fast Times At Ridgemont High*, *Colors*, and would go on to *We're No Angels*, *State of Grace*, *The Thin Red Line*, *Mystic River* and *The Interpreter* (Sydney Pollack, 2005). Penn has also proved himself an accomplished director with his films *The Indian Runner*, *The Crossing Guard* and *The Pledge*.

Also making an early career appearance in *Casualties of War* is John C Reilly who went on to work as a key performer in the 'repertory' company of writer–director Paul Thomas Anderson in his films *Boogie Nights* (1997) and *Magnolia* (1999) and who also appeared in *The Thin Red Line*.

John Leguizamo, who plays Diaz, starred as Toulouse Lautrec in *Moulin Rouge* (Baz Luhrmann, 2001). Dale Dye, the noted military adviser, takes a small onscreen role as a captain. Dye can also be seen in

Platoon and *Saving Private Ryan*. Ving Rhames, who appears as the somewhat oblique and off-the-wall lieutenant, had a recurrent role in the TV series *ER* and also appeared in *Mission: Impossible*, *Rosewood* and *Bringing Out The Dead*.

BACKUP: David Rabe had himself been a Vietnam veteran and prior to his work on the film had been most noticed for his writing on *Streamers*, about soldiers waiting to head out to Vietnam. De Palma's other key collaborator was cinematographer Stephen H Burum, who worked with him on *The Untouchables* (1987) and would again on *Carlito's Way* (1993), *Mission: Impossible* and *Snake Eyes* (1998). Burum's early career credits included the fantastic films *The Outsiders* (Francis Coppola, 1983) and *Rumble Fish* (Francis Coppola, 1983).

The production designer Wolf Kroeger has provided settings for some of the more striking films of the last twenty years, including *First Blood*, *Streamers* (Robert Altman, 1983) and *The Last of the Mohicans* (Michael Mann, 1992).

PRODUCTION/IN THE TRENCHES: *Casualties of War* was filmed on location in Kanchanaburi and Phuket in Thailand. The scenes that bookend the film were shot in San Francisco. Through the filming period, in order to strengthen the idea that Meserve and Eriksson had no common ground, the actors Fox and Penn would not spend time together off camera.

During filming, and as an indication of the close collaboration between De Palma and his cinematogarpher Stephen H Burum, Burum asked when in the production the director was going to include a 'creeper' scene. The term refers to a moment in many De Palma films when a character is followed by the camera into some eerie situation. On the *Casualties of War* set, De Palma explained there was no such scene devised. Nonetheless, Burum stood by his insinct and prepared his crew for such a scene to take place. Sure enough, several weeks after Burum's question, De Palma announced he had created a scene not included in the script of Erikkson walking to a latrine at night with the camera primed to 'creep' behind him.

MARTIAL MUSIC: De Palma, like Spielberg particularly, has always embraced the possibility for a rich and fulsome score for his films, working with Pino Donaggio and Bernard Herrman, John Williams and Ennio Morricone. For *Casualties of War*, he collaborated with the great

Italian Morricone, who had scored De Palma's *The Untouchables*. His work for *Casualties of War* is defined by its sense of aching lament. The music reaches its most intense in the extended sequence in which Eriksson attempts to liberate the girl and which is then followed by the harrowing confrontation on the railtrack above the river.

Morricone has scored around 400 films, some of the most notable of which *are The Good, the Bad and the Ugly* (Sergio Leone, 1967), *Once Upon A Time in the West* (Sergio Leone, 1969), *Once Upon A Time in America* (Sergio Leone, 1984), *The Mission* (Roland Joffé, 1986) and *Cinema Paradiso* (Giuseppe Tornatore, 1990). The music is desperate and aching, insistent in its conjuring of a sense of tragedy. For the most part it is these highly emotional moments of anguish that are given musical accompaniment rather than the combat sequences.

REIMAGINING REALITY: In her review of *Casualties of War*, Pauline Kael quoted Paul Fussell from his book *Wartime* (published around the time of the film's release) in which he wrote of World War Two, '(the American military) learned that men will inevitably go mad in battle and that no appeal to patriotism, manliness or loyalty to the group will ultimately matter'. After the publication of Lang's story, Eriksson went into hiding out of fear of being found by the soldiers he reported, who were subsequently imprisoned for five years.

HEART OF BATTLE: *Casualties of War* is less about the Vietnam War specifically and far more about where the lines of right and wrong behaviour lie and how far war can excuse those instances where a sense of decency warp out of all recognition. The film takes the line that decency can still find its place in the midst of crazed combat. The film also critiques a certain sense of masculinity and macho bravado. For Eriksson and the film, the issue is not that war excuses having to do the right thing and that it is acceptable to live by an 'anything goes' rule, but instead the fragility that war creates is exactly the reason for decent deliberate thought and action. The film dramatises the limitations of men and our capacity for unthinking violence. In *Casualties of War* men become desperate in the most appalling sense of the word, and the banality of evil is sickeningly apparent.

CHARACTER: The heartbeat of conscience in the film is Eriksson, in his refusal to obey what he considers an immoral order to partake in raping the young Vietnamese girl. He stands up to those who seek to intimidate him. Eriksson is physically less imposing than his enemy, Meserve, and so there is always the immediate and visually compelling sense that he is under threat from this Goliath figure. Eriksson is drawn as the most human of the soldiers, the only man in the unit with a family back home. 'We're supposed to be here to help these people,' he reminds the soldiers.

Eriksson's commitment to integrity and subverting the corruption of his military superiors echoes the drama and conflict found in the magnificent *Paths of Glory*, in which Colonel Dax protests and defends three of his soldiers put on court martial for apparent cowardice in adversity. Eriksson's liberal mindset is constantly under fire from those around him and ultimately the battle is not one of bullets but of character, integrity and emotional resilience.

Meserve is a brutal, unthinking and misogynist soldier who is essentially an adolescent much of the time. He is physically intimidating and, whilst his bravery in the field is admirable, he is far more defined by his amoral behaviour. He sees the world around him too simplistically.

Eriksson's fellow soldiers are shown as being intimidated by Meserve and his superiors are portrayed as wanting to avoid any complications by following up on his charge. Diaz is marked by doubt and cowardice in not challenging Meserve, even though he has explained to Eriksson how wrong he thinks Meserve's actions are. The other soldiers are less well defined, beyond being shown as unthinking. As in so many war films, the central combat is a means by which the protagonist enters something of a spiritual conflict and De Palma's film presents us with the redemption of Eriksson.

STYLE: Brian De Palma has always been recognised as an inventive and thoughtfully cinematic director. With *Casualties of War* there is a precision and intensity to the construction of the drama. De Palma favours several extreme close-ups in order to communicate emotional intensity, notably when Eriksson stands out in the rain after the rape has occurred. The lashing rain takes up one half of the frame, whilst Eriksson's eyes fill the other – he looks older, more beleaguered, destroyed.

De Palma is equally at home in creating good old-fashioned movie tension in the opening sequence when Eriksson hangs over a Vietcong tunnel. During the several skirmishes and battles the camera glides elegantly across the action.

The camera is used as a point-of-view device at critical moments such as when Meserve seeks out a young woman in the village and also in the climax of the scene in which the girl stumbles along the railtrack.

Zoom shots and long lenses are used for shots to establish military space, and on two occasions when Eriksson challenges authority he and his 'enemy' are framed equally in profile.

Perhaps the two most affecting scenes occur in the middle of the film and form the climax of the first half. Eriksson's attempt to liberate the girl and then the sequence on the railway line are both highly charged. In the moment when Eriksson's world slips and slides in his attempt to help the girl, the camera tilts to symbolise how his whole world has tilted out of balance. The image encapsulates the moral sense.

CRITICAL CROSSFIRE: For legendary film critic Pauline Kael, 'This movie about war and rape – De Palma's nineteenth film – is the culmination of his best work. In essence, it's feminist.' Over at the *Time Out Film Guide* they were less keen: 'The non-sensationalist approach seems to have taken a toll on (De Palma's) energies.' It's a similar attitude in *Leonard Maltin's Movie and Video Guide*: 'For all its good intentions, the film has a jumbled, detached feel to it.'

MEDALS OF HONOUR: *Casualties of War* was nominated at the 1990 Golden Globes for Best Score and won the Peace category at the Political Film Society awards.

OTHER BATTLEFRONTS: *Casualties of War* benefited in part from Oliver Stone's 'revival' of the Vietnam War film with **Platoon**. Like that film, De Palma's emphasises the youth of the soldiers involved and has a cherry (a new recruit) as the focus of its story. Perhaps the most useful comparison, though, is with **Saving Private Ryan**, which also uses the backdrop of war for a very intimate and small-scale story about essential morality. Released in the same year as **Born on the Fourth of July**, *Casualties of War* shares that film's sense of the eeriness of combat, the otherworldly quality of it.

THE HOMEFRONT: *Casualties of War* is available on DVD. The DVD features a 1989 featurette about the making of the film and an interview with Michael J Fox.

FINAL BRIEFING: Of the many Vietnam films made in the 1980s, *Casualties of War* is absolutely the strongest effort. It is also one of the lesser-known features. Certainly Oliver Stone dominated this body of work, but De Palma's morality play has such a narrow focus that it is all the stronger for it. The film covers the expected Vietnam War movie staples in terms of its choreography of combat and presentation of the jungle, but the film works hard to humanise the Vietnamese and to address what it is that war does to the minds of its combatants. There is a dazzling precision and economy to the film and its operatic phases contrast brilliantly with its realistic visual style.

FINAL SALUTE: The American film critic, and one of the most astute there is, Armond White, has said the film is 'as compelling and astounding as a great work of art ought to be . . . it draws you into a moral analysis of the story that is being told'.

Wars in Other Worlds

Ultimately, the war film is not and never will be confined to the most familiar frames of reference for combat, namely the Great War, the Second World War and the Vietnam War, all wars with which we have a dynamic and profound familiarity because of photography and motion pictures.

There are many war films that depict images of conflict in this world and others, for which we have no such frame of reference. These wars in other worlds endure for many of the same reasons as the other films covered in this book. They may appear less immediate to our experience, but like *All Quiet on the Western Front*, like **In Which We Serve**, like **Born on the Fourth of July,** they all use war as the prism through which to explore human behaviour in its most dynamically aggressive, compassionate and brave forms.

Ran (1985)

160 minutes

Herald Ace/Nippon Herald/Greenwich (France/Japan)
Producer: Masato Hara, Serge Silberman
Director: Akira Kurosawa
Co-Producer: Hisao Kurosawa
Screenplay: Akira Kurosawa, Hideo Oguni, Masato Ide
(based on *King Lear* by William Shakespeare)
Cinematographer: Takao Saito, Masaharu Udea and
Asakazu Nakai
Editor: Akira Kurosawa
Music: Toru Takemitsu
Production Design: Yoshiro Muraki, Shinobu Muraki
Art Direction: Yoshiro Muraki
Costume Design: Emi Wada

CAST: Tatsuya Nakadai (*Lord Hidetora Ichimonji*), Akira Terao (*Taro Takatora Ichimonji*), Jinpachi Nezu (*Jiro Masatora Ichimonji*), Daisuke Ryu (*Saburo Naotora Ichimonji*), Meiko Harada (*Lady Kaede*), Yoshiko Miyazaki (*Lady Sue*), Kazuo Kato (*Ikoma*), Masayuki Yui (*Tango*), Peter (*Kyoami*), Hitoshi Ueki (*Fujimaki*)

RATING: R/15

TAGLINE: Akira Kurosawa's *Ran*.

WAR STORY: It is an unspecified time in the sixteenth century. Lord Hidetora and his three sons are on an expedition hunting wild boar. While asleep at their hilltop camp, Hidetora has a dream in which he sees himself alone in wasteland with only his beloved sons to save him.

Hidetora then convenes his sons and counsel and announces his wish to step down as the family head and explains that from now on the family dynasty is to be headed by his son Taro. Unsure of his competence, Taro reluctantly accepts his father's plan. The youngest son, Saburo, vexes and angers his father when he states that a family can fracture and acknowledges that the sons are not united. Hidetora banishes Saburo and Saburo's counsel Tango.

Taro assumes his status as the head of the family and ruler of the kingdom, while his other brother Jiro can only look on. Immediately, though, concerns and tensions develop. At the first castle they come to Taro settles into his new position with his wife, Kaede, who is now the mistress of the castle. The court jester Kyoami playfully taunts Hidetora for his decision which will divide the kingdom. Taro holds a gathering for the transfer of power and wants Hidetora to sign a pledge of allegiance and submission, but Hidetora is angered by the proposition. Jiro is already becoming wary of Taro's apparent eccentricities and he is advised to challenge his brother and assume status as head of the family. Hidetora is still protected by thirty warriors.

Hidetora goes to find Jiro and his wife Sue, and Jiro speaks with his father. Jiro is then instructed not to let Hidetora and his men into the castle. Hidetora says that Jiro and Taro both want to banish him, and Taro does indeed cast Hidetora out into the wilderness with his jester and his guards. Local peasants have fled to the mountains having pledged allegiance to Hidetora, for which Taro has threatened to kill them.

Taro's troops arrive at Saburo's fortress and seize control of it. One of Saburo's captains says they can have the fortress but that they are going to join Saburo elsewhere. In the wilderness, Tango, now a peasant, finds Hidetora and tells him that Taro has issued an edict that anyone found supporting Hidetora will be killed, but that Saburo has sent him (Tango) to protect his father. Hidetora and his retinue ride to the castle of Fujikama, a neighbouring warlord, but Taro and his soldiers arrive and a huge battle begins. Saburo's soldiers ride into battle on behalf of Hidetora. The battle rages and Taro's soldiers take control, but Taro himself is killed.

Hidetora prepares to kill himself but then relents, choosing instead to walk away from the carnage and out into the wilderness, eventually joined by his jester. Jiro goes after his father but is stopped, and is told he now rules the land.

In the wilderness, Hidetora is besieged by visions and nightmares, doubts and regrets. Hidetora, Tango and Kyoami come across a hermit who initially resists identifying himself, but eventually reveals that he is Lady Sue's brother and has been in hiding ever since the death of their parents at the hand of Hidetora. The former warlord's bloody past is beginning to catch up with him.

Jiro returns to Taro's castle with a braid of his hair and gives it to Kaede. Kaede then persuades Jiro not to kill her too – she wants to become his wife and for him to murder Sue. Jiro agrees to Kaede's plan.

In the wilderness, Hidetora continues to deteriorate, and Tango asks if he wants to see his son Saburo.

Saburo has crossed the river with his army, ready to confront Jiro, who is being urged to avoid war with his brother. While the armies mass, ready for the final battle, Saburo rides out to his father in the wilderness. Sue is killed by Kaede, and in turn Jiro kills Kaede. Saburo reunites with his father and begins the journey to take him to safety, but Jiro has sent men to ambush Saburo on the desert plain. Saburo is killed with his father as they gallop along.

As Saburo and Hidetora are both carried in a funeral procession, Sue's brother stands alone against the setting sun.

CONCEPT/THE MISSION: There is a Japanese maxim that reads, 'War is the art of embellishing death.' Kurosawa's film dramatises this idea as fully as could be imagined. The word 'Ran' is Japanese for chaos and the acts of murder and mass carnage that develop bear out the truth of the maxim.

Writer–director Kurosawa had become a major figure in Japanese cinema in the late 1940s and even though he made numerous powerful contemporary dramas such as *Ikiru* (1952), he was most famous for his samurai movies: *The Seven Samurai* (1954), *Hidden Fortress* (1958), *Throne of Blood* (1957) and *Kagemusha* (1980). Kurosawa had spent ten years working on *Ran* prior to its release and it was another opportunity for him to fold a Shakespeare tragedy into the context of feudal, samurai Japan, as *Throne of Blood* had been an adaptation of *Macbeth*. Other Kurosawa films include *Stray Dog* (1949), *Dodes Kaden*, (1970), *Dersu Uzala* (1975) and *Rhapsody in August* (1991).

With *Ran*, Kurosawa was in effect offering the summation of his epic film style. He fused his initial concept for the film with elements of Shakespeare's *King Lear* when he saw the relationship that existed between his film idea and the play.

When *Ran* was released in 1985, Kurosawa commented on the samurai context for his film, saying, 'At the time, people were still free. If they were strong enough to fight, they could make something of their lives, they could be really human. Even a fighting peasant could do it, though the competition was fierce. People could express their personality much more than today.'

Kurosawa was 73 years old when he shot the film and he had truly begun to think that he would never get to realise his dream project. Despite his great standing in world cinema, and even though his previous film *Kagemusha* had been very popular, Kurosawa struggled to finance *Ran*. For all his great worldwide standing, Kurosawa's proposed new epic was considered just too much of a gamble for the Japanese studios. With its proposed budget of ten million dollars the film was an aberration at a time when Japanese live action films were budgeted at around one or two million. Furthermore, *Ran*'s story dictated that the majority of it be filmed on location, which mean that Toho studio would lose out on renting sound-stage space. Interestingly, after *Kagemusha*, Kurosawa and his son Hisao had set up the Kurosawa Film School and *Ran*'s interiors were ultimately filmed there.

Eventually, the project was funded by Masatoshi Hara of Herald Ace Productions and Serge Silberman of French company Greenwich Film Production. The budget was twelve million dollars.

To some degree *Kagemusha* had been a rehearsal for *Ran*. Kurosawa was not only informed by the *King Lear* narrative but also very much by his own cultural tradition and also by the cinema of Russian filmmaker Sergei Eisenstein and his film *Ivan the Terrible* (1945, 1958). For Kurosawa, *Ran* would depict human events seen from heaven.

Kurosawa's mythology of Japanese history and military class recalls the work of his great hero, the American director John Ford. As an indication of his enthusiasm and respect for Ford's kind of filmmaking, Kurosawa said that when he died he wanted to be John Ford. At Kurosawa's funeral, the golden altar used was based on his castle set for *Ran* and standing on the altar was a photo of Kurosawa in his cap and glasses.

Kurosawa had enjoyed consistent commercial success in Japan in the 1940s, 1950s and 1960s. He had innovated the Panavision camera in Japan and multi-camera coverage of action, starting with *The Seven Samurai*. He also used long lenses with great conviction and energy. The 1970s saw Kurosawa's commercial appeal take a downturn, though Russia became one source of financing for his work such as *Dersu Uzala*. Kurosawa also wrote the screenplay for the thriller *Runaway Train*, a fantastic action film made by Russian director Andrei Konchalovsky in 1985 starring Jon Voight, Eric Roberts and Rebecca De Mornay.

For Kurosawa the most effective way to structure the screenplay for *Ran* was to adhere to the Noh theatre tenets of *jo, ha, kyu*; that is to say, sequences that offer an introduction, then a range of contrasts and finally capitulation.

In part, *Ran* is based on the historical account of Lord Mori, who had three sons and got each son to break a single arrow, which they did. When he handed them three arrows together, however, they could not break them. Kurosawa appreciated the metaphor but decided that the third son would break the three arrows across his knee.

Given the warm critical and commercial reception to *Kagemusha*, Kurosawa was keen to amplify *Ran*'s drama and resonance.

CASTING/RECRUITMENT: Like many established directors, including one of Kurosawa's heroes John Ford, he had a corps of regular actors who appeared in *Ran*, notably Takeshi Kato and Jun Tazaki. For the film Kurosawa hired a pop star, Akira Terao, and a comedian, Hitoshi Ueki. For the role of the jester, Kurosawa hired the drag queen Peter, who had made his name on Japanese television.

The actress portraying Kaede had also appeared in Kurosawa's film *Dreams* (1990), in which she appears as a snow fairy coming to the aid of a team of mountain climbers.

Tatsuya Nakadai had a bit part early in his career in *The Seven Samurai* and much later in his long career appeared in Kurosawa's *Yojimbo* (1961) and *Kagemusha*.

BACKUP: Given the reluctance of any Japanese studio and distributor to invest in the film, Kurosawa found an ally in French producer Serge Silberman, who insisted that they had to be in total agreement on all the key issues in order for the project to proceed. Thankfully for Kurosawa and Silberman they enjoyed an essentially harmonious creative collaboration, given the creative latitude Kurosawa (known widely as The Emperor) had come to know over the years. Silberman worked with Kurosawa on revisions of the screenplay and in the casting process, and beyond that allowed the director to go and shoot his film.

His trio of cinematographers held an impressive track record with other Kurosawa collaborations such as *Dersu Uzala*, *Kagemusha* and *Dreams*, and would also work on his 1993 film *Madadayo*.

PRODUCTION/IN THE TRENCHES: The film's emphasis on location filming was its most logistically challenging aspect, but the decision to do so gives the story great scope, as characters are embedded in symbolic surroundings. The production, for example, had to wait for the snow to melt on Mount Fuji so that one of the fortresses could be constructed there and filmed at. This mountain set covered one square kilometre and saw 150 horses and riders charging into action around it. When the film was about to begin filming, Kurosawa invited the press to the studio for promotional purposes, and he introduced each of his actors in full make-up and costume. For *Ran*'s much celebrated battle scenes, horses smaller than regular thoroughbreds were used.

Ran filmed for thirty weeks and the third castle that features in the film was built specifically for the film at a cost of $1.6m. As the story shows, this fortress was then burned down. This lavish scale brings to mind the huge engineering effort required for **The Bridge on the River Kwai** and would have similarities with the creation of the French village set for the concluding battle of **Saving Private Ryan**. Initially, Kurosawa had wanted to shoot *Ran* at Hokkaido, where he had filmed parts of *Kagemusha*, but this time around he was denied. Another location for *Ran* was Mount Aso in southern Japan.

To ensure the historical authenticity of the beautiful costumes that Kurosawa demanded, his designer Emi Wada used sixteenth-century weaving and dyeing techniques.

A rumour circulated that 15,000 horses and 120,000 extras had been used in the film, but in reality there had been 250 horses and 1,400 extras. Kurosawa's great skill with editing had made less seem more.

MARTIAL MUSIC: With his love of Western classical music, Kurosawa elected to invoke the spirit of Mahler with the score for *Ran*. The film's composer Toru Takemitsu has gone on to create many well-regarded classical works including the piece *Tree Line* (1996).

REIMAGINING REALITY: The age of war in Japan that *Ran* is set during was the Sengoku Jidai, and it has been defined as a period of what historian Stephen Turnbull describes as 'fission and fusion'.

The term samurai means 'those who serve' and they had their roots in a military elite of mounted archers. As time passed the bow and arrow were replaced by spears to allow cavalry charges. *Ran* opens with a fast-paced wild-boar hunt in which the ageing Hidetora gracefully wields a bow and arrow. The banners that flutter and fill the frame so colourfully are named *nobori* and historically were colour-coded to define different warring factions. Kurosawa uses these colours to great visual effect. Samurai armour was leather and lacquered iron, and the helmets were lacquered iron. There were many siege battles during the Sengoku period and *Ran*'s first and brilliant battle sequence dramatises such a siege and also makes strong visual use of *yamashiro* (mountain castles).

HEART OF BATTLE: At the time of the film's release it was considered as possibly an anti-war statement for the Reagan–Gorbachev generation. When Kurosawa was asked if this *was* his message he famously replied, 'If I wanted to deliver a message, I'd write a letter.'

Ran suffuses its intense family drama of jealousy, duplicity and greed with explosions, aggression and war. Two huge battles puncture the already intense domestic conflict as loyalties and family ties are tested, broken and, momentarily, partially restored. The film charts the pains of ambition and the chaos and pain that rain down on Hidetora like the flaming arrows he is surrounded by at one moment in battle.

In this film loyalties, usually confirmed and reinforced by battle, are utterly shredded by greed and deceit, suspicion and fear. There is a sense that all of the bloodshed is fated and that the battles and conflicts are a way of testing human resolve and dignity. As the jester says, in a way that echoes so much ancient Greek tragedy, 'Are there no gods . . . no Buddha?' This sense of calling the god is as much a part of the spiritual battle in this film as it is in *All Quiet on the Western Front*, albeit differently rendered.

CHARACTER: All the characters in *Ran* are torn between their duty and their personal desire and interest.

Lord Hidetora is a character committed to a sense of honour and the belief that a family bond is unbreakable. He comes to learn that his perceived wise judgement as the head of the clan is not as strong or sure as he thought, and as the film develops he becomes increasingly crazed by betrayal within his family and also, perhaps more potently, by guilt and regret. He cannot escape his past as an apparently glorious warlord and eventually describes himself as 'wretched' and 'rejected'. His sense of guilt, of fragile humanness, overwhelms him. What Hidetora witnessed in his dream at the beginning of the film has become terrifyingly true. Hidetora's guilty conscience is apparent from early in the film. His daughter-in-law Sue was 'orphaned' when he killed her parents during one of his campaigns, and he wants Sue to now hate him. Sue does not and she simply replies, 'All is decided in our previous lives.'

Hidetora begins the film as a glorious-looking, though ageing, king who by the end is essentially a bombed-out ghost, having suffered his own personal apocalypse. Potential salvation comes too late. His war crimes will never be forgiven.

Kaede is perhaps the most lethal character in the film, a Sengoku *femme fatale* who is at first the wife of the son who inherits Hidetora's kingdom. When she is widowed she turns her savage attention to Hidetora's other son Jiro, urging him to betray his own wife.

Chaos and conflicts of the soul rage throughout the film. Kaede's father and brother were killed by Hidetora during the wars, and Kaede enjoys the fact that she is now living back in the castle of her youth. The scene in which she attacks Jiro with a dagger and then in the next instant licks blood from his neck and has sex with him takes Kaede from apparent victim to lethal hunter in the flash of light on her dagger.

Taro is reluctant to accept his father's wish that he lead the family. Soon, though, his reluctance to rule is replaced by greedy ambition. Jiro seeks to assume power over Taro and is advised to 'Sound the horn or become the quarry.' Jiro emerges as the weakest, most easily manipulated son.

Saburo, initially, appears the least dependable son, but ultimately emerges as the one who can restore the family, even though he it is who acknowledges how fragile the idea of a family together can be when he breaks the cluster of arrows over his knee. Early in the film Saburo comments that the world is 'barren of loyalty and feeling'. Of his son's apparent lack of family honour Hidetora says, 'When flesh is rotten, even our own cut it away.'

In the midst of this sea of destructive, super-serious emotion is the playful jester Kyoami. He functions as something like a Greek chorus in drama, offering commentary on the action. Kyoami is a holy fool, perhaps the wisest character of them all, ever ready with an insightful comment such as the not too optimistic line, 'Hell is ever at hand, which you cannot say of Heaven.' The bleakness that characterises so many war films is no less in place in this very distinct film, seemingly far removed from the films of America and Britain, yet still using the template of war to explore the same ideas and emotions.

STYLE: In his book *The Films of Akira Kurosawa*, Donald Richie writes, 'The visuals are often Noh-like. The costumes, for example, are, like those of Noh, particularly and ostentatiously gorgeous.' By contrast to many war films that seek to immerse the viewer in the immediacy of war through 'point of view' shots, Kurosawa opts for a more aloof stance where the symmetry and expanse of the frame shows us individuals helpless amidst the hell of war. This is no more clearly shown than when Hidetora sits in a room of a fortress, passive and perhaps demented as fiery arrows cascade in around him. The images of war are run mute, with very mournful music playing over them. Colours enrich the frame as banners and blood swirl and guns explode with red firepower. There is an immense theatricality to the battles and yet Kurosawa always seeks to plainly show the blood and death of combat, bodies heaped on one another, faces racked in pain.

Throughout the film Kurosawa makes very telling cuts to images of clouds, in blue skies and darkening skies; the natural world is a metaphor for the seasons of the heart, from its capacity for glory to its capacity for terror and moral darkness.

Against the huge visuals for the film are the equally powerful details. Consider the framing of shots and incidental detail that Kurosawa deploys to spike the action. During the first battle, heaped bodies frame the image across its base and right corner. Consider also the use of mute images in depicting much of the first battle, and the contrast between bloody battle and the image that follows not so long after of Hidetora gathering up beautiful flowers. The brutal and the delicate exist side by side, just as they do in the final image of *All Quiet on the Western Front*.

The film is rich with bursts of colour against the landscape. Cinematographer Takao Saito commented that Kurosawa 'devised special costumes based on colour schemes found in Noh . . . We meddled very little with the colours, but we sometimes used colour reflectors for character delineation.'

CRITICAL CROSSFIRE: Everyone loved this film. *Time Out* magazine wrote that it was 'a huge, tormented canvas . . . A *Lear* for our age, and for all time.' Vincent Canby in the *New York Times* said, '*Ran* has the

terrible logic and clarity of a morality tale seen in tight close-up.'
Leonard Maltin's Movie and Video Guide comments that *Ran* is
'beautifully filmed . . . Slowly paced and overly expository at the start,
(the) epic picks up with two superb battle scenes.'

MEDALS OF HONOUR: The film won the Best Costume Design award
at the 1986 Oscars and was nominated for Best Art Direction, Best
Cinematography and Best Direction. At the 1986 BAFTA awards the
film won Best Make-up and Best Foreign Film.

OTHER BATTLEFRONTS: Two other Kurosawa films offer further
evidence of his use of cinema to engage with the issues of conflict, firstly
with *The Seven Samurai* and then *Kagemusha*. *Kagemusha* was released
in 1980 with the backing of Francis Ford Coppola and George Lucas,
both of whom had made highly 'American' films that found inspiration
and influence from Kurosawa's movies. *Kagemusha* told the story of a
warlord who, for his protection, uses a body double. As such the film's
title (it means 'Shadow Warrior') becomes clear. The film interweaves
the personal drama and anxiety of the Shadow Warrior with expansive
battle sequences. As with *Ran*, *Kagemusha* was rejected by Japanese
studios and hence Kurosawa looked to North America for support and
encouragement.

Kagemusha received the backing of Twentieth Century Fox, where
Alan Ladd Jr backed the film as a favour to George Lucas. The film won
the Palme d'Or at Cannes. Interestingly, Kurosawa fired his lead actor on
Kagemusha when he brought his own film crew with him. This lead
actor was Shintaro Katsu, who was famous for *Zaitoichi* (Takeshi
Kitano, 2003). The lead roles of the warlord and his peasant
impersonator had been written specifically for Katsu, but eventually the
role went to Tatsuya Nakadai. *Kagemusha* is set in the 1570s, a period
when rival clans battled to control Japan.

The film that Kurosawa made after *Ran* was *Dreams* and this
anthology film included two short pieces that concern themselves
separately with nuclear devastation and also with the army and death.
For an astonishing exploration of Kurosawa's career and his work with
Toshiro Mifune, with whom he collaborated so many times, read the
immense book *The Emperor and the Wolf* by Stuart Galbraith.

Beyond Japanese shores there are countless other old-world war film
epics, for instance *El Cid* (Anthony Mann, 1961). More recently Ridley

Scott has directed *Kingdom of Heaven* (2004), a dramatisation of aspects of the Crusade in the Holy Land.

THE HOMEFRONT: *Ran* is available as a DVD. Complementing the film is one of the strongest and most impressionistic 'behind the scenes' films yet made entitled simply *AK*. The piece is a long way from the kind of film documentaries we might normally be used to. It is directed by Chris Marker, director of the classic short film *La Jetee* (1962). Marker's film dwells on moments and details in the filming process and becomes a work of expressive art in its own right as it focuses on *Ran*'s shoot on the slopes of Mount Fuji.

FINAL BRIEFING: *Ran* is replete with immense, widely framed shots of wasteland that symbolise the emotional state of Hidetora. He is a man who has paid the price for losing his humanity and the film, in its various smaller, interweaving dramas, charts this loss across the span of characters as the result of wars in the past and the present.

The story is clearly told and unfussily presented. The emphasis on wide shots to frame most of the action, not just the battle scenes, gives the film a super simplicity and symbolic quality. The battle sequences depict war as partly unreal and also as a bloodbath. The scene of blood raining down through the floorboards of the fortress interior is particularly hard to forget. This is a film that connects most powerfully as it uses its war story to ultimately deal with one of the great human emotional wars: the feeling of regret for things said and done, and those things not said and done. *Ran* is a war film and urgent domestic drama about fathers and sons.

FINAL SALUTE: For Kurosawa *Ran* was his definitive epic statement, one that would be 'more richly conceived, more deeply personal'.

Aliens (1986)

148 minutes (Special Edition)

Twentieth Century Fox
Producer: Gale Ann Hurd
Executive Producers: Gordon Carroll, David Giler, Walter Hill
Director: James Cameron

Screenplay: James Cameron, based on a story by James
Cameron, David Giler and Walter Hill, based on characters
created by Dan O'Bannon and Ronald Shusett
Cinematographer: Adrian Biddle
Sound Recordist: Roy Charman
Editor: Ray Lovejoy
Music: James Horner
Production Design: Peter Lamont
Art Direction: Ken Court, Bert Davey, Fred Hole, Michael
Lamont
Costume Design: Emma Porteous
Visual Effects: Stan Winston (Creature Effects), Alex Gillis
(Creature Effects), Tom Woodruff Jr (Creature Effects) John
Richardson (Visual Effects Supervisor), Dennis Skotak
(Visual Effects Supervisor), Robert Skotak (Visual Effects
Supervisor), Brian Johnson

CAST: Sigourney Weaver (*Ripley*), Carrie Henn (*Rebecca 'Newt'
Jorden*), Michael Biehn (*Corporal Dwayne Hicks*), Lance Henriksen
(*Bishop*), Paul Reiser (*Carter Burke*), Bill Paxton (*Private Hudson*),
William Hope (*Lieutenant Gorman*), Jeanette Goldstein (*Private
Vasquez*), Al Matthews (*Sergeant Apone*), Mark Rolston (*Private
Drake*), Ricco Ross (*Private Frost*), Colette Hiller (*Corporal Ferro*),
Daniel Kash (*Private Spunkmeyer*), Cynthia Dale Scott (*Corporal
Dietrich*), Tip Tipping (*Private Crowe*), Trevor Steedman (*Private
Wierzbowski*)

RATING: 18

TAGLINE: There are some places in the universe you don't go alone.
This time it's war.

WAR STORY: The following synopsis refers to the Special Edition.

Space. A small space vessel drifts through the stars. Within it sleeps
Ellen Ripley, the only person aboard the ship which is then detected by a
larger vessel picking up salvage. The salvage team are surprised to find a
woman on board who is still alive, albeit in deep space sleep.

Ripley awakes in a medical unit on board a massive space station. She
is met there by a man named Carter Burke who works for the massive
Weyland Utani company, an organisation in the process of colonising
planets. Burke informs Ripley that she has been asleep for 57 years.

Anxious and afraid, Ripley experiences one of her many vivid nightmares about confronting the alien that she had been hunted by 57 years previously. Burke visits Ripley again and tells her that the daughter she had is now dead. Ripley has outlived her. Deep space sleep has deprived Ripley of a real life.

Ripley attends a hearing about her experiences and reports about the alien that had wiped out the Weyland Utani crew (as seen in the first film *Alien*). The board does not believe her stories and says she is unfit to work for them any more as a commercial flight officer. Ripley is stripped of her duties and ordered to undertake a psychometric probation period. Ripley insists on the terror of the alien being very real and her anger and concern is amplified when she is told that the planet of LV426 (where she had originally confronted the alien) has been colonised for twenty years and that up to seventy families now live there.

On the surface of LV426, stormy and dark, stands the colony, a working, industrial complex. Out on the wasteland a truck drives across the terrain. Inside the truck are a family: parents, a little boy and a little girl. The father sights a huge, unusual structure and goes to investigate leaving his children Timmy and Rebecca (nicknamed Newt) in the truck. Night falls and there is no sign of their parents returning. Newt looks worried. Her mother returns to the vehicle to call for help. Lying on the ground is Newt's father. He is dead. An alien face-hugger is wrapped across his face.

In her apartment on board the space station Ripley sits quietly, pensively. She is visited by Burke who brings with him Lt Gorman of the Colonial Marine Corps. They inform Ripley that contact with the LV426 colony has been lost. They want to investigate and they want to take Ripley with them as she knows the terrain. Burke and Gorman explain that they fear the return of the alien Ripley had described. Ripley is reluctant to accept the mission. She has been given a job in the cargo dock as a loader but Burke says that if she agrees to the mission she will be reinstated as a flight officer. Ripley does not accept the mission immediately and, again, she is haunted by her nightmares of the alien. Ripley contacts Burke and asks if the mission will only be to destroy the alien lifeforms and not to bring them back for study. Burke reassures Ripley that the mission is solely to destroy any aliens they may find. Ripley agrees to join the mission and accompany the Marine combat force.

Space. On board a mighty ship are the Marines and Ripley, all in deep space sleep en route to LV426. They awake from their chambers and eat.

Ripley observes the crew of soldiers and is clearly not a part of their tightly knit cadre. Some of the soldiers appear more ready for action than others. The soldiers talk about the rescue mission ahead of them to protect colonists and destroy aliens. When Ripley realises that one of the crew is an android she becomes sceptical.

In the holding bay of the vessel, Gorman addresses the troops and Ripley informs them of her experiences combating the alien previously. All that the soldiers are interested in is where the enemy will be when they land. The troops prepare to be dropped onto LV426 and load their weaponry and hardware.

The drop-ship rockets the crew and Ripley to the surface of LV426. The troops disembark and approach and enter the colony. It is a ghost-town and once inside there has evidently been a showdown between humans and aliens. Ripley remains on board the armoured truck with Gorman and Burke to monitor the soldiers' progress. The area seems to have been secured by the unit and so Gorman, Burke and Ripley go in too.

Inside a laboratory the unit come across several alien fetuses in tanks. They were removed from victims. Concern for the unit's safety begins to mount. Ripley and Hicks find a young girl in hiding. It is Newt. Her parents and brother are dead.

Hudson says he has detected survivors and so the unit head towards them. The unit go straight into an alien lair and there is an intense battle during which Apone, Crow, Frost and Drake are killed. Taking swift emergency action, Ripley drives the armoured vessel to rescue the remaining soldiers from the aliens' lair.

Tensions boil over. Ripley, Hicks and the other soldiers agree that they should detonate a nuclear charge to totally destroy the colony and eliminate the alien threat. Burke objects to this plan saying the site is financially valuable. The unit call for the drop-ship to come in and pick them up but there is an alien on board and it kills the two-person crew and the ship crashes. Ripley and the others are now marooned and it will be seventeen days until they can be rescued. Ripley instigates a plan to counter the alien attack.

Bishop sets about remotely calling down the second drop-ship from the cruiser in orbit over LV426. Ripley and Newt find themselves cornered by two face-hugger aliens. Ripley tries to alert the others but Burke stops the signal in the hope that Ripley and Newt will be killed by the alien which will then use their bodies as hosts to grow in. Ripley and Newt are rescued by the Marines just in time from the facehugger's grip.

The situation immediately worsens when the power supply cuts out and the aliens close in. Burke and Hudson are both killed by the aliens. Ripley, Hicks, Newt, Gorman and Vasquez head for the landing area. Gorman and Vasquez are killed by aliens and Newt is separated from her protectors Hicks and Ripley who then witness an alien move in for the kill on Newt. Ripley and Hicks run for the drop-ship as it comes in to land. Bishop takes Hicks on board and Ripley arms herself. She goes back in to find Newt.

Ripley finds the nest of the queen alien and sets about torching her and all of the eggs she has laid. There in the nest is Newt. Ripley rescues her and they run. They board the drop-ship and it rockets away as the entire colony explodes. The drop-ship docks with the *Sulaco* in orbit. An alien is on board the drop-ship and it kills Bishop. Newt hides from the creature and Ripley confronts the alien once and for all with the energy and anger of a gladiator. Ripley ejects the alien into space and reunites with Newt. They go into hypersleep, the nightmare of combat over.

CONCEPT/THE MISSION: Two Vietnam films were released in 1986 – one was *Platoon* and the other was *Aliens*.

Writer–director James Cameron had begun his filmmaking career in the early 1980s, prompted to focus on his filmmaking ambitions after viewing *Star Wars* in 1977 and recognising that a way of telling stories using technology and a certain kind of narrative dynamism and energy was now in place. For Cameron one of the critical films in his developing film enthusiasm had been *Alien*, with its futuristic 'house of horror' intensity.

Cameron began his film career as a production designer for Roger Corman's New World Pictures, working most notably on *Battle Beyond the Stars* (Jimmy T Murakami, 1980). Cameron eventually secured a position as the director of *Piranha 2* (1981), the sequel to the original Joe Dante cult classic, *Piranha* (1978). This debut directorial effort proved frustrating for Cameron, who then invested his energies in the development of the film that was to be his breakthrough and which became a classic of modern science-fiction cinema, *The Terminator* (1984). With this film (about a robot sent from the future to prevent the birth of a saviour of tomorrow) a bona fide, low-budget blockbuster hit, Cameron was able to pursue his dream project of the time, a sequel to *Alien*.

Like *The Terminator*, *Aliens* would pit a woman against an otherworldly force in a typically male-dominated genre. Prior to *Aliens* becoming a reality Cameron had been approached by the producers of the original *Alien* film about his interest in making a futuristic version of *Spartacus*. Cameron was not especially keen on the concept but did ask what other projects Walter Hill and David Giler were developing. One of the films they proposed was a sequel to *Alien*. By the mid-1980s several efforts had been made at crafting a screenplay that would creatively extend the *Alien* story, but nothing gelled until Cameron entered the frame with his explosive idea for a follow-up.

An accomplished screenwriter, Cameron wrote the screenplay for *Aliens*, electing to centre on Ripley and return her to the zone of her original nightmare. In effect, she was being placed back into combat on a scale she could never have imagined. In *Alien*, Ripley emerged gradually as the focal character, and by the end of the film was the only one left alive. *Aliens* would place her front and centre from the start, and this new film galvanised the significance of Sigourney Weaver to the developing and long-running *Alien* series.

For Cameron the *Aliens* concept built on an interest that had evidenced itself a year earlier when he had been the screenwriter on *Rambo: First Blood Part 2*. This film had been hugely popular and also widely criticised for its violence. The film reimagined the Vietnam conflict and clearly made America the victor through the personality of John Rambo, an all-powerful one-man arsenal. Vietnam was a significant reference point for Cameron who, in developing *Aliens*, set out to 'do a film that was . . . more intense, and I do like to use the word . . . exhilarating'.

For Cameron, *Aliens* was an opportunity to move the sequel away from the original film's 'monster hiding in the shadows' scenario. It was wise not to compete with the particular tension that Ridley Scott's film had achieved. With *Aliens*, Cameron elected to develop the story as a combat film, and his affinity for military codes and hardware were on full display throughout. In *The Terminator* the future-world battle sequences between man and machine had indicated Cameron's war-movie flair, and *Aliens* would let it be writ large.

The film was conceived on an expansive scale as a unit of Marines are sent in to combat a 'hive' of aliens. In *Aliens*, the enemy have an elusive quality that recalls the way in which the Vietcong were described in the jungles of Vietnam. Cameron's interest in tough, resourceful women under extraordinary pressure would later result in the screenplay for the science-fiction thriller *Strange Days* (Kathryn Bigelow, 1995).

CASTING/RECRUITMENT: Cameron had been asked by the studio to write a screenplay based around Ripley yet, bizarrely, the studio had not been especially keen on recalling Sigourney Weaver for the role. Cameron and his producer Gale Anne Hurd had to insist that she return. For each character, Cameron wrote a background dossier to aid the actors in enriching their performance. In Cameron's notes, Vasquez has been recruited from juvenile prison for the Marines, along with Drake (Mark Rolston). Cameron also encouraged the actors to embellish and personalise their military uniforms and artillery, and the onscreen result is a corps of distinct, quirky, and very endearing 'grunts'. Several Cameron 'veterans' returned to work with him on the film.

Aliens returned Sigourney Weaver to the bio-mechanoid war zone. Since *Alien*, Weaver had established herself as a major and accomplished screen actress with her role in *The Year of Living Dangerously* and then as Dana in *Ghostbusters* (Ivan Reitman, 1984). In the wake of *Aliens*, Weaver went on to a winning streak that included *Working Girl* (Mike Nichols, 1988), *Gorillas in the Mist* (Michael Apted, 1988) and *The Ice Storm* (Ang Lee, 1995).

Michael Biehn had starred in *The Terminator* (1984) and went on to appear in Cameron's *The Abyss* as the nervy and intense Coffey. Initially Biehn had felt that the character of Corporal Hicks in *Aliens* was a little too similar to Reese in *The Terminator*. It transpired that Cameron thought the same, so together they developed character traits for Hicks that would be immediately distinctive. Biehn went on to play screw-loose subaqua saboteur Coffey in *The Abyss*, and has also appeared in *The Lords of Discipline* (Frank Roddam, 1983), *Tombstone* (George Pan Cosmatos, 1993) and *The Rock* (Michael Bay, 1996).

Like any sequel worth its storytelling salt, *Aliens* needed to strike a balance between the new and the familiar, and Cameron's concept featured an android to succeed the creepy Ash portrayed by Ian Holm in the original film. The role of the android Bishop in the sequel was taken on by Lance Henriksen. Henriksen had appeared in *Close Encounters of the Third Kind* and also in *The Terminator*, where he played the police detective Vukovich. As a touchstone for how best to portray a very human robot, Henriksen felt that Rutger Hauer's portrayal of Roy Batty in *Blade Runner* was the high-water mark. Henriksen called it 'a beautiful piece of work' and realised he would have to develop certain characteristics for Bishop that made the character its own.

Aliens marked the second collaboration between Bill Paxton and James Cameron. Paxton had appeared as a punk in *The Terminator* and went on to portray the goofy secret service colleague of Harry Trasker (Arnold Schwarzenegger) in Cameron's *True Lies* (1994), an astronaut in *Apollo 13* (Ron Howard, 1995) and a tornado chaser in *Twister* (Jan De Bont, 1996). Paxton also featured in the modern-day sequences of *Titanic* (James Cameron, 1997) and Cameron's 3D film *Ghosts of the Abyss* (2002). Very early in his career, Paxton had been an art director on several Roger Corman films.

Aliens also featured as Private Vasquez the diminutive and memorable Jeanette Goldstein, who had most of her waist-length hair cut off for the role. She also appears in *Lethal Weapon 2* (Richard Donner, 1989), *Terminator 2: Judgement Day* and *Titanic*.

BACKUP: *Aliens* was one of a number of large-scale fantasy and science-fiction films to have been made in the UK between the mid-1970s and the late 1980s. With *Aliens*, Cameron collaborated to stunning effect with British cinematographer Adrian Biddle to create a smoky, claustrophobic world, redolent of the original film but also more visually elaborate. Biddle went on to work on *The Princess Bride* (Rob Reiner, 1987), *Willow* (Ron Howard, 1988) and *Thelma & Louise* (Ridley Scott, 1991).

Cameron's other key creative compadre on *Aliens* was Stan Winston. Winston had begun his career as an actor but had moved into make-up and then with *The Terminator* (creating the Terminator's endoskeleton) and *Aliens* began his now famous 'creature feature' legacy, creating believable and visceral creature effects. In the early 1980s Winston had provided the facial make-up effects for Andy Kauffman and Bernadette Peters in the hardly seen robotic rom-com *Heartbeeps* (Alan Arkush, 1981), and also crafted the dog-thing beast in *The Thing* (John Carpenter, 1982). With *Aliens*, Winston and his crew were responsible for creating numerous of the fiendish critters, basing their creatures on HR Giger's iconic design for the original film.

The most astonishing alien effect in the sequel was the arachnid-like, regal alien queen. It was designed by James Cameron and sculpted by Stan Winston and makes for a terrifying yet somehow elegant beast for Ripley to ultimately confront. Winston and his studio have gone on to define movie monsters, handling the creation of the baby in the underseen *Starman* (John Carpenter, 1984); the disintegration of Mr Dark in *Something Wicked This Way Comes* (Jack Clayton, 1983); the titular creature in *Predator* (John McTiernan, 1987); Edward Scissorhands in *Edward Scissorhands* (Tim Burton, 1990); The Penguin in *Batman Returns* (Tim Burton, 1992); dinosaurs in *Jurassic Park*, *Jurassic Park: The Lost World* (Steven Spielberg, 1997) and *Jurassic Park III* (Joe Johnston, 2002); the toys in *Small Soldiers* (Joe Dante, 1998); and the dazzling robot and talking teddy bear in Spielberg's genius effort *AI: Artificial Intelligence* (2001).

The optical visual-effects team on *Aliens* was extensive, with both British and American crews making the imaginary so totally believable. Briton Brian Johnson had begun his career as Les Bowie's assistant and then moved into features on Kubrick's *2001: A Space Odyssey* before winning an Oscar for his work on *Star Wars: The Empire Strikes Back*. He supervised the effects for *Dragonslayer* (Matthew Robbins, 1981), *The Neverending Story* and *Legend* (Ridley Scott, 1985), with a powerful and frightening moment when Darkness finally reveals himself and emerges from a mirror. On *Aliens*, Johnson served as post-production visual effects supervisor responsible for the filming of spacecraft and other miniatures. *Aliens* had twice as much miniature work as *Alien* and a number of shots were achieved with rear projection because of the amount of atmospheric effects. Motion-control shots were focused on shots of the ship that carries the troops to the planet, the *Sulaco* (a reference to Joseph Conrad's novel *Nostromo*) in space.

Editor Ray Lovejoy had collaborated with Kubrick on *2001: A Space Odyssey* and *The Shining*. Production design for *Aliens* was handled by Peter Lamont, whose credits include Cameron's films *True Lies* and *Titanic*.

Producer Gale Anne Hurd collaborated with Cameron on *The Terminator* as his producer, did so again on *The Abyss* and finally with *Terminator 2: Judgement Day*. Hurd went on to specialise in producing science fiction and fantasy with films such as the tense and very funny *Tremors* (Ron Underwood, 1990) and the recent adaptation of *The Hulk*.

PRODUCTION/IN THE TRENCHES: *Aliens* was shot through the autumn of 1985 in west London on location at a disused site that had been Acton Power Station, where large and intricate sets were built.

For Vasquez's gun, prop designers connected an anti-aircraft gun to a steadicam rig. The lifter that Ripley dons (rather like a high-tech gladiatorial suit) with which to combat the alien at the end had originally been a concept from a film that Cameron never had the chance to make.

At Pinewood Studios, miniature effects were shot concurrently with the live-action shoot at Acton. Many of the miniature effects were handled by the LA Effects Group. A model was built of a corridor in the processing station. The model was around eighteen inches high, four feet wide and twenty-five feet long, and a miniature Armoured Personnel Carrier was filmed on this set – a one-twelfth scale model of the real vehicle on location at Acton.

MARTIAL MUSIC: For the important score, Cameron brought in another Roger Corman alumnus who had begun to secure his place on major studio films. James Horner had broken into the mainstream with his scores for *Star Trek II: The Wrath of Khan* (Nicholas Meyer, 1982). His credits now include *Cocoon* (Ron Howard, 1985), *An American Tail* (Don Bluth, 1986), *Willow*, **Glory**, *Field of Dreams*, *The Rocketeer* (Joe Johnston, 1991), *Legends of the Fall*, *Apollo 13* and *Troy*.

Horner's score for *Aliens* gave him the chance to create a kinetic and percussive score regarded as a classic among his immense output. Amidst the action cues were a range of more tender and melancholy themes that express the relationship between Ripley and Newt as they fight to survive and as they bond as adoptive mother and daughter to endure the trauma of combat. Horner has had one of the most prominent film-composing careers of the last 25 years.

REIMAGINING REALITY: Though science fiction in its orientation, *Aliens* is also very much a combat film marked by a fidelity to military code and a symbolic connection to the Vietnam War.

Cameron has commented, 'The sense of the dramatic relationships from those 1940s, 1950s war films, which sort of portrayed the common soldier, was more what I was looking for. The dialogue itself, the idiom, is pretty much Vietnam War.'

HEART OF BATTLE: *Aliens* uses its science-fiction format to explore the code of honour that exists between men and women in combat. It also posits a critique of corporate culture in the weaselly character played by Paul Reiser. Amidst the sound and fury of battle, the film's other key thematic issue is the development of Ripley as a mother figure to Newt. For Cameron the key concept underlying the action, horror and tension is that 'In a way almost everyone in this film is a hero . . . It's about being pushed to the limit and finding the resources to act.'

CHARACTER: In *Alien*, Ripley was the lone female in a sweaty, oily macho world of intergalactic truck drivers. By the end of the trauma,

Ripley emerged as the sole survivor, her resourcefulness and courage seeing her through, together with a dose of primal ferocity. With *Aliens*, Ripley returns to the site of her trauma only to find it intensified the second time around, and complicated further by the need for her to protect a young girl. Ripley is a committed woman of integrity who, amidst the battleground of human and alien combat, finds fragile opportunities in which her maternal instincts are foregrounded. Amidst all the destruction she creates a bond with Newt. At the time of the film's release Weaver commented that 'the emotional content of the part is much greater in *Aliens* . . . Ripley's personal situation is so bleak . . . In that group of marines, because she's from another time, she feels like an alien.' Ripley is the only non-soldier in the team that goes up against the aliens.

The Marines are introduced economically when Ripley first meets them and they all emerge as lovable and idiosyncratic. What comes through most powerfully, as in all of the war films discussed in this book at least, is the intensity of their camaraderie. Vasquez and Drake are tight and Apone clearly enjoys commanding his mouthy, cocky troops. Lieutenant Gorman, the newest of the unit, is rendered the least effective once in the field and the true movie heroics are saved up for the character of Hicks. He is a cool, reserved and considerate character. When all the other soldiers are talking, fretting and smart-mouthing on the drop-ship as it rockets towards the planet, Hicks just sleeps.

The most memorable of the Marines, though, is surely Hudson. Way too talkative, easy to worry and also extremely funny, he makes the group of high-tech, super-sharp professional soldiers that bit warmer. Hudson also delivers what is on the surface a funny line as the drop-ship races down to LV426. He describes it as 'an express elevator to hell'. Sure enough, the experience the crew confront is beyond hellish.

The villain of the piece is not the alien but Burke, the corporate lackey who is all too willing to eject his morals into outer space in pursuit of a fast buck.

Newt, the little girl, is first seen as a clean, well-cared-for little girl. In the period following the death of her parents and her discovery by Ripley she has become a feral child in appearance, but she is resourceful and forms the most meaningful relationship in the film as she bonds with Ripley. Newt becomes the daughter that Ripley never knew.

Against the crucible of the bloody and intense showdown with monsters and nightmares, the source of hope for Ripley and Newt is their growing mother–daughter love.

STYLE: James Cameron has often been regarded as a post-Vietnam film director, drawing on images and tropes of that televised war to inform his own stories and connect with audiences with a similar frame of reference. For Cameron the overarching style for *Aliens* was dictated not so much by Ridley Scott's design on *Alien* but rather Cameron's own work on *The Terminator*. The camera movement and compositions owe more to combat films than horror films for much of the time, as we track with the combat team through corridors and shafts. Marked by blue light cut through by beams of torchlight and a roving, drifting steadicam, *Aliens* suitably achieves its need for suspense and anxious energy as the troops enter enemy territory – a futuristic jungle – and go up against their unseen enemy.

The film plays on our familiarity with nervy camerawork from battle-zone TV reports and the capturing of point-of-view video footage by troops as they carry their own cameras attached to their helmets.

Two particular sequences stand out in the use of war-movie style, namely the very first attack and battle with the aliens once the soldiers enter the wrecked township, and secondly when the alien embryos, in their face-hugger form, attack Ripley and Newt. It's the anticipation of seeing the monster at that point that terrifies. The latter sequence, in which the Marines and Ripley realise that the aliens are above them and closing in, is ferocious and again flips the film from suspense into all-out combat. As Ripley helps the injured Hicks along the corridor to escape the enemy they could be in the jungle. Fuelling this war-movie sensibility all the more is the ever-present horror-film sensibility, with the monsters out to get the innocent. One of the best images in the film is when Newt, up to her neck in water, does not see the alien rise up menacingly behind her.

When Ripley enters the lair of the queen alien the image is seared with a heat haze and flame. The world is alight with apocalyptic terror.

CRITICAL CROSSFIRE: For *Time Out*, 'After a slow build-up, Cameron scores a bull's-eye with a sequel which manages to be more thrilling than *Alien* (but less gory) . . . One helluva rollercoaster ride.' *Leonard Maltin's Movie and Video Guide* succinctly comments that this is an 'intense, exciting sequel'.

MEDALS OF HONOUR: *Aliens* was recognised substantially for its superior craft, and in 1987 it won the ASCAP Film and Television Music Awards for James Horner's score. At the Academy Awards in 1987 the film won the Oscar for Best Effects (Sound Editing) and Best Effects (Visual Effects). It was also nominated for Oscars in Best Actress in a Leading Role, Best Art Direction (Set Decoration), Best Film Editing, Best Music and Best Sound. At the Saturn Awards (Academy of Science Fiction, Fantasy and Horror Films) in 1987 Sigourney Weaver won the Saturn Award for Best Actress, James Cameron won for Best Director, Carrie Henn won for Best Performance by a Younger Actor, and the film also won Best Science Fiction Film, Best Special Effects, Best Supporting Actor (Paxton), Best Supporting Actress (Goldstein) and Best Writing. It was also nominated for Saturns in Best Actor (Biehn), Best Costumes and Best Make-up. At the 1987 BAFTAs the film won Best Special Visual Effects and was BAFTA nominated for Best Make-up, Best Production Design and Best Sound. At the 1987 Golden Globes Sigourney Weaver was nominated for Best Actress and at the Hugo Awards the film won Best Dramatic Presentation. In 2004, *Aliens*, along with the other titles in the quartet, was nominated for a Saturn Award for Best DVD Collection.

OTHER BATTLEFRONTS: *Aliens* stands as the second of the quartet of *Alien* films. The most action orientated, it possesses a kinetic fury that established an approach to action over the ensuing years. *Aliens* was Cameron's opportunity to expand on the small-scale hints of battle in the future in *The Terminator*, which he then amplified in the opening sequence of its sequel *Terminator 2: Judgement Day*.

In 1987 Twentieth Century Fox released a very popular earthbound monster combat film called *The Predator*, starring Arnold Schwarzenegger during his glory days as a major action-movie star. The film was if anything an even more direct appropriation of war-film dynamics than *Aliens* was, using a science-fiction monster as the unseen enemy.

In 1997 a far more satirical film than Hollywood might normally permit was released. On the surface a mega-budget action-horror futuristic film, *Starship Troopers* was based on a novel of the same name by Robert A Heinlein, though the film was considered to diverge perhaps too wildly from the source material. Director Paul Verhoeven had made the visceral and vital science-fiction film *RoboCop* and *Total Recall*.

As of this writing, James Cameron has been developing a new war-themed, futuristic feature film entitled *Battle Angel Alita*, based on the manga title of the same name created by Yukito Kishiro in 1991. Given the growing popularity in mainstream pop culture for Japanese and Korean cinema Cameron's idea for an adaptation seems timely. An anime film of the title has already been made. Clearly Cameron is an anime and manga fan given his enthusiasm for the film *Ghost in the Shell* (Mamoru Oshii, 1995). The story's other Japanese title is *Gunm*, which translates from the Japanese characters that denote the words gun and dream.

The *Battle Angel Alita* concept as it exists in the manga format centres on a world called the Scrapyard and tells of the relationship between robot physician Doc Ido and the robot he tends to, Alita. Alita becomes a crime fighter of sorts, eliminating the Scrapyard's criminal activity as she also pieces together her past. With its fusion of combat and a compelling female protagonist, the concept ties in with Cameron's work on *Aliens*. Cameron has also proposed the Alita character being realised as a computer-generated character.

Alongside *Aliens* another 1980s science-fiction combat film that has stood the test of time is *Le Dernier Combat* (Luc Besson, 1983). Besson has gone on to direct *Subway* (1985), *Nikita* (1990), *Leon (1994)*, *The Fifth Element* (1997) and *Joan of Arc* (1999). *Le Dernier Combat* is a post-apocalyptic film in which nobody speaks.

THE HOMEFRONT: *Aliens* is available on DVD in its Special Edition format of 137 minutes. Supplementing the movie are a commentary track and a range of incisive documentaries about the conceptualising of the film and the intense production of the film. The film is also available in a box set of the quartet of *Alien* films.

FINAL BRIEFING: *Aliens* stands alongside *The Abyss* as the high point of James Cameron's work. Kinetic, intelligent and chilling, it succeeds in its mission to be a combat film in space. Released at a time when Vietnam War movies were beginning to experience a resurgence (***Platoon*** was released in 1986), *Aliens* tapped into that same zeitgeist and anxiety around American soldiers fighting in a distant wilderness and being totally uncomfortable with the terrain.

This is an astonishing film that hasn't dated at all and is surely a touchstone for how to create an action-adventure film that is not only big on spectacle but also on primal emotion. Probably one of the best films of the 1980s of any genre or style, *Aliens* is a supercharged fairy tale wrapped up in a war movie.

FINAL SALUTE: '*Aliens* takes clichés – the bonding between them, what happens, what disintegrates, what gets stronger, all that, which creates an emotional crucible out of a combat situation.' James Cameron.

Glory (1989)

122 minutes

Tri-Star
Producer: Freddie Fields
Director: Edward Zwick
Co-Producer: Pieter Jan Brugge
Screenplay: Kevin Jarre (based on the books *Lay This Laurel*
by Lincoln Kerstein, *One Gallant Rush* by Peter Burchard
and the letters of Robert Gould Shaw)
Cinematographer: Freddie Francis
Editor: Steven Rosenblum
Music: James Horner
Production Design: Norman Garwood
Art Direction: Keith Pain and Dan Webster
Costume Design: Francine Jamison-Tanchuck
Visual Effects: Kevin Yagher and Carl Fullerton

CAST: Matthew Broderick (*Colonel Robert Gould Shaw*), Denzel Washington (*Trip*), Cary Elwes (*Cabot Forbes*), Morgan Freeman (*John Rawlins*), Jihmi Kennedy (*Sharts*), Andre Braugher (*Searles*), John Finn (*Sergeant Mulcahy*), Donovan Leitch (*Morse*), John David Cullum (*Russell*), Alan North (*Governor Andrew*)

RATING: R/15

TAGLINE: Their innocence. Their heritage. Their lives. Nothing would be spared in the fight for their freedom.

WAR STORY: The film begins with a title card explaining how young Robert Gould Shaw wrote letters home from the battlefront as he led the 54th Massachusetts regiment against the Confederate army in the American Civil War.

The sun rises over a Union camp. Robert Gould Shaw, in his early twenties, marches along. The Union army are suffering defeats against

the Confederates, and at the battle of Antietam Shaw falls to the ground
wounded and survives the carnage. In a field hospital, Shaw is treated
and then returns home to his affluent family home in Boston. He is
introduced to the great black writer Frederick Douglass and also
Governor Andrew, and is told about a plan to raise a black regiment and
that his name has been put forward to lead it. Shaw accepts and wants
his lifelong friend Cabot Forbes to go with him. Another childhood
friend of Shaw's, the young black man Thomas, is the first to enlist, with
an eagerness and sincerity that will be tested soon after.

Shaw inspects a crowd of freed slaves who have come to sign up for
duty in the newly created 54th. At Readville Camp the black recruits are
trained and disciplined, though racial tensions inevitably arise. The
recruits Trip, Rawlins, Sharts and Shaw's friend Thomas share a tent,
and tensions among the black men are rife with Trip the most
hot-headed and furious of the men.

The black soldiers want to know when they will get their uniforms
and concern grows that they will only ever be used for manual labour.
Shaw informs the black soldiers that if they are caught by Confederate
soldiers they will be killed, as will any white Union soldiers. Shaw offers
the new recruits the chance to discharge themselves from service the next
morning if they so wish. The next morning, not one soldier has elected to
leave.

The recruits are armed with rifles and begin training. There is evident
conflict between Forbes and Shaw, as Forbes believes Shaw is treating
the black soldiers too harshly.

Christmas comes and, as the Union army continues to suffer defeats,
Shaw is increasingly sensing that his soldiers will never actually fight.
Relations between Shaw and his men strain further. Trip is considered a
deserter, though all he was doing was running off to find a decent pair of
boots, and is flogged as an example to the other men. Subsequently,
though, Shaw ensures that all the men have boots. Aware of his difficulty
in communicating with the trainee soldiers, Shaw asks the older recruit
Rawlins to serve as an intermediary between him and the men.

The struggle to unify the 54th continues when Shaw is informed that
his recruits will not be paid the same as white soldiers. Shaw addresses
the regiment en masse about the payment issue, and when the black
soldiers, led by Trip, tear up their pay cheques, Shaw tears up his own in
solidarity with his men.

Finally the blue uniforms arrive for the 54th and the soldiers parade
with pride before making their way south, joined by a reporter from

Harper's Weekly magazine. Shaw's men are then teamed with the Union guerillas under the dubious command of Jayhawker, Colonel Montgomery. When the soldiers arrive at the Confederate town of Darien, Montgomery's soldiers loot the community and then burn it to the ground while Shaw and his soldiers look on in bewilderment. Montgomery tells Shaw that he will be court-martialled if he does not follow orders to burn the town. By now Shaw is convinced the 54th will only be used for manual labour.

Shaw and Forbes go to Montgomery and the other General (Gunton) and 'blackmail' them into commissioning the 54th into military action with the threat of reporting Montgomery's looting. The regiment are finally commissioned to engage in battle.

The scene moves to James Island, South Georgia, 1863. The 54th are involved in a fierce forest skirmish where Thomas saves Trip from death, the Confederates retreat and the pride and confidence of the regiment surges. Thomas is seriously injured but refuses to go home. Shaw and Trip talk alone – Shaw wants to award Trip the regimental colours, an award for exceptional courage in the field of battle.

Fort Wagner is a coastal defence for the Confederates that the 54th are to lead an attack on. The night before battle the men gather to prepare themselves for combat, and they sing and pray together.

The next day Shaw leads his men along the beach and they attack Fort Wagner. The battle is furious and many of the 54th are killed, including Shaw and Trip, and the dead are heaped in a mass grave.

The final image is of a bas-relief sculpture showing Shaw leading the 54th Massachusetts to glory.

CONCEPT/THE MISSION: In the *BFI Companion to the Western* the American Civil War is described as 'the great prism of nineteenth-century American history'. As with any past event it can be reshaped and made newly relevant and compelling for today and tomorrow. *Glory* was to be a film that celebrated a relatively unknown aspect of the American Civil War.

Ed Zwick, the writer–director, had made his name with *thirtysomething* on American television and had directed the contemporary drama *About Last Night* (1986). *Glory* would be the first of several large-canvas films that Zwick would specialise in making. He has directed the romantic and melodramatic western *Legends of the Fall*, the Iraq War-set *Courage Under Fire* (1995), the prescient thriller *The Siege* (1997) and the historical drama *The Last Samurai*.

The American Civil War was not unusual in being a war fuelled by many colliding issues, none more immediate and fundamental to it than the fact that where the northern states were capitalist, industrial and forward looking, the southern states were regarded as rural and against progress, an image (and now a stereotype) which continues today. For the north, the Civil War assumed the quality of a moral battle against the culture of slavery.

The Civil War, then, has always been a rich vein for storytellers either as a backdrop or as something more central to the drama. John Ford's cavalry trilogy had a Civil War backdrop in the films *Fort Apache* (1948), *She Wore A Yellow Ribbon* (1949) and *Rio Grande* (1950). *The Outlaw Josey Wales* (Clint Eastwood, 1976) similarly used the Civil War as a context for its story. *Glory*, though, continues to stand as one of the few major studio releases that has explored an aspect of the Civil War itself. Perhaps the most famous Civil War film of all, with a romance front and centre, is *Gone With The Wind* (Victor Fleming, 1939).

Zwick's filmmaking career began with study at the American Film Institute, where he made an award-winning short called *Timothy and the Angel*. Zwick moved into television, where he directed TV pilots and dramas, his major TV piece being *Special Bulletin*, which was framed as a quasi-documentary about nuclear attack by terrorists.

Zwick went on to direct *About Last Night* but it is the films made since that have all dramatised combat to a greater or lesser degree. His film *Legends of the Fall* includes a sequence set during the First World War and *The Last Samurai* begins its story with a Union soldier being offered the chance to go to Japan and train recruits there. *Courage Under Fire* had as its backdrop the Gulf War and concerned itself with the court case to determine a friendly fire fatality. The film was based on the military experience of Medevac helicopter pilot Karen Walden, who was the first woman to be awarded the Medal of Honor (posthumous), for rescuing a downed chopper crew and then fighting against Iraqis in a standoff during which she was killed. *The Siege* dealt, uncannily and unnervingly, with terrorist attacks on Manhattan.

CASTING/RECRUITMENT: For *Glory*, Zwick cast three young actors, all of whom were beginning to break through and who would go on to enduring careers. Matthew Broderick, who stars as Robert Gould Shaw, had established his movie-star credentials in two films that had been immensely popular with teens in the 1980s: *WarGames* (John Badham, 1983) and *Ferris Bueller's Day Off* (John Hughes, 1986). *Glory* was a chance to subvert that image to some degree but also draw on it. Broderick has also starred in the brilliant *You Can Count On Me* (Kenneth Lonergan, 2000). Morgan Freeman had broken through in middle age in a film called *Street Smart* (Jerry Schatzberg, 1987) and then starred alongside Jessica Tandy in *Driving Miss Daisy*. The warm paternal quality Freeman exudes in *Glory* has continued to define a number of his other performances and Freeman has become one of the major actors of American cinema, more often than not offering a calm maturity amidst often hysterical situations, notably in *Se7en* (David Fincher, 1995) *Amistad* and *Deep Impact* (Mimi Leder, 1998).

Glory was also the breakthrough moment for Denzel Washington. Washington has gone on to star in *Mo Better Blues* (Spike Lee, 1990), *Malcolm X* (Spike Lee, 1992), *Philadelphia* (Jonathan Demme, 1993), *The Pelican Brief* (Alan J Pakula, 1993), the fantastic and little seen *He Got Game* (Spike Lee, 1995) and more recently *Man on Fire* (Tony Scott, 2004).

Cary Elwes had starred in *The Princess Bride* and went on to *Bram Stoker's Dracula* (Francis Ford Coppola, 1992) and more recently *Cradle Will Rock* (Tim Robbins, 1999) and *Saw* (James Wan, 2004).

BACKUP: Freddie Francis, the cinematographer on *Glory*, was a veteran of feature films. His other credits include *Room at the Top* (Jack Clayton, 1959), *Sons and Lovers* (Jack Cardiff, 1960), *The Elephant Man* (David Lynch, 1980) and *The French Lieutenant's Woman*. Francis also directed horror films such as *The Creeping Flesh* (1973) and *Legend of the Werewolf* (1975). The final film that Freddie Francis served as cinematographer on was the beautiful and gentle *The Straight Story* (David Lynch, 1999).

The film's writer Kevin Jarre has also penned *Tombstone* and the screen story for *The Mummy* (Stephen Sommers, 1999).

PRODUCTION/IN THE TRENCHES: *Glory* was filmed largely in Massachusetts at locations such as Beacon Street, Boston, the Appleton Farm and Old Sturbridge village. Savannah, Georgia also served for the sequences in the South that are the setting for the film's final act.

Ed Zwick was brought onto the project by producer Freddie Fields and the film shot through the latter part of 1988 for its release in autumn 1989. Production on the film was overseen for authenticity by Civil War authorities Shelby Foote and Ray Herbeck Jr. In the film's pursuit of authenticity the set dressing for the Shaw family home scenes at the beginning included the use of silver candlesticks that had once been in the Shaw family. Also, *Glory* recruited 1,500 Civil War enthusiasts for the crowd and battle scenes. In turn, these re-enactment specialists trained up other extras in the arts of battle.

MARTIAL MUSIC: The musical score for *Glory* is central to its dramatic impact, complementing much of the drama whether on a large or small scale. It is one of James Horner's finest efforts, with its use of the Harlem Boys' Choir against a rich orchestral backing. By the late 1980s, Horner had made his name and would go on to produce numerous affecting scores for films such as *Legends of the Fall*, *Titanic* (James Cameron, 1997) and *The Perfect Storm* (Wolfgang Petersen, 2000).

The score for *Glory* does not eschew the use of music over the final battle and in the moment preceding it the music is especially effective in further ennobling the characters, rather like the goosebump-inducing moment earlier when Shaw realises that none of his soldiers have chosen to leave the regiment.

REIMAGINING REALITY: *Glory* faithfully chronicles and dramatises the period in the real Robert Gould Shaw's life when, aged 26, he agreed to recruit and organise the 54th Massachusetts regiment. Shaw came from a prestigious abolitionist family in Boston, and as the 54th was the first black cohort to be created it was a genuine source of interest to people, either as novelty or a useful indication of the future. Most of the 54th were free black men from Pennsylvania and Massachusetts. The great American ex-slave and writer Frederick Douglass (author of the vital prose pieces *The Narrative of Frederick Douglass* and *What to the Slave if the Fourth of July?*) saw his two sons Lewis and Charles enlist.

The 54th's most noted battle was its attack on the Confederate coastal stronghold of Fort Wagner, depicted at the end of *Glory*. Shaw was killed in this battle shouting, 'Forward, fifty-fourth!' and 281 of the black soldiers were among the casualties, including 54 dead or terribly wounded and a further 48 unaccounted for. Perhaps unsurprisingly, the valour of the 54th was instrumental in fostering black recruitment to the Union armies. They went on to be the Union's rearguard with the 35th United States Colored Troops, and may well have stopped the Union army from being brought down.

In the film Robert Gould Shaw is shown clothed as he falls into the burial pit, but in truth his body was stripped by the Confederate army. In the final battle the flag bearer for the 54th was killed and the flag was picked up by Sergeant William Carney, who returned to his lines with bullets in his head, chest, right arm and leg. Carney was the first of 23 black soldiers to win the Congressional Medal of Honor, though it was a posthumous honour granted 37 years after the Civil War ended.

Free black men were keen to enlist in the US military when the Civil War began, but they were stopped in their tracks by a 1792 law that barred 'persons of colour from serving in the militia'. For all its abolitionist tendencies, though, the Northern states considered that black people might not be intellectually capable for warfare. Unsurprisingly, then, most of the black soldiers who enlisted found themselves not in combat but instead driving wagons, laying railroads and burying those killed in battle. However, when the Union began experiencing defeat, white men were less prepared to enlist and suddenly there were numbers that needed filling. On 17 July 1862, Congress passed the Confiscation Act, stating that all slaves of southern masters were free the moment they crossed into Union territory. President Lincoln also ensured that he was able to recruit as many black Americans as he felt necessary to the Union forces and the 1792 law was repealed. The inclusion and integration of black men into the Union army was opposed by many, including Union General William Tecumseh Sherman. General Ulysses S Grant, though, who was to become President in 1869, was very much in favour. Abraham Lincoln refuted any opposition to black soldiers and wrote of those white Americans 'with malignant heart and deceitful speech' who 'strove to hinder it'.

Frederick Douglass had written *The Narrative of Frederick Douglass, American Slave* and in the years after securing his freedom he committed himself to the abolotionist cause. The American Civil War began at 4.30 a.m. on 12 April 1861 when the Confederate General Beauregard opened fire on Fort Sumter. The only casualty that day was a horse, but the Civil War saw the mass slaughter of so many Americans. The most celebrated modern-era historian of the Civil War, the late Shelby Foote, wrote: 'The Civil War defined us as what we are and it opened us to being what we became, good and bad things. And it is very necessary, if you're going to understand the American character in the twentieth century.' The Civil War was also known as the War Between the States, the War Against Northern Aggression, the Second American Revolution, the Lost Cause, the War of the Rebellion, the Brothers' War and the Late Unpleasantness. The great American poet, Walt Whitman, called it the War of Attempted Secession.

Whitman stands as one of America's great poets, even though in his day he was not widely celebrated. Whitman's poetry selection

Drum-Taps gives expression to the loss that war constitutes. He worked as a clerk in Washington during the war and was also a volunteer hospital visitor and wound dresser. He wrote powerfully of the war that 'Future years will never know the seething hell and the black infernal background, the countless minor scenes and interiors of the secessionist war and it is best they should not. The real war will never get in the books.' Suffice to say alongside the several hundred films that have been made about the Civil War, this number is dwarfed by the roughly fifty thousand books that have been published on the subject.

The Jayhawkers referred to in the film were guerilla soldiers of the free states who opposed the pro-slavery 'border ruffians' during the fight over Kansas in the years that ran up to the American Civil War. During the Civil War, Jayhawkers was the name given to the 7th Kansas Cavalry led by Colonel Charles R Jennison

Glory acknowledges the American Civil War as perhaps the first media war. Towards the end of the film, as the soldiers move towards Fort Wagner, a wide shot includes painters and reporters observing the imminent final battle. During the war reporters from the *London Illustrated News*, the *New York Illustrated News*, *Leslie's Weekly* and *Harper's Weekly* all reported on the war, and whilst wet-plate cameras were too slow to capture battle scenes, countless artists painted and sketched scenes, including two British brothers William and Alfred Waud. The great American painter Winslow Homer also offered up 'reportage' images. In later life Homer would paint a number of celebrated pictures including *The Veteran in a New Field* (1865), which even made the cover of the album *Southern Accents* by Tom Petty and the Heartbreakers (1985). That particular painting alludes specifically to the American Civil War, being painted in the year it finished.

HEART OF BATTLE: *Glory* concerns itself not only with the racial intolerance and tension around the creation of a black regiment but also with the developing bonds of interracial honour. The film attempts to honour the communal, religiously informed spirit of the ex-slaves, never more clearly than in the spirituals they sing the night before their final and fateful battle.

Like *Saving Private Ryan*, *Glory* references the writings of the American transcendentalist Ralph Waldo Emerson.

The film also alludes to corruption within the higher echelons of military command in a way that recalls *Paths of Glory* and *Casualties of War*.

CHARACTER: The drama of *Glory* and the historical and social
dynamic at play are represented and filtered through young Robert
Gould Shaw's witnessing of war and in his letters home. In this respect
Shaw, as a film character, is consistent with an observation made by
twentieth-century American poet and novelist Robert Penn Warren, who
wrote that in the Civil War '. . . all the self-divisions of conflict within
individuals become a series of mirrors in which the plight of the country
is reflected'. As with so many other war films the story also charts the
growth of young men in the crucible of combat. Shaw matures and Trip
comes to a calmer sense of self and the world around him. Shaw is
initially an idealist who writes home that 'this time we must make it a
whole country'. He also struggles to understand the men he commands.

The character of Thomas is compelling, as he is the most impassioned
and least effective soldier in the unit, a literary, scholastic man who finds
army life tough on his more delicate soul. Finally, though, he is able to
rise to the need of combat just as Upham does in *Saving Private Ryan*.

Rawlins emerges as the father figure of the black soldiers, calm and
wise at all times, countering the abrasive, hot-headed Trip who alerts his
fellow soldiers to the economic value of having black soldiers serve when
he says 'Uncle Abe got himself a real bargain here!'

Forbes, a more dashing and apparently confident soldier than Shaw,
goes from being unsure of his military efficiency to being someone with
responsibilities and authority. His story echoes the narrative line of so
many war films that take a young protagonist to a point of maturity.

Glory transforms the 54th Massachusetts regiment into a universal
symbol of an evolving spirit of community and commitment to an idea.
Where *Glory* excels is not only in its 'human' drama but in its effort within
the great limitation of a two-hour running time to acknowledge certain
tensions and social resonances around the creation of a black army unit.

STYLE: *Glory* is a small-scale epic; that is to say, it focuses on character
relationships and interweaves a number of larger-scale battle scenes in
order to galvanise the comradeship. Zwick's film does not shun the
visceral – a soldier's head explodes in silhouette in the first few moments
of battle at Antietam.

Amidst the occasional moments of grandstanding, *Glory* downplays
what could easily have been the more obvious expression and uses the
close-up as the most emotionally direct expression, for instance in the
moment when Trip is flogged, and the look he exchanges with Shaw as a
tear rolls down his face as he fights not to scream out.

One of the most telling images, though, is a refrained close-up on the face of impassioned black soldier Thomas. Wearing glasses at all times, on several occasions we see the reflection of a campfire in the lenses. Thus there really is fire in Thomas's eyes, and this throwaway detail packs a quiet punch.

CRITICAL CROSSFIRE: Well received all around, *Time Out* wrote: 'It's an ambitious and purposeful film, but complexities have been pared down.' *Leonard Maltin's Movie and Video Guide* says the film is 'exceptional . . . Grand, moving, breathtakingly filmed . . .'

MEDALS OF HONOUR: *Glory* won the 1990 Oscars for Best Supporting Actor, Best Sound and Best Cinematography. It also received Oscar nominations for Best Art Direction and Editing. At the Grammy awards in 1991 the film's composer James Horner won for his stunning score.

OTHER BATTLEFRONTS: In 1951 John Huston (who also directed a trilogy of highly accomplished documentaries about aspects of American World War Two experience) directed an adaptation of Stephen Crane's classic American Civil War novel *The Red Badge of Courage* starring Audie Murphy. In 1997 Steven Spielberg directed *Amistad* about a slave court case that predated the Civil War. Then, too, there is the epic-length feature *Gettysburg*.

In 2003 the Charles Frazier novel *Cold Mountain* was adapted into a well-regarded feature film directed by Anthony Minghella and starring Jude Law, Nicole Kidman and Renee Zellwegger. In one sense a retelling of Homer's *The Odyssey*, to some degree the film used the Civil War as the context in which a love story unfolds.

Other notable Civil War films are *Shenandoah* (Andrew McLaglen, 1965), *Gods and Generals* (Ronald F Maxwell, 2003), *Andersonville* (John Frankenheimer, 1966), *The Beguiled* (Don Siegel, 1971), *North and South* (Richard T Heffron, 1985), and *Ride with the Devil* (Ang Lee, 1999).

Whilst not 'fiction' (though perhaps the distinction between factual and fictional film is far less clear than we sometimes lazily allow), in 1990 a phenomenal documentary film was made simply entitled *The Civil War*. Directed by Ken Burns, who has gone on to become the Homer of America with his other documentary films, the series was expansive and melancholy. The core of the film is guided by a sense of the importance of a sense of home in our lives, both literally and figuratively. The series frames much of its visual material around accounts, letters and diary entries being read out by a number of notable American voices.

In its inclusion of the character of Frederick Douglass, *Glory* acknowledges a wide-ranging literary world of discourse about the war and the issue of slavery. *Glory* is one more title in the vast expanse of stories and responses to the American Civil War. As well as the previously mentioned *Drum-Taps*, Walt Whitman wrote a prose piece *Memoranda During the War* (1875) and also the elegy for Lincoln entitled 'When Lilacs Last at the Dooryard Bloom'd'.

THE HOMEFRONT: *Glory* is available as a Special Edition DVD, which contains a number of featurettes and a director's commentary.

FINAL BRIEFING: *Glory* is one of the most notable of historical dramas at a time when so many have been produced. The film confidently combines characterisation with the expected fidelity to recreating moments of historic combat.

FINAL SALUTE: 'There is great dialogue in movies, but the things one takes away from movies are a set of images, a set of juxtapositions . . . beyond the story itself.' – Ed Zwick

Land and Freedom (1995)

109 minutes

BBC Films and Canal Plus
Executive Producer: Sally Hibbin, Marta Estaban, Ulrich Fesberg, Gerardo Herrero
Producer: Rebecca O'Brien
Director: Ken Loach
Screenplay: Jim Allen
Cinematographer: Barry Ackroyd
Editor: Jonathan Morris
Music: George Fenton
Production Design: Martin Johnson

CAST: Ian Hart (*David Carr*), Rosanna Pastor (*Blanca*), Iciar Bollain (*Maite*), Tom Gilroy (*Lawrence*), Marc Martinez (*Juan Vidal*), Frederic

Pierrot (*Bernard Goujon*), Eoin McCarthy (*Connor*), Suzanne Maddock (*Kim, David's granddaughter*)

RATING: 12

WAR STORY: In mid-1990s Liverpool an old man (David Carr) is taken to hospital. His granddaughter remains at his home and begins reading through his old newspaper cuttings and photos. She discovers that her grandfather had fought in the Spanish Civil War. Throughout the film we will return to this young woman reading his letters home, providing detail and information about the context.

The film goes back to a young David Carr at a Communist Party meeting in Liverpool in the 1930s where a Spanish communist is recruiting British allies. David signs up and tells his girlfriend Kit that he is going to fight the fascists in Spain.

David rides across Spain on a train to the Aragon Front, befriending several other fighters as he travels. Arriving, David is put into training with POUM, the Workers' Party militia, and soon after David finds himself with one of the POUM units in the Spanish countryside, and we see them engaging in a skirmish. David begins talking to Blanca, but she is not easy to talk to, as she is with a man called Coogan. The unit receive their mail and one of the soldiers runs off, wanting to go home to sort out his marriage. He is encouraged to stay with the fight rather than give up the political for the personal.

The unit attack a village being held by the Fascists and are successful, though Coogan is killed. The POUM militia take over a large house and a furious debate ensues amongst the fighters about whether or not to collectivise. The decision is made to collectivise though not everyone agrees and tensions rise. The unit march across the terrain to another camp and, realising that they need more arms and support, they begin to train up some peasant boys. Lawrence, the American fighter, is angry and leaves the POUM, considering it ineffective. David, meanwhile, has been wounded by a faulty rifle, so Blanca ensures that David gets to Barcelona to be treated for his injury. She gives him the name of a boarding house she knows, and David leaves the POUM.

In Barcelona David is treated and goes to the boarding house, where he meets Blanca. They are getting close, but an argument breaks out when she realises that David has left the militia and joined the professional army, the International Brigade. She calls him a traitor and leaves him to return to the Aragon Front. In a café, David gets into a fight and then tears up his Communist Party card. He returns to POUM and reunites with his old comrades and with Blanca, and they fight another battle against the Fascists.

Several truckloads of soldiers turn up, Lawrence being one of them, and say that the POUM is an illegal militia and is to be disbanded. When the militia refuse to be arrested Blanca is shot, and David goes with her dead body to her village, where she is buried.

Back in present-day Liverpool, David is buried and his granddaughter scatters the Spanish earth that he had always kept onto his coffin.

CONCEPT/THE MISSION: Ken Loach has marked himself out as perhaps the most important British filmmaker, and certainly the most politically engaged, of the last 35 years, directing numerous feature films that are dramatically compelling and take a committed stance to advocate the lives and aspirations of the marginalised. Loach's left-wing politics have occasionally caused him to fight battles to save his career, but he endures. *Land and Freedom* was his first period film, set as it is during 1936 and the Spanish Civil War. Loach had made his name with British social realist films for television such as *Cathy Come Home* (1966) and *Up the Junction* (1965) and then, perhaps most famously, the lyrical and melancholy *Kes* (1969), based on Barry Hines's novel *A Kestrel For A Knave*. *Land and Freedom* allowed Loach to engage directly with a particular historical moment of combat with the fictional account of a young man who is a member of the British Communist Party who goes to Spain to fight for the Second Republic.

Loach developed the *Land and Freedom* screenplay with writer Jim Allen in the early 1990s in the wake of the collapse of communism in Eastern Europe. Loach and Allen had many political affiliations to delineate in the narrative, but made the political personal and, in doing so, highly accessible to a mainstream audience. More than a dozen drafts of the screenplay were written in an effort to focus the large social and political canvas of the film. At one point, rather in the style of *Reds*, the film would have intercut between the recreation of the film drama and interviews with people still alive who had fought in the Spanish Civil War against the fascists and General Franco.

One of Loach's key sources of inspiration was George Orwell's *Homage to Catalonia* and also Felix Morrow's *Revolution and Counter-Revolution in Spain*. For an age in which cinema is not regarded as being able to contain any genuine political dialogue, *Land and Freedom* is a brave and successful project.

For some the film was regarded as placing too much emphasis on what is considered an incidental moment in the conflict, namely the crushing of the POUM. Surely, though, no event is ultimately minor in the fabric of a civil war. Loach's approach was regarded as being too narrow and he certainly took understandable dramatic licence by having English-speaking POUM militia.

CASTING/RECRUITMENT: Starring in *Land and Freedom* was one of the upcoming British actors, Ian Hart, who had starred in *Backbeat* (Iain Softley, 1994), and went on to star in *Hollow Reed* (Angela Pope, 1996), *Wonderland* (Michael Winterbottom, 1999), *The End of the Affair* (Neil Jordan, 1999) and *Liam* (Stephen Frears, 2001). He also went on to feature in *Harry Potter and the Philosopher's Stone* (Chris Columbus, 2001).

BACKUP: Loach's screenwriter Jim Allen has also written Loach's *Hidden Agenda* (1990) and *Raining Stones* (1993). Barry Ackroyd, the cinematographer for the film, has collaborated with Ken Loach on *Ladybird, Ladybird* (1994), *My Name is Joe* (1998), *The Navigators* (2001), *Sweet Sixteen* (2002) and *Ae Fond Kiss* (2004).

PRODUCTION/IN THE TRENCHES: Logistically, *Land and Freedom* represented Loach's largest-scale film to date. The film was shot on location in Spain in the Aragon region and also in Liverpool for the sequences that book-end the film.

MARTIAL MUSIC: British composer George Fenton composed the orchestral score for the film. His music functions as a support for the action and offers both a sense of optimism and energy and also a softness for the scenes where the developing relationship between David and Blanca is shown. Most affectingly, he couches the music in a specifically Spanish tone. Fenton is a major figure in modern British film music, having also composed scores for *Gandhi*, *The Company of Wolves* (Neil Jordan, 1984), *Dangerous Liaisons* (Stephen Frears, 1988), *Shadowlands* and *My Name is Joe*.

REIMAGINING REALITY: Spain in the nineteenth and twentieth centuries experienced repressive governments and in 1936 an intense and bloody civil war erupted. The war was led by an army officer named General Francisco Franco. Despite the challenge to his right-wing government he won out and remained in power as dictator until his death in 1975. The Spanish Civil War lasted from 1936–39 and ultimately saw the victory of fascism over communism, with the fascist propaganda claiming they were liberating Spain.

George Orwell's novel *Homage to Catalonia* condemned the communists' destruction of anarchist militia forces (such as the POUM in the film). There had been a long relationship between Russia and Spain and in the early 1930s, through the organisation Friends of the Soviet Union, the Russian ideal was promulgated across Spain. Moscow even used the Spanish Civil War as material for Russia's own domestic and international propaganda and in late 1936, for a short period, Russia intervened militarily in the Civil War.

In Catalonia and Barcelona especially the CNT (Anarcho Syndicalist) fought against the fascists and there was a general strike. The republican government would not allow arms to get to the militia forces, which led Orwell, who served in the POUM militia, to say the government was more afraid of revolution than the fascists were. The POUM were anti-Stalinist communists.

One of the most significant aspects of the Civil War, and a feature that *Land and Freedom* (by its very title) explores and acknowledges, is that the war was very much supported by the rural poor as peasants seized the land. The peasants collectivised the land (pooled their resources) and the debate midway through *Land and Freedom* deals with this issue. There were five to seven million peasants involved in the revolution and the Aragon region, where *Land and Freedom* is set, was the most successful area for collectivism.

One of the outcomes of this movement was that the uneducated poor saw education for their children for the first time. What compromised the courage and commitment of the militia forces was a lack of arms. Moscow sold arms to the militia but they never reached them.

As a feature film *Land and Freedom* can only offer indications of the political complexities that surround any war, but the film begins by offering us onscreen title cards that give some context. The film was especially popular in Spain, but did not really find much favour in Britain.

On October 19th 2005 David Ronald Marshall died. Who was he? David Ronald Marshall arrived in Barcelona on September 4th 1936. He was one of the first British volunteers who made the journey to fight in the Spanish Civil War. After returning to Britain from the war, Marshall wrote poetry, his most enduring piece was entitled 'Retrospect'. It gave a poetic voice to the ongoing fight against Fascism.

HEART OF BATTLE: *Land and Freedom* wears its political affiliation boldly and clearly. The film does indeed dramatise the sense of brotherhood and sisterhood in combat but it also takes its time to linger on the politics of the situation and the intricacies of political tension and interest. Perhaps the most important battle in the film is one of ideas and not of bodies. The midpoint of the film focuses on a heated meeting of the POUM militia after taking a fascist-held village, during which they discuss whether to collectivise or not. The meeting begins to hint at ideological tensions that will ultimately be shown to lead to the militia's end. Ultimately, though, the film celebrates the POUM and the anti-fascist movement. The earth and the community that can be built on it are what the film celebrates.

Holding on to integrity in the midst of political affiliations and personal relationships is shown as a battle in itself, but David is victorious and is warmly received when he returns to the POUM having doubted their efficacy and walked away from them for a short period. The film is a war film that is a rallying cry for the revolutionary spirit, and by framing the story with David's granddaughter reading his letters the sense is that the spirit of revolution must stay alive in the young. As David's voice-over at the end of the film says, 'Revolutions are contagious.'

Land and Freedom shares with other Loach films, very powerfully it must be said, what has been described as 'the pleasures and tensions of living as part of an oppressed or underprivileged community'.

CHARACTER: In his landmark book about the films of Ken Loach, Jacob Leigh writes about *Land and Freedom*: 'Each character represents part of a larger whole, and the film uses David's interaction with Lawrence and Blanca to show his moral growth in Spain.'

David starts the film as an eager, enthused young man with a self-acknowledged romanticism about going to fight in the war. 'Maybe I'll see some action,' Dave writes home to his girlfriend Kit as he crosses Spain. Late in the film, David says to Blanca that when he joined the International Brigade he 'saw a lot of things with my own eyes. Things I didn't want to see.'

STYLE: Ken Loach's cinema has always been marked by its quiet naturalism. For him, style is something that should not be apparent and yet, inevitably, every film he makes is presented in a certain way. Most notable is Loach's understated approach to the filming of the battle sequences, all of which are shot with a documentary-like, slightly distanced quality. Yet they still draw us into the emotional dynamic of combat through well-placed close-ups (shot with long lenses) of the protagonists. The action sequences are not supercharged and kinetic in the way that so many war films present them, as adventures, even as games to some degree. There is a plain, unfussy style to Loach's war film and it is one that is enriched all the more by the structural decision to weave into the story accessible discussions about what is at stake in the war. The film's visual palette is naturalistic, with no particularly arresting visual designs. We are simply there in the trenches or behind the sandbags. There is a delicacy to the images, and sound is used in a very realistic way also. There is not really a hyper-reality to the storytelling, and as such it is all the more immediate and affecting.

CRITICAL CROSSFIRE: *Time Out* wrote that the film was 'complex', containing 'muscular performances' and that it 'packs an emotional punch'. *Leonard Maltin's Movie and Video Guide* commented that the film was a 'perceptive, passionate account of the Spanish Civil War' but 'a bit too moralistic at times'.

MEDALS OF HONOUR: *Land and Freedom* won the FRIPESCI Award at the 1995 Cannes Film Festival, and also the Festival's Ecumenical Jury Prize. In France at the 1996 Cesar Awards the film won for Best Foreign Film. At the 1996 BAFTA awards the film was nominated for the Alexander Korda Award for Best British Film.

OTHER BATTLEFRONTS: There is a thoughtfulness to *Land and Freedom* that is not always to be found in war films, and a willingness not only to focus on sustained combat. Stone's ***Born on the Fourth of July*** has the same commitment to a sense of social responsibility and Terrence Malick's ***The Thin Red Line*** is equally contemplative, though more in spiritual terms than social matters. Specific to the Spanish Civil War there is the Hollywood adaptation of Ernest Hemingway's *For Whom The Bell Tolls* (Sam Wood, 1943) and Attenborough's *In Love and War* (1996).

In the 1930s nations became increasingly aware of the impending threat of fascism and efforts were made in many countries to make films that reflect this and so help to counter fascism. In 1937 in America John dos Passos, Ernest Hemingway, Archibald MacLeish and Lillian Hellman backed a film about the Spanish Civil War. The film was called *Spanish Earth* (Joris Ivens, 1937) and was a documentary that made associations and connections between the government and the need to improve Spanish agriculture, with these elements in stark contrast to the bombing being deployed by Franco's forces.

Other Spanish Civil War documentaries were made by Herbert Kline and were entitled *Heart of Spain* (1937) and *Return to Life* (1937), which was a collaboration with photographer Henri Cartier Bresson. In Britain in 1938 Thorold Dickinson and Sidney Cole directed *Spanish ABC*, a documentary about the admirable effort of the Spanish republican government's commitment to education during the Civil War.

THE HOMEFRONT: *Land and Freedom* is available on VHS home video and DVD.

FINAL BRIEFING: *Land and Freedom* is a stunning war film that makes great efforts to take its time and give some sense of the political and ideological context for the Spanish Civil War and the issues that were at stake. Not many war films stop the fighting and plunge the audience into a battleground of ideas. The film is certainly on the side of the people, which is no surprise with Ken Loach. *Land and Freedom* holds its elements artfully in balance, moving between the story of David's developing sense of the complexities of the war, his burgeoning romance with Blanca and the fury of combat. What is striking about the film is how the battle sequences do not carry the hysteria of so many war-film battles but are affecting, and the emotional, immediate response to conflict is shown. Whereas so many war films feel very much like action-adventure films that do not make enough effort to pause and offer the audience some consideration of context, *Land and Freedom* satisfies on all fronts, its final image a call to people to remain revolutionary, either internationally or, to paraphrase singer–songwriter Steve Earle, in their 'own backyards and their own home towns'.

FINAL SALUTE: 'This was an extraordinary film on which to work.' – Ken Loach

Welcome to Sarajevo (1996)

103 minutes

FilmFour
Producer: Graham Broadbent and Damian Jones
Director: Michael Winterbottom

Screenplay: Frank Cottrell Boyce
Cinematographer: Daf Hobson
Editor: Trevor Waite
Music: Adrian Johnston
Production Design: Mark Geraghty
Art Direction: David Minty
Costume Design: Janty Yates

CAST: Stephen Dillane (*Michael Henderson*), Woody Harrelson (*Flynn*), Marisa Tomei (*Nina*), Emira Nusevic (*Emira*), Kerry Fox (*Jane Carson*), Goran Vinjic (*Risto Bavic*), James Nesbitt (*Gregg*), Emily Lloyd (*Annie McGee*), Igor Dzambazov (*Jacket*), Gordana Gadzic (*Mrs Savic*), Juliet Aubrey (*Helen Henderson*), Drazen Sivak (*Zeljko*)

RATING: 15

TAGLINE: To get the story they'll risk everything.

WAR STORY: Archive footage of Sarajevo draws us into the war zone. In the town of Vukovar the Serbians have taken control and the refugees from the city head for Bosnia. A family prepare for a wedding, but en route to the church the mother of the bride is shot dead in the street. One of the journalists, the American Flynn, carries the dead woman into a building with help from the priest. Filming the event are British news reporter Michael Henderson and his cameraman Gregg.

Back at their news-broadcaster base in Sarajevo, where reporters from around the world are based, Michael and Gregg edit their story.

Out on the streets a young Bosnian man named Risto runs through the streets and trenches with bottles of water and returns to the bombed-out building that he and his people are hiding out in. Risto gets help from his friends to dress smartly for an interview – he is hoping to work as a driver for the ITN news crew that Michael, Gregg and Jane, their producer, are part of. Risto arrives for the interview only to immediately drive the crew to the site of a mortar attack, and sure enough he gets the job. Soon after they head out to cover another story, where the street is filled with dead and injured people.

At the local hospital Michael is approached by a little girl, who tells him that her parents are dead. Michael is at a loss it seems, increasingly changed by the war zone, and he argues more with Jane about what news they should be reporting. Risto, Gregg and Michael visit an orphanage where many children are buried, each with a makeshift gravestone. Back at base Michael tries to convince Jane to cover the news story about the orphanage, and he returns to the orphanage once again.

Risto and Jane spend some time with Risto's friends at his flat. At night the crew return to the orphanage and Michael chats with Flynn back at the base.

Michael is incensed when a plane leaves Sarajevo without taking any children to safety. He and the crew visit a prisoner-of-war camp, filled with emaciated men. Michael becomes ever more caring about the plight of the orphans and Flynn tells Michael that he is not responsible for them. He is then introduced to an aid worker named Nina who is looking to maybe get news coverage about her work.

Michael goes to the orphanage with Nina, where they are preparing to take the youngest children out of Sarajevo. He has bonded with a little girl named Emira and asks if she could go to him in England, but Nina is not sure, so he asks Emira directly and she says yes. Michael is advised to keep his plan quiet, as it is illegal to take children out of the country. Michael files another report, this time about some of the children getting out.

A bus takes the children across Yugoslavia towards Italy, and Michael, Gregg and Nina are all on board. They stop overnight and the next morning Michael wanders through a ravaged, bloody village. On a country road the bus is stopped by Serbian soldiers, who take some of the children. There is nothing anyone can do to stop them, and the bus continues on to Split. The children board the ferry with Nina, but Emira stays in Split with Michael, who calls home and explains to his shocked wife that he is bringing Emira with him.

Back in England, Emira is beginning her new life when Michael is called by Jane, who explains that Michael must return to Sarajevo. Emira's mother wants her daughter back.

Michael returns to Sarajevo and reunites with Risto, who takes Michael to try to find Emira's mother, but they are unsuccessful. Risto is then killed. A piece of good fortune strikes when an old acquaintance of Michael's, a young man named Jelko who worked in the hotel where the news crew lived and worked, offers to help Michael find Emira's mother. When Michael meets the woman he plays her a videotape of Emira in London, and then she speaks to Emira on the phone. Emira does not want to return to Sarajevo and her mother accepts this.

Michael follows a crowd on the street to a concert being given by a cellist, who plays a mournful piece on high ground overlooking Sarajevo. The cellist has sadness and defiance in his eyes.

CONCEPT/THE MISSION: In the mid-1990s British director Michael Winterbottom emerged as one of Britain's most accomplished filmmakers, able to work across a range of genres and hence of styles. He was at once both socially committed in a way that recalled Ken Loach and Mike Leigh, and also had a dynamic visual sensibility. A particular quirk of the filming, and a sobering one, is that each location had to be checked for landmines. Winterbottom's concept was that 'I wanted audiences to make up their own minds about how to react and respond honestly to the characters and the stories in the film.' In part the film was intended to compel the West to engage with a war that many considered it had walked away from. The screenplay was based on true stories from the siege. One of the key stories was inspired by British correspondent Michael Nicholson, who smuggled a child out of Bosnia and adopted her. Nicholson covered this experience in his book *Natasha's Story*.

Graham Broadbent and Damian Jones, the producers, sent Winterbottom a copy of Nicholson's book. At this stage, Winterbottom had made an impact with his film *Jude*, an adaptation of Thomas Hardy's *Jude the Obscure*.

Of Nicholson's reaction to the war, Winterbottom commented, 'The balance between what he could do personally as an individual and what he could achieve as a journalist is extremely interesting.'

In creating the screenplay, with Sarajevo too dangerous to enter, Cottrell Boyce researched by talking to journalists and refugees. Available online was video footage that had not been broadcast. For Boyce, 'As I . . . thought about the story, the city seemed to me to be the main character . . . The people of Sarajevo resisted the siege by trying to carry on as normal, shopping and socialising with style and grace in the teeth of this monstrous inhumanity.'

CASTING/RECRUITMENT: Winterbottom was keen to combine well-known actors with unknowns in an attempt to reflect the Sarajevo scenario where some very prominent journalists were working side by side with less familiar ones.

Of actor Stephen Dillane, Winterbottom commented in the production notes for the film, 'We wanted someone who has the kind of intellectual strength to be believable as a journalist and also that kind of neutrality and seriousness which Stephen has.'

Many of the Sarajevan characters and roles were cast with people from Sarajevo and the surrounding region. For the production it was important to cast a Sarajevan child as Emira, and more than 3,000 children from the city auditioned for the role. The young girl who was cast was also called Emira and she was five when the war began, living in the All Pasinopolje area of the much-bombed city.

Stephen Dillane has also appeared in *Spy Game* (Tony Scott, 2001), *The Hours* (Stephen Daldry, 2002) and *King Arthur* (Antoine Fuqua, 2004).

James Nesbitt has gone on to a major television career in Britain starring in *Cold Feet* and *Murphy's Law*. He has also appeared in the feature films *Hear My Song* (Peter Chelsom, 1991), *Jude, Bloody Sunday* (Paul Greengrass, 2002) and *Millions* (Danny Boyle, 2005).

Emily Lloyd, as the freelance journalist, made her name in the film *Wish You Were Here* (David Leland, 1987) and has also appeared in *Cookie* (Susan Seidelman, 1989), *In Country* (Norman Jewison, 1989) and *A River Runs Through It* (Robert Redford, 1992).

Woody Harrelson began his career in the American sitcom *Cheers*, alongside Ted Danson (who appears in *Saving Private Ryan*). Harrelson has also starred in *Doc Hollywood* (Michael Caton-Jones, 1991), *White Men Can't Jump* (Ron Shelton, 1992), *Natural Born Killers* (Oliver Stone, 1994), *Sunchaser* (Michael Cimino, 1996), *The Hi Lo Country* (Stephen Frears, 1998) and *The People Versus Larry Flynt* (Milos Forman, 1997).

Marisa Tomei featured in *My Cousin Vinny* (Jonathan Lynn, 1992) for which she won an Oscar. She has also appeared in *Chaplin, Untamed Heart* (Tony Bill, 1993), *The Paper* (Ron Howard, 1994) and *In The Bedroom* (Todd Field, 2001).

Goran Visnjic is very well known via his weekly TV appearance as Luka Kovac in the still strong *ER*. He has also appeared in *The Peacemaker*.

Kerry Fox starred alongside Ewan McGregor and Christopher Ecclestone in *Shallow Grave* (Danny Boyle, 1994) and *Intimacy* (Patrice Chereau, 2001).

BACKUP: The screenplay for *Welcome to Sarajevo* was written by Frank Cottrell Boyce, who has also scripted the films *Hilary and Jackie* (Anand Tucker, 1998), *The Claim* (Michael Winterbottom, 2000), *24-Hour Party People* (Michael Winterbottom, 2002), *Revengers Tragedy* (Alex Cox, 2002), *Code 46* (Michael Winterbottom, 2003) and *Millions*.

In addition to those films above scripted by Boyce, Michael Winterbottom has also directed *Jude, Wonderland* and *Nine Songs* (2005).

Editor Trevor Waite has worked on the Michael Winterbottom films *Wonderland, The Claim* and *24-Hour Party People*.

PRODUCTION/IN THE TRENCHES: Channel Four Films and Miramax financed the film, and it was shot in Sarajevo in the summer of 1996. It was the first summer after the conflict and the city was marked by its apocalyptic landscape. Location filming lent the project immediacy and authenticity that recalls *Rome, Open City* (Roberto Rossellini, 1945). Given the sensitive aspect of 're-creating' a very recent combat zone, the production found that the Sarajevans were willing to participate in the traumatic scenes.

MARTIAL MUSIC: In pursuit of creating an atmosphere of unease, Winterbottom chose to run pop music over some of the intense images in pursuit of a sense of life carrying on amidst the trauma and destruction.

Throughout the film pop music plays, never more powerfully than when the Rolling Stones' fantastic 1981 song 'Waiting on a Friend' plays over the image of the dead Risto in his flat and on over the image of him being buried by his friends and allies.

The film's final sequence is based almost entirely around the effect of music as one of Risto's friends plays his cello on a hilltop. As with the end of *Paths of Glory*, music absolves a war zone of pain, if only momentarily, and acts as an emotional release.

Adrian Johnston, who composed the original music, also scored Winterbottom's film *Jude*.

REIMAGINING REALITY: Sarajevo was a multicultural, cosmopolitan city, where different faiths and cultures lived side by side. Bosnian Muslims in the city wanted Bosnians in Sarajevo and Bosnian Serbs wanted to stay in Yugolsavia. However, major problems developed that resisted and countered this mix of cultures. The Bosnian Serbs encircled Sarajevo and began firing at the Muslims and the siege of Sarajevo had begun. Initially the Muslims held the city even though they were the weaker force. The chilling Serb order was given: 'Bomb them until they're on the edge of madness.' On the walls of war-torn Sarajevo were the words 'Welcome to hell'. The ethnic cleansing of the Muslims had been long in the planning and plotting. The subsequent siege of the city would become the longest running in the history of the modern era. Sarajevo never fell. The people of the city endured.

Mark Geraghty, the production designer on the film, commented, 'It would have been virtually impossible to re-create Sarajevo anywhere else. We had access to places that people hadn't been in for three to four years and they were fantastic, a designer's dream.'

HEART OF BATTLE: During their time spent reporting, Western journalists holed up in hotel rooms would make music videos of their footage.

The film testifies to the toll that war takes on families and communities. *Welcome to Sarajevo*, amidst all of the horror it shows, also suggests the immense goodness that war can compel, from Michael's decision to take one of the children home to the UK and away from the war, to the sense of loyalty that one of the young Sarajevan men shows Michael. Using archival news footage of politicians the film makes straightforward, pointed comments about the absence of support for the victims of the war, repeating an image of David Owen stating that Western help is a dream.

The film is very strong in its small details that say so much, such as when Risto brings three eggs back to his friends, which means they can make an omelette that several of them then all share.

One of the children in the orphanage has a little picture of Constable's painting *The Haywain*. The little boy asks if that is what England is like. It is a telling moment about a perception of England as an idyll, a place without tensions and strains. We know this is not actually true.

CHARACTER: Michael Henderson is an intense committed reporter who experiences a moment of massive change when he realises that he wants to adopt one of the children at the orphanage. This sense of wanting to save at least one child is prompted by the moment in the hospital when he meets a young child who has lost both her parents to the war. He goes from being distanced from the emotional impact of the war to being totally consumed by it. At the beginning of the film he says to Gregg, 'We're not here to help, we're here to report.'

Jane is the news producer with whom Michael has a tense relationship, her pragmatism contrasting with Michael's idealism. Flynn, the American reporter, is the maverick among the central characters. Gregg, the Irish cameraman, copes with the war zone with a sense of humour, always wearing his lucky hat.

Nina is a committed aid worker who appeals to Michael and Jane when she sells the story of the children to them as an exodus. As such, the film's Eastern European setting gives the film an affinity with *Schindler's List*, a very different film in many ways but quite similar in its focus on everyday people affected by war and the scourge of racism.

Risto is a useful local ally who shifts from being innocent to wiser and less certain in the aftermath of having killed someone.

Haroun, the cellist, is the last face we see in the film and in a sense he represents all those enduring the war as he plays his music with pride. The sound of gunfire and bombs will not defeat identity.

STYLE: In a way that recalls Oliver Stone's work and Coppola's style in *Gardens of Stone*, Winterbottom interpolates into his re-creation of a warzone excerpts from actual news coverage. In doing so this makes the drama that much more immediate and powerful. Winterbottom's stylistic concept in terms of structure was to give the film a sense of being divided into chapters that were terse, tense and affecting. The intercutting of the news footage with the film material creates a jolting effect as the story flips back and forth between the drama and the wider context. This style roots the film in an affecting emotional landscape so that news footage of young mothers and orphan children alongside the tragically familiar image of emaciated men held prisoner behind barbed wire very directly expresses the tragedy of war.

The film is replete with wide shots and images taken from inside cars and along roadsides of Sarajevo, bombed to pieces. The film's opening sequence includes archival images of Sarajevo as host to the 1984 Winter Olympics.

The camera often stands low to the ground, emphasising vast stretches of road littered with bombed-out cars and, in one striking image, a wide shot of a dead body just lying on the highway as cars drive by.

Early in the film a street is bombed and the journalists witness the devastation as people, bloody and injured, either lie on the ground or stumble around in a daze.

The film takes off from the naturalism of Ken Loach's cinema but Winterbottom invests the film with a slightly more generic approach.

There are also moments of silence. Michael walks through a decimated village, covering his mouth at what he sees. When the children, en route to new lives in Italy (temporarily at least), stop off at a beach for a break, the camera holds on a close-up of a little girl simply enjoying some food. As the children splash in the sea the contrast with the bleak and fiery world that was home is all too clear.

Like Oliver Stone, Winterbottom, in a more understated way, uses various cinematic devices for effect, such as when a freeze-frame is used to accentuate a particular moment of horror.

Winterbottom also repeats an image of an altar boy wearing a bloody vestment running through the streets. Late in the film, there is a 'dream' image of a young girl with her back to the camera walking the war-torn streets, pushing a pram filled with wood.

For all the horror, perhaps the most emotional image and moment is when the little girl in the hospital, having just been told she has lost both her parents, walks off down a corridor alone. She can only be six or seven years old.

CRITICAL CROSSFIRE: *Time Out* commended the film for the way it 'captures a powerful sense of the jogging, jagged rhythms of life and death under siege'. *Leonard Maltin's Movie and Video Guide* describes the film as: 'Achingly realistic, unsentimental . . . told with a compelling blend of genuine and staged footage.'

MEDALS OF HONOUR: The film was nominated for the Golden Palm at the Cannes Film Festival and at the Chicago International Film Festival in 1997 the film was nominated for Best Film.

OTHER BATTLEFRONTS: More recently released than *Welcome to Sarajevo* is the film *No Man's Land* (Danis Tanovic, 2001), a small-scale film in which Serbian soldiers find themselves sharing a trench with a Bosnian soldier, the trench lying between the Bosnian and Serbian front lines. During the real war Tanovic spent two years filming documentary footage with the Bosnian Army.

The Bosnian commander drags what he thinks is a dead body over a mine, but the body is not dead it transpires, and is a friend of the Bosnian fighter in the trench. The duel of character defines the film's drama. This is not a war film about expansive terrain but rather about the impact of combat on one's sensitivity and common sense. It is a film marked by its sense of humour amidst the trauma of the bizarre combat situation. The film won the award for Best Screenplay at Cannes in 2001. Another film about this conflict is the more austere and 'real' film *Pretty Village, Pretty Flame* (Srdan Dragojevic, 1996).

In stark aesthetic contrast and intent to *Welcome to Sarajevo*, another film that concerns itself with a 1990s combat zone is the assault on the senses that is the 2001 Ridley Scott film *Black Hawk Down*, based on the account of the same name by Mark Bowden. The narrative relates American troop intervention in Mogadishu in 1993 to depose the local warlords. The film is highly kinetic, even if it does not offer a particularly rounded sense of context. Remember, though, that the Hollywood, popular-cinema tendency is to make the personal political. This caveat aside, the film dazzles as an action piece, immersing the audience in battle.

Then, too, there is *Three Kings* (David O'Russell, 1999) and Ed Zwick's *Courage Under Fire*, both of which use the Gulf War as their backdrop.

THE HOMEFRONT: *Welcome to Sarajevo* is available on DVD.

FINAL BRIEFING: This dynamic and soulful film is both wonderfully cinematic and also deeply affecting, both in whole and in very particular moments where images do more than any dialogue could. The film presents and dramatises the war with an understated quality that makes it all the more powerful, and the sense of life going on against the backdrop of conflict is very memorable. Winterbottom's film and *Land and Freedom*, another British-made war film of the 1990s, stand as two of the best British films of many years. In 2002, Winterbottom directed *In this World*, set in Afghanistan.

FINAL SALUTE: Winterbottom commented that 'I used footage . . . that would be familiar to the audience . . . I wanted to make the point that we had watched this war on television, but very often just switched channels.'

War of the Worlds (2005)

117 minutes

DreamWorks SKG-Paramount Pictures
Producer: Kathleen Kennedy and Colin Wilson
Director: Steven Spielberg
Screenplay: Josh Friedman and David Koepp
Cinematographer: Janusz Kaminski
Editor: Michael Kahn
Music: John Williams
Production Design: Rick Carter
Costume Design: Joanna Johnston
Visual Effects: Dennis Muren, Industrial Light and Magic,
Stan Winston

CAST: Tom Cruise (*Ray Ferrier*), Dakota Fanning (*Rachel Ferrier*), Justin Chatwin (*Robbie Ferrier*), Tim Robbins (*Ogilvy*), Miranda Otto (*Mary Ann*), Morgan Freeman (*Narrator*), Gene Barry (*Grandfather*), Ann Robinson (*Grandmother*)

RATING: 12

TAGLINE: They're already here.

WAR STORY: The setting is present-day America. A dockworker named Ray Ferrier comes home from work to look after his son and daughter, who are being dropped off by Ray's ex-wife, as he is having them for the weekend. Ray is not the most accommodating father and there is tension with his children. A storm strikes and knocks out all the power. Ray goes into town where he witnesses the revelation of alien forces, who have been lying in wait below the ground, and huge tripods begin bestriding America and the rest of the world. Ray takes his children to escape the immediate trauma as the entire East Coast is in chaos. They race furiously to his ex-wife's house but she has gone up to Boston to her parents. Ray and his children sleep in the basement and at night hear a horrific noise. The next morning they discover that the tripods have downed a commercial aeroplane in suburbia.

The family make the journey from the city and into the country, bickering but beginning to bond. Robbie watches a military convoy pass by and wants to join so that he can take part in fighting back at the aliens. They drive on towards a ferry point where mass hysteria is rife as people frantically attempt to board the boat in the hope of escaping. Ray is attacked for having a vehicle and held at gunpoint. The ferry fills with people and Ray and his children just about make it on board as the aliens close in.

The tripods strike again, capsizing the ferry. Ray, Rachel and Robbie make it to safety and flee on foot, joining hundreds of other refugees as the tripods continue to decimate the human race.

The military engage in ground and aerial combat against the tripods but it is no use. Robbie separates from Ray and Rachel, who find shelter with a crazed middle-aged man named Ogilvy. Ogilvy is convinced that he and others should fight back at the aliens, but Ray resists. As they sleep one of the alien tendrils enters the basement and searches for life forms. Ray, Rachel and Ogilvy avoid being detected initially. The scanner pulls out of the basement and then three aliens enter, but do not see the humans. Ogilvy sees the aliens using human blood as fertiliser for their weed and freaks out. Ray kills Ogilvy to prevent him from alerting the aliens.

The scanning device returns again and locates Rachel, the tendril face to face with the terrified little girl. Ray destroys it and in her terror Rachel runs. Ray rushes outside to find her, but he cannot see his daughter.

The terrain in every direction is suffocated by red weed. Ray looks for Rachel but when he finds her he is confronted by a tripod, which grabs Rachel and drops her into one of its baskets alongside other humans. Ray is then also dumped in the basket, before being grabbed and pulled up inside the machine. He succeeds in escaping by planting two grenades inside the machine. As the machine rocks and explodes, the humans fall to safety, and Ray, Rachel and many others walk into Boston where they discover the alien invaders are beginning to perish. The birds are carrying some kind of virus that the aliens cannot counter. One final tripod attacks and the army bring it down. Ray goes to his ex-wife at her parents in Boston to find his son is already there. The children are reunited with their mother and Ray embraces Robbie.

CONCEPT/THE MISSION: HG Wells's 1898 source novel has become a classic of science fiction (or scientific romance, as the genre was then labelled) being widely regarded as a fantasy that reflects the perils of British imperialism. At the same time the growing power of the German Kaiser was causing Britain concern just as in this post 9/11 world there is the threat of the unseen attack. The film's tagline, 'They're already here', hot-wires into our collective sense of unseen enemies within our midst, ready to reveal themselves abruptly and violently. The story was adapted for radio with terrifying effect by Orson Welles several years before America became embroiled in World War Two, prompting some people to actually flee their homes for fear of an alien invasion. Director Byron Haskin teamed up with producer George Pal in 1953 for a classic feature-film version of the story that was true to the novel's Edwardian setting.

For Steven Spielberg's screen version the setting has been relocated to the eastern seaboard of contemporary America, but many of the motifs and thematics of the novel remain true and honest. Spielberg described the film as being about 'the American refugee experience' and some of the images of lines of ragged, everyday people recalls *Empire of the Sun*, *Schindler's List* and even the train sequence in *Close Encounters of the Third Kind*.

Perhaps the most obvious issue in relation to the new film has been how it sits as part of America's stories it tells to itself, about itself, in the shadow of the tragedy of 11 September 2001.

An important concept, and key to selling the film, was that the aliens were already here on Earth and, we assume, waiting to strike, rather like terrorists.

For designer Doug Chiang 'It could be a World War Two film because it's about refugees and these aliens could be an invading other force.'

Spielberg commented, 'It's about the basic elements of human nature set against an extraordinary unnatural event.'

Interestingly, in the early 1980s Spielberg had collaborated with writer John Sayles on a project called *Night Skies*, in which aliens would have besieged a house. That concept morphed into what became *ET* but it is compelling to wonder if any of the images and concepts in this version of *War of the Worlds* might once have made it into the *Night Skies* project.

Up to thirty designs were considered for the aliens and Spielberg would merge elements together. Ryan Church, who had been designing for *Star Wars Episode 3: Revenge of the Sith* (George Lucas, 2005) nailed the look of the tripods, which Spielberg envisioned as being jellyfish-like. The tripods resemble the ships in *Close Encounters of the Third Kind* and are most terrifying in the sounds they make, especially their calling sound.

CASTING/RECRUITMENT: Tom Cruise had worked with Spielberg before on *Minority Report* and had also starred in *Risky Business*, *Top Gun*, *Rain Man*, **Born on the Fourth of July** and, more recently, *Magnolia* and *Eyes Wide Shut*.

Dakota Fanning had appeared in Spielberg's miniseries *Taken* and also *The Cat in the Hat* (Bo Welch, 2003).

Tim Robbins has appeared in *Howard the Duck* (Willard Huyck, 1986), *Bull Durham* (Ron Shelton, 1988), *Short Cuts* (Robert Altman, 1993), *The Player*, *The Hudsucker Proxy* (Joel and Ethan Coen, 1994) and has directed *Bob Roberts* (1992), *Dead Man Walking* (1995) and *The Cradle Will Rock* (1999).

Miranda Otto has appeared in **The Thin Red Line** in the flashback sequences to Bell's wife at home. Otto also appeared in the *Lord of the Rings* films.

Gene Barry and Ann Robinson cameo at the end of the film as the grandparents. They had originally starred in the George Pal/Byron Haskin version as Forrester and Van Buren respectively.

BACKUP: The preproduction period for such a large-scale film as *War of the Worlds* was very brief, with the project moving into action in the summer of 2004 for a summer 2005 release.

Key collaborators of Spielberg's in the abbreviated preproduction phase were designer Doug Chiang and production designer Rick Carter. Chiang had designed concept art for *Star Wars: Episode 1: The Phantom*

Menace (George Lucas, 1999) and *Star Wars: Episode II: Attack of the Clones* (George Lucas, 2002) as well as working on *The Abyss, The Polar Express* (Robert Zemeckis, 2004) and *Beowulf* (Robert Zemeckis, 2007). Rick Carter has worked with Spielberg since the *Amazing Stories* TV series of 1985–6, and designed *Jurassic Park, The Lost World: Jurassic Park, Amistad, What Lies Beneath, Cast Away* (Robert Zemeckis, 2000) and *AI: Artificial Intelligence.*

Chiang commented during its production that 'this would be more akin to Orson Welles's version than to George Pal's'. Rick Carter added, 'It's both sociological and broad but it's also in a few instances very personal . . . Let me just say it would be the opposite of the little fingers going and getting candy. It would be the opposite of touching a flower that's dying and making it come alive.'

Spielberg collaborated with designer Dan Gregoire to pre-visualise *War of the Worlds*. Supervising the Industrial Light and Magic visual effects work was the legendary effects artist Dennis Muren. He is the only practitioner in his field to have been granted a star on the Hollywood Walk of Fame. Muren had supervised effects work on *ET: The Extra Terrestrial, Indiana Jones and the Temple of Doom, Jurassic Park, The Lost World* and *AI: Artificial Intelligence* and has become a key collaborator of Spielberg's. Overseeing animation of the tripods was Randall Dutra, who had animated the dinosaurs for *Jurassic Park*. Dutra had also animated on *RoboCop, Willow* and *The Lost World: Jurassic Park.*

Producing the film were Kathleen Kennedy and Colin Wilson. Kennedy has worked with Spielberg since the film *1941*, beginning as his assistant before progressing to producer with him on *ET: The Extra Terrestrial*. Her other credits include *Indiana Jones and the Temple of Doom, Back to the Future* (Robert Zemeckis, 1985), *The Goonies* (Richard Donner, 1985), *Who Framed Roger Rabbit?* (Robert Zemeckis, 1985), *The Color Purple (1985), Empire of the Sun* (1987), *Hook* (1991), *Jurassic Park* (1993), *The Sixth Sense* (M Night Shyamalan, 1998) and *Signs* (M Night Shyamalan, 2002). Wilson had produced *The Flintstones* (Brian Levant, 1994) and *Casper* (Brad Silberling, 1995).

PRODUCTION/IN THE TRENCHES: *War of the Worlds* was shot in 72 days across the autumn and winter of 2004–05. Spielberg and Cruise had both planned to be at work on *Mossad* and *Mission Impossible 3* by this time, but both projects went into further development and there was a window of opportunity. The film was rapidly prepared, with the pre-visualisation technology used on *Star Wars: Revenge of the Sith* used to block out *War of the Worlds*. Spielberg had collaborated with Lucas on the two intercutting duels that round out the final *Star Wars* prequel. This process of predetermining locations, camera set ups and staging benefited a fast turnaround production like *War of the Worlds*. The film was shot largely on location in Bayonne, New Jersey, California and Virginia, all three locations grounding the fantasy and making it all the more terrifying.

Several military units were enlisted, namely New York's 10th Mountain Division, Marines from Camp Pendleton and soldiers from Fort Irwin. The film is piled high with striking images of mass destruction through which characters move in bewilderment and terror. No image is more affecting than that of the downed aircraft. For this scene, a commercial plane no longer in use was purchased for the film and then cut up so as to be strewn across the Universal Studios back lot.

In a full-circle moment of moviemaking history, the second-unit filming and stunt co-ordination on the film was supervised by Vic Armstrong, who had choreographed the energetic stunt work on Spielberg's *Indiana Jones and the Temple of Doom* (1984) and *Indiana Jones and the Last Crusade* (1989).

MARTIAL MUSIC: For *War of the Worlds* composer John Williams created an atonal, abrasive score that emphasises the bleakness of the situation the characters and general populace experience. The score offers a pounding abrasive accompaniment to the hysteria of the ferry sequence. Much of the music, though, features brooding, downbeat and eerily sliding strings with occasional traces of warmth. The most melodic piece in a largely dissonant score is the music that represents the relationship between father and daughter.

REIMAGINING REALITY: Whilst the central conflict is science-fiction fantasy, at its best the film's post-9/11 subtext is where the reality of it lies. The film comprises moments that reverberate with our shared, recent memories of mass tragedies.

HEART OF BATTLE: Perhaps the most disturbing sequence in the film is the scene around Ray's van as he approaches the ferry, where mob rule has taken over and the people are at war with themselves. The core of the story, though, is the battle Ray must confront to protect his family from the invaders. The assumption the audience must make is that what Ray is experiencing is what the other American families and communities are engaged in, namely surviving their own homefront, backyard war. Hence Ray represents Everyman and Everywoman in classic Spielbergian tradition.

There is a gripping sequence in the middle of the film where the American military fight the tripods to little avail, and a sequence near the end of the film where the army bring down the last tripod has the hand-held energy of a *Saving Private Ryan* combat scene. As the final narration explains, all the technology in the world was not what stopped the aliens from continuing their campaign. Nature ultimately proved the victor, human endeavour meaningless against the power of a virus.

Very early in the film Rachel goes to her father with a splinter under her skin. This apparently throwaway scene is the concept of the film in super concise form.

The ending of the film recalls *The Searchers* (John Ford, 1956) with Ray rescuing Rachel from danger and returning her home, but to a home that he is excluded from. *War of the Worlds* does not clarify whether or not Ray goes indoors with his children or whether he walks away. All we see is an expression of exhausted relief on his face.

CHARACTER: The protagonist, Ray Ferrier, is an adult who lives more like a kid, and the invasion of alien forces compels him to become far more paternal than he has previously been. Screenwriter David Koepp stated, 'Tom's played so many characters that are capable and cocky, and I thought it would be fun to write against that.' For costume designer Joanna Johnston, when Ferrier sheds his hoodie and leather jacket, 'To me, it's like an old-fashioned hero emerging.'

Ray's son Robbie is transfixed by the horror around him and is on the verge of attempting to enlist in the army as it rumbles by without jingoistic fervour. Ray's daughter, Rachel, is an anxious child.

Ogilvy, the slightly crazed man who takes Ray and Rachel into the basement of his country home is conceived in the spirit of an American frontiersman, with his rifle permanently at the ready. Ferrier, though, does all he can to prevent Ogilvy using the gun. Eventually though, Ray becomes feral and takes an axe to the alien probe when it sights Rachel face to face. Ray hacks at the tendril like a caveman hacking at a snake. Worse still, Ray murders Ogilvy. All of the things that made sense in life have slipped away, just as they have done to other characters in other war stories.

STYLE: *War of the Worlds* is a fraught film that features some of Spielberg's strongest evocations of mass hysteria and the anticipation of doom. Spielberg takes the most anxious, domestic scenes of *Close Encounters of the Third Kind* and *Poltergeist* and amplifies them as the home becomes the most potent battlefront of all. Spielberg has always excelled at small visuals that anticipate bigger scares to come, for instance a ripple in the water that floods Ogilvy's basement, and falling debris as the aliens come down into the basement to investigate. The sequence where the tripods are first seen is one of the greatest Spielberg set pieces of his incredible career. The cat-and-mouse chase around the cellar with the tripod's probe recalls the velociraptor showdown with the children in the kitchen in *Jurassic Park*.

Spielberg also conjures a number of 'understated' moments of terror, the best of which is when Rachel goes to the riverside. The image of clothes falling from the night skies is also beautiful and terrifying.

Spielberg's camera tracks through wilderness, drawing us along the adventure. When the tripods first strike the camera immerses right in amongst the running crowds and twice Spielberg appeals to our familiarity with video-recorded images of war to help tell his story of the attack. The alien tripods are indeed phantom menaces.

Perhaps the most shocking image is the long take of Ferrier emerging from the remains of his wife's house to find a downed jumbo jet in pieces across the town. The apocalyptic quality of this is in many ways more accessible than the wide shot of devastation that concludes the film.

CRITICAL CROSSFIRE: Matt Soller Zeitz in the *New York Press* wrote, 'The director's knack for primal terror remains unsurpassed: this film does for lightning what *Jaws* did for beaches . . . Spielberg is a humanist who looks for community and decency.' For Peter Bradshaw in the *Guardian*, though, the film was a travesty: 'This *War of the Worlds* is a fundamentally unambitious and often quite dull film.'

MEDALS OF HONOUR: In autumn 2005 the film was nominated in the category of Movie of the Year at the Hollywood Movie Awards.

OTHER BATTLEFRONTS: Spielberg's version of HG Wells's novel is notably distinct from the George Pal/Byron Haskin version, and tonally it may have more in common with the Orson Welles radio dramatisation. Ridley Scott's film *Alien* was a key influence on Spielberg, and he acknowledges it as his favourite science-fiction scare film.

Whilst stylistically and thematically and tonally very different, *Red Dawn* tells a story of American soil under attack from communism. The film's right-wing impulse sees America's youth arming itself against the invading force. Written and directed by bellicose maverick and underappreciated 'Movie Brat' John Milius, the film is oozing with male bonding and the American frontier spirit. The film was co-written with Kevin Reynolds, who went on to direct a barely seen action film set in Afghanistan called *The Beast* (1988) about a Russian tank. *Reds* was seen as rather lacking in subtlety as it pitched America against communism.

Rather closer to the idea of Earth under alien attack is *Independence Day* (Roland Emmerich, 1996), which puts a far more humorous spin on the prospect of such an event. The film used a now iconic image of the White House being immolated by an alien ship hovering just above it.

THE HOMEFRONT: The *War of the Worlds* DVD was produced in a single and two-disc format. The two-disc format including a comprehensive range of features including mini features entitled *Revisiting the Invasion, Designing the Enemy* and *Steven Spielberg and the Original War of the Worlds*.

FINAL BRIEFING: *War of the Worlds* is marked by a sense of desperation. This is a film in which what saves the world is not military firepower or even human resilience but birds carrying viruses that ultimately infect the aliens. The sense of terror and helplessness is what the film excels in portraying, that sense of being at the grassroots level when war strikes. The film has the immediacy of several key moments of combat in *Saving Private Ryan*. The monster movie is a combat zone in which the common man rises to the challenge presented.

FINAL SALUTE: 'I think there are politics certainly underneath some of the scares and some of the adventure and some of the fear.' – Steven Spielberg

Appendix 1 – War Documentaries

As long as there have been moving pictures there have been documents about war and combat and soldiering and the price of war and the administrative entanglements that often lead to war.

The Second World War presented fiction filmmakers with a chance to move into documentary, perhaps none more effectively than John Huston with his three pieces: *Report from the Aleutians* (1943), *San Pietro* (1944) about American infantry men struggling in Italy, and finally *Let There Be Light* (1945), which was banned from being screened by the US War Department because it explored rehabilitating soldiers and shell-shocked troops. The film was finally released in 1980.

Report from the Aleutians showed the construction of a landing strip. The *New York Times* reviewed this first documentary very favourably, writing, 'It is imperative that (the film) be seen by anyone intent on knowing something of the labour, the hazard, and the importance – both real and potential – of one long-forgotten theatre of war.' *San Pietro* was made by John Huston with a crew of six Signal Corps cameramen, with Huston providing most of the voice-over narration. Huston went into the US Army Signal Corps as a lieutenant and was commissioned to record American combat for the War Department. The Aleutian project was to go to that part of Alaska to record the building of a landing strip for B-24 Liberator bombers so they could fly out on raids in the Pacific. Huston even went filming on several bombing missions. The film went to cinemas in 1943 and was considered one of the ten best films of the year.

Huston then did some filming in North Africa, and another film was shot but not released because it lacked authenticity – the crew had had to restage tank battles in California and air battles in Florida. After this Huston's focus was Europe, and Italy in particular. The small mountain town of San Pietro saw a battle between US forces and German troops who had fortified the route into Rome. The finished film was considered very powerful by the War Department, who cut almost thirty minutes to make it more palatable.

Huston's final documentary was *Let There Be Light*, where he interviewed recovering soldiers. For Huston the film was 'the most hopeful and optimistic and joyous thing I ever had a hand in', but the film was only first shown in 1980 at the Los Angeles County Museum. In

1981 all three films were broadcast in one slot on American television, with Huston interviewed between each film.

Another interesting factual film from World War Two is *Hiroshima-Nagasaki: August 1945*, comprising footage shot during that period by a Japanese documentary crew commissioned by the Japanese government to record the effects of the Hiroshima and Nagasaki bombs. The footage was held back for 25 years before being released.

In Britain the films *Fires Were Started* (1943) and *Listen to Britain* (1942) are notable for their documentary–drama fusions as pieces of propaganda, and both were directed by Humphrey Jennings. For pure drama, perhaps, Laurence Olivier's adaptation of Shakespeare's *Henry V* (1944) was the most striking, with its emphasis on the Battle of Agincourt. It is interesting to contrast this film's presentation with Kenneth Branagh's bloody, messy, brilliant rendition in his version of 1989.

Other documentaries that explore the machinations, implications and pains of war include *The Fog Of War* (Errol Morris, 2003), *The Civil War* (Ken Burns, 1990), *Shoah* (Claude Lanzmann, 1985), *The World At War* (Lowell Mullett, 1942), *Lessons of Darkness* (Werner Herzog, 1992) and *Dear America* (Bill Couterié, 1987).

The following films are documentaries about war; with an emphasis on Vietnam. As with the 'fiction' film, many of the issues that arise in one war can be applied to others in terms of the human cost and the legacy left for future generations to contend with. The titles are *The Anderson Platoon* (1946), *The Battle for Dien Bien Phu* (1979), *Battlefield Vietnam* (1998), *Be Good, Smile Pretty, Ecocide: A Stratgy of War* (1988), *Faces of the Enemy* (1987), *Four Hours in My Lai, Hearts and Minds* (1991), *Rising Above: Women of Vietnam* (1996).

Appendix 2 – War and Satire

As long as there have been wars and mass media there has been satire.

A number of films have been made, still readily available, that take a satirical view of war and conflict in an attempt to make a larger comment and critique and to indicate the absurdity of it all. Satire has always sat well with history and military endeavour, and one of British cinema's most expansive films embodied this tradition with confidence. The film was *Charge of the Light Brigade* (Tony Richardson, 1968), which dramatised those events leading up to the British involvement in the Crimean War. The film hits the target as a critique of nineteenth-century British imperialism. Richard Attenborough's *Oh! What A Lovely War* is another film from the same period that takes a satirical view on combat and conflict. Another film of the 1960s, though not a satire, that presented the British at war in Africa was *Zulu* (Cy Endfield, 1964) in which the British fought the Zulus at Rorke's Drift. The Rorke's Drift battle yielded the most Victoria Crosses for one engagement.

Perhaps one of the most enduring satires of war and the administration of it is the Stanley Kubrick film *Dr Strangelove or How I Learned To Stop Worrying And Love The Bomb* (1964).

Stanley Kubrick's filmmaking career has been distinguished by his commitment to inventive and memorable adaptations of novels to the screen, and *Dr Strangelove* was no exception to this. Based on a straightforward thriller novel by RAF pilot Peter George called *Red Alert*, Kubrick's resulting film was originally to have been equally straight-arrow. However, as the writing process developed, 'one had to keep leaving out of it things which were either absurd or paradoxical, in order to keep it from being funny; and these things seemed to be close to the heart of the scene in question'. Kubrick continued redrafting the screenplay throughout filming, with improvisational sessions informing the dialogue.

The film deals with the brinkmanship that marked the Kennedy–Khrushchev Cold War dynamic of the early 1960s and that came to a head with the Cuban missile crisis, and the film was made during this period. Intriguingly, the film seems to play to something that an American air-force psychiatric officer observed at the base he was stationed at, namely a sense of exhilaration in the air due to the mounting tension and the constant stimulation of combat possibilities.

Ironically, Kubrick used the song 'We'll Meet Again', reigniting the wartime song's popularity and also the profile of Gracie Fields.

Far more recently, one Hollywood-made war movie with a satirical impulse has made its mark. Very different in style and tone to a *Dr Strangelove*, for example, the film has developed something of a cult following, though it never really made much of an impact at the box office. The film, released in 1999, is called *Three Kings* and to date (in part, one imagines, because it was not especially successful commercially) has been one of the very few American films to set their drama against the backdrop of the Gulf War.

The writer–director of the film was David O Russell, who felt that the American military had failed the Iraqi people by not protecting them against Saddam Hussein. For Russell the story was a chance to analyse and satirise the Gulf War. Advisers on the film were plentiful to ensure military and cultural accuracy. Lieutenant John Rottger (an ex-Navy SEAL) and Colonel King Davis worked on the film, as did a number of Iraqi consultants in America who read the screenplay and worked on dialogue and expression, such as Al No'mani, an Iraqi filmmaker from Chicago.

For George Clooney, starring in *Three Kings* offered an opportunity to galvanise his emerging star status. Clooney had been a contract actor with Warner Brothers for a number of years and had made occasional TV appearances on *Roseanne* before breaking through as Doug Ross in the medical drama series *ER* (1994 to present). Clooney soon began developing a feature-film career, starring in *From Dusk Till Dawn* (Robert Rodriguez, 1996), *One Fine Day* (Michael Hoffman, 1997), *The Peacemaker, Batman and Robin* (Joel Schumacher, 1997), **The Thin Red Line**, *Out of Sight* (Steven Soderbergh, 1998), *Solaris* (Steven Soderbergh, 2002), *Ocean's Eleven* (Steven Soderbergh, 2001). For Clooney the script for *Three Kings* '. . . in a weird way, it had elements of several great films like *Lawrence of Arabia* and *Schindler's List* because . . . you start out doing something for mercenary reasons and personal gain, and eventually you do what's right'.

Also cast in the film was music promo director Spike Jonze as Private Conrad Vig. Jonze went on to direct *Being John Malkovich* (1999) and *Adaptation* (2002).

For David O Russell, 'I wanted the visual style of the film to mirror (the) craziness; to startle you.' Critical to this concept was a sense of dislocating the characters from anything they might otherwise know and understand.

Going further back we can also namecheck *M*A*S*H* (Robert Altman, 1970) with its Korean War setting.

What all of these films do, perhaps more definitively than anything else, is remind audiences of the tragic absurdity of war. It's a simple intent and it can generate mixed feelings.

What the war film satire does is alert audiences to failings and misjudgements, often of the superstructures that serve as a backdrop to the battlezone bravery of men and women in all eras.

WAR FILMS Appendix 2 – War and Satire

Appendix 3 – The Historical Epic

War films are virtually countless. One of the more popular forms has been the historical epic, a subdivision of the war film that still endures. Of course, most war films are to some degree historical, but over the years there has been an affinity between the epic scale that cinema can render and the war story.

In 1925 Sergei Eisenstein's film *Battleship Potemkin* was released. Immensely controversial at the time, the film was produced as a way to celebrate the unsuccessful 1905 revolution against the Russian Tsar. Rather than re-create the revolution in its entirety, Eisenstein opted for a more dynamic focus, electing to dramatise the incident in which there was a mutiny on the battleship *Potemkin* followed by a civilian massacre on the steps of Odessa harbour. The film is shot in a way that suggests documentary and yet it had been meticulously designed and staged. The film is filled with now iconic images, such as the woman with her glasses broken on her bloody face. Even Brian De Palma's *The Untouchables* (1987) references the Odessa steps with the shoot-out at Chicago railway station as the pram bounces down the steps.

Throughout *Battleship Potemkin*, Eisenstein flexes his montage muscles to create meanings by juxtaposing apparently unrelated images. At the end of the film he uses montage to create a symbol of the revolution and the spirit of defiance as he cuts together three shots of marble lions. Edited at a fast pace, the three differently posed sculptures create the illusion of a lion standing up. The spirit of animation informs artistic protest.

Whilst Eisenstein was reacting to fairly immediate history, in France epic filmmaker Abel Gance released his 'biopic' *Napoleon* (1927), a sprawling black-and-white silent film that dramatised key aspects of the military leader's life.

In 1939, Hollywood producer David O Selznick adapted Margaret Mitchell's novel *Gone with the Wind* into a full-colour romantic drama set in the Confederate South against the backdrop of the American Civil War.

Through the 1960s and early 1970s there were a number of massively scaled World War Two films such as *The Longest Day*, which sought to re-create, restage almost, the D-Day landings in Normandy. In 1971 the Sergei Bondarchuk epic *Waterloo* was released, dramatising Napoleon's defeat in that pivotal battle. The original Russian version of the film ran to almost four hours.

More recently, in the era of digital cinema and the more affordable creation of crowds and battles that computer imaging allows, the epic war movie has returned, for instance with *Troy* (Wolfgang Petersen, 2004) and *Kingdom of Heaven* (Ridley Scott, 2005).

The historical epic, for all its rooting in the usually distant past, still does what all the other war films do, which is to forefront characters marked by courage in the face of numerous kinds of adversity.

Appendix 4 – War Scores

Where there is a film about war there is often a music score that is fated to become part of the public imagination and popular-culture memory. The 'Colonel Bogey March' from *The Bridge on the River Kwai*, the theme music from *The Dam Busters*, the title track from *The Great Escape*, the signature piece *Hymn To The Fallen* from *Saving Private Ryan* – all these pieces have moved beyond the movies they were created for and encapsulate courage and stoicism under immense pressure.

The great British composer Ralph Vaughan Williams, he of the powerhouse *The Lark Ascending* and countless dazzling orchestral pieces inspired by English folk tunes, turned his hand to film-music composition and in the process provided incredible scores for the war film *49th Parallel* (Michael Powell, 1941).

In America one of the key contributors to the war-film score was Hugo Friedhofer, not a name as familiar to us as, say, Elmer Bernstein or Jerry Goldsmith, but Friedhofer offered up a number of affecting themes and pieces. Films such as *Above and Beyond* (Melvin Frank, Norman Panama, 1952) about Colonel Paul Tibbets (pilot of the *Enola Gay*, the plane that dropped the bomb on Hiroshima), *Between Heaven and Hell* (Richard Fleischer, 1956) and *Never So Few* (John Sturges, 1959).

In Britain the composer most associated with the war-movie sound was Ron Goodwin. He provided scores for *633 Squadron* (Walter Grauman, 1964), *Operation Crossbow*, and *Battle Of Britain* (Guy Hamilton, 1969). Goodwin's standout contribution might well be that for *Where Eagles Dare*.

More recently we can look to the efforts of John Williams, James Horner and Gabriel Yared, amongst others, for compelling musical expressions of the combat zone and the price of conflict.

John Williams has been composing film scores since the mid-1960s, and several war-themed films are contained in his body of work. There is the World War Two soundtrack for *Midway*, the often choral and ethereal-sounding score for *Empire of the Sun* and the violin-led lament of *Schindler's List*. Williams's music for *Saving Private Ryan* centres on a self-contained concert piece entitled *Hymn to the Fallen*, only heard in full over the end credits of the film. Music is used relatively sparingly in the film, typically at its best when underscoring a quiet moment of contemplation or loss, as in the sequence when Mrs Ryan is visited by the military and a priest. Williams also scored the American Revolution film *The Patriot* (Roland Emmerich, 2000), the main theme of which begins beautifully with a violin solo by Mark O'Connor that is wistful and sets the score in a sense of period. By contrast, Williams's score for *1941* is loud, crazily energetic and parodic.

Since the mid-1980s James Horner has stood as a leading composer for Hollywood films. His choral score for *Glory* is one of his most exemplary pieces of work. Then, too, there is his music for *Enemy At The Gates* (Jean-Jacques Annaud, 2001) and his sinister and kinetic contribution to the science-fiction war film *Aliens*.

Gabriel Yared might be less immediately recognisable a name but he has contributed music to the American Civil War film *Cold Mountain* and the wartime romance *The English Patient*.

Staying in Europe, and with a film that explores the landscape of the war-torn Balkans of the mid-1990s, is the score to the mesmerising film *Ulysses Gaze*. Composed by Eleni Karaindrou, the music is elegiac in the extreme.

Appendix 5 – Web Resources

Inevitably, there are countless war-related websites online.
Some that are worth starting out from are:
www.iwm.org.uk/ – website of the Imperial War Museum
http://www.firstworldwar.com/
www.filmscoremonthly.com
www.spielbergfilms.com
www.filmjournal.com
www.imdb.com – for an immense amount of information about films
www.sensesofcinema.org – one of the finest film websites; wise and
wide-ranging
www.bfi.org.uk – the website for the British Film Institute
www.screenonline.org – a fascinating offshoot of the British Film
Institute website
www.film-philosophy.com

Picture Credits

The following pictures are reproduced courtesy of the Ronald Grant Archive:

Page 1 (top) Universal Pictures; Page 1 (bottom) RAC; Page 2 (top) R&R Films; Page 2 (bottom) ABPC; Page 3 (bottom) Zespol Filmowy; Page 4 (top) United Artists; Page 4 (bottom) DreamWorks SKG; Page 5 (top) 20th Century Fox; Page 5 (bottom) Universal Pictures; Page 6 (bottom) Columbia Pictures; Page 7 (bottom) 20th Century Fox; Page 8 (top)C4; Page 8 (bottom) Columbia Tristar

The following pictures are reproduced courtesy of the Kobal Collection: Page 3 (top) Columbia/The Kobal Collection; Page 6 (top)Universal/The Kobal Collection/Neveu, Roland; Page 7 (top) Herald Ace/Nippon Herald/Greenwich/The Kobal Collection

Index of Quotations

THE GREAT WAR/WORLD WAR I
All Quiet on the Western Front

26   'These guys thought . . .' Arthur Gardner quoted by Duncan Campbell, 'The Unknown Soldier', 2 November 2003, The *Guardian Online*, www.guardianonline.co.uk

26   'whole societies were engaged . . .' JM Roberts, *The History of the World*, Penguin Books, 1990, p. 819

27   'And don't forget . . .' *Punch* magazine, 25 April 1917

27   'scenes suggest that war is hell . . .' Jeanine Basinger, *The World War Two Combat Film: Anatomy Of A Genre*, Wesleyan University Press, Connecticut, 2003, pp. 89–90

30   'the film's strength now derives . . .' The *Time Out Film Guide*, Penguin Books, 1991, p. 14

30   'be shown to every nation . . .' *Variety*, 1930

30   'vivid, moving . . .' *Leonard Maltin's 2002 Movie and Video Guide*, Plume/Penguin, 2001, p. 27

La Grande Illusion

38   'I toed the line absolutely . . .' Jean Renoir quoted by Raymond Durgnat, *Jean Renoir*, Studio Vista Books, Cassell and Collier Macmillan, London, 1975, p. 147

39   'deploys a European complexity . . .' Raymond Durgnat, *Jean Renoir*, Studio Vista Books, Cassell and Collier Macmillan, London, 1975, p. 147

39   'La Grande Illusion . . .' Pauline Kael, review from the collection *I Lost It At The Movies* by Pauline Kael, Little Brown and Co, Boston, 1965 (review originally written 1961) p. 108–111

39   'The Grand Illusion, often cited . . .' The *Time Out Film Guide*, Penguin, 1991, p. 265

39   'Beautiful performances . . .' *Leonard Maltin's 2002 Movie and Video Guide*, Plume/Penguin, 2001, p. 546

41   'If I had to save . . .' Orson Welles, quoted at www.rottentomatoes.com/m/grand_illusion/about.php

Paths of Glory

45   'There are even signs that . . .' JM Roberts, *The History of the World*, Penguin Books, 1990, p. 812

47   'The fact that some favourably compared . . .' Alexander Walker, Sybil Taylor and Ulrich Rudick, *Stanley Kubrick: A Visual Analysis*, WW Norton and Co., New York and London, 1999

48   'an impact of hard reality . . .' Bosley Crowther, The *New York Times*

48   'unusually trenchant for its time . . .' The *Time Out Film Guide*, Penguin, 1991, p. 508

48   'shattering study . . .' *Leonard Maltin's 2002 Movie and Video Guide*, Plume/Penguin, 2001, p. 1045

51 'The soldier is absorbing because . . .' Stanley Kubrick quoted by Jonathan Stang, 'Film Fan to Film Maker' by Jonathan Stang, The *New York Times Magazine*, 12 October 1958 reprinted in *The Cinema of Stanley Kubrick*, by Norman Kagan, Roundhouse, Oxford, 1995

Gallipoli
53 'By approaching the subject obliquely . . .' interview with Peter Weir, *Literature/Film Quarterly*, vol. 9, no. 4, 1981
53 'graduation film' Peter Weir quoted by Don Shiach, *The Films of Peter Weir: Visions of Alternative Realities*, Letts and Co., London, 1993
54 'getting at what this thing was . . .' interview with Peter Weir, *Literature/Film Quarterly* , vol. 9, no. 4, 1981
58 'a well executed . . .' Pauline Kael, *Taking It All In*, Arena, London, 1987, p. 455
58 'buoyed up by a fulsome naturalistic fervour . . .' The *Time Out Film Guide*, Penguin Books, 1991, p. 248
58 'engrossing human drama . . .' *Leonard Maltin's 2002 Movie and Video Guide*, Plume/Penguin, 2001, p. 504
59 'I wanted to give . . .' Peter Weir interviewed by Sue Matthews, 1982, www.peterweircave.com

WORLD WAR II
In Which We Serve
66 'it is wrong to have . . .' The *Daily Express* quoted by SP Mackenzie, *British War Films 1939–1945*, Hambledon and London Ltd, 2000, p. 75
68 'I wish I could find words . . .' *Picturegoer* editor quoted by SP Mackenzie, *British War Films 1939–1945*, Hambledon and London Ltd, 2000, p. 80
68 'Human deeply moving . . .' Ernest Betts, *Daily Express*, 24 September 1942, quoted by Kevin Brownlow in *David Lean*, Faber and Faber, 1996, p. 167
68 'If this in so many respects . . .' Roger Manvell, *Films and the Second World War*, AS Barnes and Company, London, 1974
68 'Staged with what passed at the time . . .' The *Time Out Film Guide*, Penguin, 1991, p. 326
68 'Unlike many . . .' *Leonard Maltin's 2002 Movie and Video Guide*, Plume/Penguin, 2001, p. 679
69 'Toward the end there was . . .' Noel Coward quoted by SP Mackenzie, *British War Films 1939–1945*, Hambledon and London, 2000, p. 80

The Dam Busters
72 'somewhat simplified treatment . . .' producer of *The Dam Busters* quoted by John Sweetman, *The Dambusters Raid*, Cassell Military Paperbacks, London, 1982, 2002, p. 14

73   'The Dam Busters raid, visually so . . .' John Sweetman, *The Dam Busters Raid*, Cassell Military Paperbacks, London, 1982, 2002, p. 14

74   'inaccuracies and embellishments . . .' John Sweetman, *The Dam Busters Raid*, Cassell Military Paperbacks, London, 1982, 2002, p. 13

75   'a beloved child' Barnes Wallis quoted by John Sweetman, *The Dam Busters Raid*, Cassell Military Paperbacks, London, 1982, 2002, p. 257

75   'The recovery from low level . . .' quoted by John Sweetman, *The Dam Busters Raid*, Cassell Military Paperbacks, London, 1982, 2002, p. 172

77   'an attempt to express a more . . .' *Monthly Film Bulletin*, vol. 22, no. 257, June 1955, pp. 82–82

78   'slips some thoughtful reservations . . .' The *Time Out Film Guide*, Penguin Books, 1991, p. 150

79   'We had this . . .' Gary Kurtz quoted by Stephen Zito, 'George Lucas Goes Far Out', *American Film*, April 1977, pp. 8–13, reprinted in *George Lucas: Interviews*, University of Mississippi Press, edited by Sally Kline, pp. 51–52, 1999

The Bridge on the River Kwai

82   'He thought about film as a Jesuit . . .' Anthony Havelock-Allan quoted at www.lean.bfi.org.uk

88   'I'm fascinated by these . . .' David Lean quoted by Alain Silver and James Ursini, *David Lean and his Films*, Silman James Press, USA, 1992, p. 144

88   'Colonel Nicholson, David felt . . .' Kevin Brownlow, *David Lean*, Faber and Faber, London, 1996, p. 349

89   John Milius, *An Appreciation*, DVD interview on *The Bridge on the River Kwai* DVD

90   'Bridge on the River Kwai . . .' Lindsay Anderson, review of *The Bridge on the River Kwai*, *New Statesman and Nation* review, 2 October 1957 quoted by Kevin Brownlow in *David Lean*, Faber and Faber, 1996, p. 385

90   'A classic example of . . .' The *Time Out Film Guide*, Penguin Books, 1991, p. 85

90   'psychological battle . . .' Leonard Maltin, *TV and Video Guide*, Plume Books, 2001, p. 179

92   'It has incredible . . .' John Milius quoted from the short interview 'An Appreciation' with him on The Bridge on the River Kwai DVD'

Kanal

95   'on the one hand . . .' Andrzej Wajda commenting about his early years as an aspiring artist, at his website www.wajda.pl

96   'was largely concerned with . . .' Boleslaw Sulik, Introduction to *The Wajda Trilogy Scripts*, Lorimer Publishing, London, 1973, p. 16

96   'We chose to create cinema from scratch . . .' Andrzej Wajda, Introduction to *The Cinema of Andrzej Wajda*, edited by John Orr and Elzbieta Ostrowska, Wallflower Press, London, 2003, p. xii

117　'concerns itself not only with . . .' ibid. p. 31

118　'Even though the screenplay wasn't . . .' Steven Spielberg, *Directors Close Up*, edited by Jeremy Kagan, Focal Press, 2000, p. 43

118　'you're a kid and you hear . . .' ibid. p. 43

119　'There is nothing unconventional . . .' Louis Menand, 'Jerry Don't Surf: *Saving Private Ryan*', from *Critical Essays: Steven Spielberg*, edited by Charles LP Silet, The Scarecrow Press, Maryland, Oxford, 2002, p. 251

119　'in a face hunt . . .' Steven Spielberg, *Directors Close Up*, edited by Jeremy Kagan, Focal Press, 2000, p. 56

121　'formal dressing down . . .' Steven Spielberg, *Directors Close Up*, edited by Jeremy Kagan, Focal Press, 2000, p. 164

122　'This is a movie about a company . . .' Steven Spielberg talking to Richard Dyer, *Sounds of Spielberg, Boston Globe*, 24 February 1998

125　'I was concerned about deconstructing . . .' Steven Spielberg, *Directors Close Up*, edited by Jeremy Kagan, Focal Press, 2000, p. 162

125　'I deliberately gave some scenes . . .' Janusz Kaminski in *Cinematography: Screencraft* by Peter Ettedgui, RotoVision Books, 1998, p. 191

125　'Why a new Spielberg . . .' *Newsweek* cover, 13 July 1998

125　'A masterpiece . . .' *Entertainment Weekly*, 14 July 1998

125　'trenchant World War Two drama . . .' *Leonard Maltin's 2002 Movie and Video Guide*, Plume/Penguin, 2001, p. 1192

127　'For moviegoers . . .' Sam Fuller quoted by Kent Jones, 'Battle Fatigue', *Film Comment*, May/June 2004, p. 22

127　'The spirit of the film . . .' Kent Jones, *Battle Fatigue, Film Comment*, May/June 2004, p. 22

128　'When people see World War Two movies . . .' Steven Spielberg interviewed by Stephen Hunter, 'Steven Spielberg's Road to War', The *Washington Post*, 27 July 1998

The Thin Red Line

130　'loves to speak in metaphors . . .' John Toll on Terrence Malick, 'The War Within', *American Cinematographer* online article, February 1999, www.theasc.com

136　'the graphic and visceral aspects . . .' John Toll, 'The War Within', *American Cinematographer* online article, February 1999, www.theasc.com

136　'ethereal, moodily philosophical . . .' *Leonard Maltin's 2002 Movie and Video Guide*, Plume/Penguin, 2001, p. 1388

137　'a genuinely epic . . .' The *Time Out Film Guide*, Thirteenth Edition, Penguin Books, Geoff Andrew, www.timeout.com/film/79249

137　'Where [*Saving Private Ryan*] had been . . .' Martin Flanagan, *Everything A Lie: The Critical and Commercial Reception of Terrence Malick's* The Thin Red Line, *The Cinema of Terrence Malick*, Wallflower Press, London, 2003, p. 128

176 'At a deeper level . . .' Michael Klein, *Hollywood and Historical Memory: The Road to Platoon, From Hanoi to Hollywood*, edited by Linda Dittmar and Gene Michaud, Rutgers University Press, 1990 p. 25

176 'It was in Southeast Asia . . .' JM Roberts, *History of the World*, Penguin Books, 1990, p. 972

177 'Men on the crews . . .' Michael Herr, excerpt from *Dispatches* reprinted in *The Heath Anthology of American Literature, Volume Two*, DC Heath and Company, Massachusetts, 1990, p. 2089

179 'It's a *Moby Dick* type thing . . .' Oliver Stone quoted by Nigel Floyd, 'Radical Frames of Mind', *Sight and Sound*, vol. 54, January 1987, pp. 10–11, reprinted in *Interviews: Oliver Stone*, edited by Charles LP Silet, University Press of Mississippi, 2001, p. 13

180 '*Platoon* is very assured . . .' Pat McGilligan, 'Point Man', *Film Comment*, January/February 1987, pp. 11–14, 16–20, 60 reprinted in *Interviews: Oliver Stone*, edited by Charles LP Silet, University Press of Mississippi, 2001, p. 17

180 '. . . a savage yet moving account . . .' The *Time Out Film Guide*, Penguin Books, 1991, p. 522

180 'the best work of any kind . . .' Vincent Canby, The *New York Times*, 1986

180 'harrowingly realistic . . .' *Leonard Maltin's 2002 Movie and Video Guide*, Plume/Penguin, 2001, p. 1070

181 'In *Platoon* . . .' Oliver Stone quoted in *History in the Movies* transcript of University of Berkeley conversations between Oliver Stone and Harry Kreister, 27 April and 27 June 1997. Transcript available at www.globetrotter.berkeley.edu/stone_con5.html

Born on the Fourth of July

185 'It was as if we had been linked by destiny . . .' Oliver Stone quoted by Norman Kagan, *The Cinema of Oliver Stone*, Roundhouse, Oxford, 1995

187 'I never put out a history . . .' Oliver Stone, 1997, Berkeley archive online, *Conversations with History*, Institute of International Studies, 1997

187 'the aloof kid . . .' Oliver Stone quoted by Pat McGilligan, 'Point Man', *Film Comment*, January/February 1987, pp. 11–14, 16–20, 60, reprinted in *Interviews: Oliver Stone*, edited by Charles LP Silet, University Press of Mississippi, 2001, p. 17

187 'Ron's story is a coherent vision . . .' Oliver Stone interview, 'The War Within' by Alan Mirabella, *New York Daily News*, 20 January 1990, reprinted in *The Cinema of Oliver Stone* by Norman Kagan, Roundhouse, Oxford, 1995, pp. 162–3

188 'I just think I like the way . . .' Oliver Stone from *Conversations with History*, 1997. University of Berkeley website

191   'relentlessly . . .' *Leonard Maltin's 2002 Movie and Video Guide*, Plume/Penguin, 2001, p. 161

191   'intense depiction of . . .' The *Time Out Film Guide*, Penguin Books, 1991, p. 80

192   'I may have lost . . .' Jane Fonda quoting Ron Kovic, The *Guardian* online from discussion with Lord David Puttnam, 3 June 2005, National Film Theatre.

Casualties of War

196   'it expresses the Vietnam dilemma . . .' Brian De Palma quoted by Kenneth Von Gunden, *Postmodern Auteurs*, McFarland and Company, 1991, p. 101

198   '(the American military) learned that men . . .' Pauline Kael quoting Paul Fussell, in *Movie Love*, Marion Boyars, London, 1992, p. 170

200   'This movie about war and rape . . .' Pauline Kael, *Movie Love*, Marion Boyars, London, 1992, p. 175

200   'The non-sensationalist approach . . .' The *Time Out Film Guide*, Penguin Books, 1991, p. 106

200   'For all its good intentions . . .' *Leonard Maltin's 2002 Movie and Video Guide*, Plume/Penguin, 2001, p. 221

201   'as compelling and astounding . . .' Armond White, www.depalma.net, interview

WARS IN OTHER WORLDS
Ran

206   'At the time, people were still free . . .' Akira Kurosawa, *Ran* press conference, First International Tokyo Film Festival, 1985, quoted by Gerald Peary at www.geraldpeary.com/interviews/jkl/kurosawa.html

209   'fission and fusion' Stephen Turnbull describing feudal Japan, *War In Japan: 1467–1615*, Essential Histories, Osprey, 2002, p. 30

209   'If I wanted to deliver a message . . .' Akira Kurosawa, *Ran* press conference, First International Tokyo Film Festival, 1985, quoted by Gerald Peary at www.geraldpeary.com/interviews/jkl/kurosawa.html

211   'The visuals are often Noh-like. The costumes . . .' Donald Richie, *The Films of Akira Kurosawa*, 3rd Edition, University of California, 1998

211   'devised special costumes . . .' Stuart Galbraith, *The Emperor and the Wolf*, Faber and Faber, 2002, p. 579

211   'a huge tormented canvas . . .' The *Time Out Film Guide*, Penguin Books, 1991, p. 549

211   '*Ran* has the terrible logic . . .' Vincent Canby, *New York Times*, 20 December 1985

212   'beautifully filmed . . .' *Leonard Maltin's 2002 Movie and Video Guide*, Plume/Penguin, 2001, p. 1119

213 'more richly conceived . . .' Akira Kurosawa, *Ran* press kit (1985) quoted by Stuart Galbraith, *The Emperor and the Wolf*, Faber and Faber, 2002, p. 577

Aliens
218 'do a film that was . . .' James Cameron, 2001 interview with Randy Lofficier, www.perfectworldusa.com
219 'a beautiful piece of work' Lance Henriksen quoted by Adam Pirani, 'Life Among the Aliens', *Starlog* issue 106, May 1986
222 'The sense of the dramatic . . .' James Cameron, 2001 interview with Randy Lofficier, www.perfectworldusa.com
222 'In a way almost everyone . . .' James Cameron, *Starlog*, issue 110, September 1986, p. 9
223 'the emotional content . . .' S. Weaver, *Starlog*, issue 109, August 1986, p. 36
224 'After a slow build-up . . .' The *Time Out Film Guide*, Penguin Books, 1991, p. 13
224 'intense, exciting . . .' *Leonard Maltin's 2002 Movie and Video Guide*, Plume/Penguin, 2001, p. 24
226 '*Aliens* takes clichés . . .' James Cameron, *Starlog*, issue 110, September 1986, p. 9

Glory
229 'the great prism . . .' *The BFI Companion to the Western*, Andre Deutsch, London, 1988, p. 88
233 'with malignant heart . . .' Abraham Lincoln quoted by Geoffrey C Ward, Ken Burns and Ric Burns, *The Civil War: An Illustrated History of the War Between The States*, Pimlico, 1992, p. 247
233 'Civil War defined us . . .' Shelby Foote, ibid. p. xvi
234 'Future years will never know . . .' *The Real War Will Never Get in the Books*, from *Specimen Days* by Walt Whitman, p. 483, *The Portable Walt Whitman*, edited by Mark van Doren, Penguin, 1973
235 '. . . all the self-divisions of conflict . . .' Robert Penn Warren, ibid. p. xix
236 'It's an ambitious and purposeful film . . .' The *Time Out Film Guide*, Penguin Books, 1991, p. 258
236 'exceptional . . .' *Leonard Maltin's 2002 Movie and Video Guide*, Plume/Penguin, 2001, p. 529
237 'There is great dialogue . . .' Ed Zwick discussing his sense of what makes a film work, www.bbc.co.uk

Land and Freedom
242 'the pleasures and tensions . . .' Martin Stollery, profile of Ken Loach in *The Critical Guide to Contemporary Irish and British Film Directors*, Wallflower Press, 2002, p. 202

APPENDICES

Documentaries

War and Satire

Index